MW01092139

Kocal

Burning Bears
Fall
From the Sky

My amusing story about relocating from a
desk in San Francisco to a remote mountain
in Northern California

By Peter Edridge

This book is a memoir, however, to protect people's
privacy, and me from lawsuits, the names of the places
and the characters have been fictionalized.

(V-1.6)

Dedicated to my loving wife Sheila, who everyday makes true on her boast that she's married to a lucky man.

Contents

The End of the Beginning	1
Starting a New Life	10
The Igo Beer Bar	21
Those First Weeks	28
The Mouse-House	40
Gotta Go Feed	44
The Well	57
The First Winter	68
A Glimmer of Hope	85
Manly Activities	93
The Day the Wheels Fell Off	102
A Semblance of Normalcy	109
Burn Piles	120
Pol Pot	134
Don't Play With Snakes	139
The North Wing	148
Dirty Burt	158
An Ordinary Day	164
It's a Matter of Assimilation	174
I Just Work Here	181
Character is Fate	186
A Man and his Derelicts	192
Nothing's Ever Easy	197
The Unimportance of Importance	205
It's a Good Life After All	213
Life's Little Unpredictabilities	218
Summer of Fire	223
A Quiet Worth Hearing	235
A Part of the Community	241
Burning Bears	250

Acknowledgements

Starting with the first of too many to thank is Mary Mihalka, my tireless supporter. Nisa Donnelly who patiently explained to me what a book was, and Annette Rardin who pulled me over the finish line. My sister, Elizabeth, and her daughter, Nicki, as well as every one of my friends and relatives that have supplied encouragement enough to swamp my doubts, and without whom I'm sure this book would have never wavered beyond the first few scribbled thoughts. Finally, I would also like to thank the wonderful people of Igo, who have added so much to my life.

The End of the Beginning

What on Earth had I been thinking? I was standing high on the side of a mountain outside an uninhabitable wreck that in some distant past had been a house, surrounded by as profound a silence as I had ever experienced. There wasn't a sound. I was alone, miles from anyone or anything, staring at a mountain range stretching out as far as the eye could see. An inanimate vista of rocky peaks and towering trees, without a sight or sense of human presence, and, for someone as hopelessly urban as myself, this was about as alien a world as I could have imagined. I stood dumbfounded, thinking back through all the events and the unlikely story of how I came to be there. I realized it had all started with one, ill-considered decision.

Just a year before, I had been living comfortably with my wife Sheila in a privileged and upscale community north of San Francisco. It was 2002, and I was an early boomer reveling in the latest variation to the California Dream—effortless consumption—entranced by the siren's song of the good life. My house had a view, a fine German automobile wore out my garage, I dined well of the best, enjoyed an unhurried glass of wine, and basked comfortably in the knowledge that I could be found in the top few percentiles of anything that really mattered.

This had been an unlikely improvement to my life, which had never known success like this, and more like the complete opposite. I had grown up in the East End of London, in the devastation left behind by World War II, playing with other grubby-faced kids in bombed-out houses, and then running home at the end of the day to a meager meal and a cold-water bath. It was a different world.

A thoroughly good English education lifted me out of these bleak surroundings, and in spite of my worst efforts I was accepted into a prestigious university. However, three years later on the afternoon of my last exam, my tattered suitcase sat propped up against the side of the wooden desk.

On dotting the last sentence to the last answer, I put my pen down, picked up the suitcase, caught a train to Heathrow airport and was gone: Trading in the memories of a childhood in post-war England for the promise of California—its endless blue skies, vast open spaces, hope and opportunity. I landed in San Francisco with an obscure academic degree and thirty-seven dollars; wearing a pair of flip-flops, powder-blue bell-bottom jeans, a sunshine-yellow shirt and a simple-minded smile. It was 1971, and I had chosen the West Coast because of its reputation for sex, drugs and rock-n-roll.

This wasn't exactly a well-thought out start to a life, and though I never found the carefree hedonism I had fantasized, I was still clueless and lost my most promising and fruitful years to a string of stunningly naïve attempts at making a living. Even "Have a nice day" (made occasionally quaint by an unintelligible British accent) had lost its meaning, and by my mid-thirties I had reached the end. I was broke and broken, driving a former gardener's mini-truck (that, in a testament to its manufacturer, I still drive today) without a thought of what to do next.

These were bleak times, indeed. But sometimes God smiles on the truly stupid, and, after years of focusing on what not to do, I stumbled across computer programming. To the astonishment of all, I'd finally found something I was good at and started a career.

There couldn't have been a better time to be a programmer, with the industry hiring anyone able to recognizably mouth the word *computer*. My obscure academic degree had become a personalized invitation, and instead of standing on the outside of life looking in, I was in its deepest warmest places, coddled and gently bumping along in its most vital bloodstream. It felt as if some beneficent being had taken pity on me, reached down and handed me the Map to Life. What I had stared at in disbelief from the outside for so many years was now as easily attainable as sitting in a comfortable chair, thinking what I was finding were easy thoughts, doing what I found enjoyable, and then being very paid well for it. At last, life finally made sense.

I spent the next few years enjoying success, choosing between whatever high-tech company offered the best prospects, but ending up at a small biotech start-up, not because of the money but because of the people. It didn't pay as well, but it was a fun little company and from the first day it felt like I had found a home. I was hired as its only programmer and, as much as a job can ever be, this became my dream job. It would have been for anyone else for that matter. Not only did I enjoy what I was paid to do, as nobody else in the company had a clue what that was, I was left alone to do it—whatever *it* was.

I was given a small office that became my sanctuary. In it I crammed two obstinately large desks, which took up almost all the space, and by arranging them so the door could hardly open I made sure that only the most determined could squeeze in and disturb me. To further discourage visitors, the desks were stacked precariously high with dead computers and oversized monitors, scoured from across the little company, and the only light in the room came from the glow of computer screens. Between the near darkness and the carefully placed obstructions, I stayed essentially invisible.

To add to this purposeful image of an eccentric computer guru, I'd hung a poster of Bora Bora across the back wall of my office. A plastic palm tree with fake fronds arched over my desk and in the gloom a three-foot tall teddy bear I'd named Algernon sat next to me, attentive, on his very own chair. There was worse. For the entire time I worked there, I wore the same pair of faded blue jeans and T-shirt, every single day, the same thing for years. I actually kept drawers full of identical T-shirts and jeans, which was typical of my childish British humor that, along with a deep-seated anti-establishmentarianism, has never done me much good.

Over many years, having stared at a few too many lines of computer code, I developed a need for a nap after lunch, to help me get through the day. When I first started taking these naps I leaned all the way back in my leather executive chair, but found that caused me to snore, which gave the game away. So I retreated under my desk with a pillow, hobbit-like in the gloom, curing the snoring problem along with most of the afternoon. And in case you were feeling a bit sorry for me about now, I was also exceptionally well paid. Yes, it was the dream job.

For ten wonderful years my work life remained idyllic, but that all changed when our small company achieved sudden success. The halcyon days of being chased around the building for perceived slights by an overly sensitive herd of slow-moving lab rats, or "lab technicians" as they preferred to be called, were over. Also gone were friendships built out of years of respect, swept away by waves of anonymous management teams, made up of very important and very gray people flown in from somewhere back East. I started to miss the old place.

The company org-chart, which had been as flat as the mat inside Macy's front door, now towered up from its broad base to a distant pinnacle in the clouds. Decisions rained down on the merely earthbound; I stood at the bottom, with my head cranked way back, staring up as this content-free management made nonsense of the bright little technology company. I soon became convinced that the new management had little interest in understanding what our little company actually did, but were filled with self-loathing for being associated with whatever that was.

The workplace changed from a collegiate frat house into something normally found lodged in the bowels of an insurance company—only less fun. Humorless interactions were required, and as more old friends started to leave the few of us remaining resembled survivors, living memories of better times. We talked amongst ourselves in lowered voices. Making matters worse, the Overly Structured have always sensed the presence of the enemy in me. I don't actually have to say or do anything, and even without overt acts, they can sense me through office doors and cubicle walls. I began thinking that beady eyes were watching me and, of course, they were.

One day my undersized office was re-assigned to a twelve-year-old with an accounting MBA, one of the thirty new-hires in accounting that week. My still dusty desk was moved to a wide spot in the hallway, conveniently beside the men's bathrooms and, expansive as the hallway was, there was no place for a palm tree or a bear. So, thinking I looked rather old and pathetic sitting out there, I borrowed a coffee mug from the lunchroom and placed it on the corner of my desk with a scrawled note taped to it, asking for donations. The push out had started. My desk might as well have had a set of wheels on it as it headed towards the backdoor and out into the parking lot.

I still had my moments though, at least enough to cause management to screech and flail, and that's always been good enough for me. For years I had been expected to find new insights into the annual re-teachings of what I called the "Church of Sexual Harassment." It was the worst of all worlds, where lawyers surpassed the clergy as the definers of all things evil. But no matter how many years management compelled us to hone our understanding of its teachings, I was still expected to find new and over-looked insights. Being quite bored with the premise to the whole thing, while also old enough to be a more or less neutral observer, I always did my best.

The last time my presence was required I sat in the front row of folding chairs, disarmingly attentive. The service was hosted by a couple of smart and attractive young attorneys, and soon after they started their expansive pre-amble about the history of sex in the workplace, without warning, I turned to squarely face some unfortunate corporate male thing that happened to be sitting beside me and, in a loud and completely outraged voice, declared: "I was NOT staring at her breasts!" Then I faced forwards again as if nothing had happened. It was an announcement to the remnants of the rebel band that I was alive and well and in the house.

Towards the end of this corporate enema, after hours of humorless preaching, the moment I had been waiting for arrived. A particularly puerile example of the evil was demonstrated in a slide. It showed a female supervisor inappropriately touching a male co-worker standing by the water-cooler.

I don't know where these thoughts come from but this one appeared as a revelation. I waited until the eager-to-please in the audience had put up their hands and proudly explained that yes, this too was sexual harassment. I waited for the obvious to be repeated in a mind-numbing number of ways. I waited patiently, waited for the full meaning of this lesson to sink in. Then, just before the next slide was put up, the time was ripe to add an alternative reading of the situation. I put up my hand and was, of course, invited to share. In a measured and thoughtful voice I delivered my latest insight on the subject to a hushed room, already exquisitely sensitized to even the faintest trace of workplace harassment.

"I would just like to point out, if some nincompoop hadn't promoted the woman to a position of power in the first place, this sorry mess would never have happened."

I've never quite understood the concept that some things are better not said. About half the auditorium knew me and burst out laughing, but the other half, mostly rows of fresh-faced professionals recently released from grad schools and trained in the evils of the workplace, were in a state of shock. Horror was more like it. This was a deadly serious matter and that hideous old man in the front row had revealed his foul, porcine inner-self.

This was one of my last public offerings of humor, and it did nothing to convince the corporate undead, several of who were floating wraith-like in the back of the auditorium observing, that I was one of them. To tell the truth, it was futile trying to stay in a place I could never, ever fit in. The past was gone, the future was something I could never be happy with, and like a periwinkle I was being levered out of my extremely comfortable, leather executive chair. The gig was up. And yes, I could have stayed on to make their lives as miserable as they were trying to make mine, but I could never have been corporate and there's not much point to staying where you are not wanted. Life's too short as it is.

So I joined nearly all my friends from the smart little start-up company and left, but only after a very complete and emphatic outburst of my truest and deepest feelings to a spindly thing that had apparently been my boss for the last year, though I was never sure. These final words made no difference, they weren't meant to, and I landed on the street.

Unfortunately, I hadn't bothered to check the street before landing on it. The year was 2002 and the dot-com bomb had just wiped out the entire tech industry. Gone. Having grown accustomed to never being out of work, even when I had wanted to be, this came as a shock. And after six months of a futile job search there didn't seem to be another good reason to email another blizzard of resumes or even turn up to one of the rare interviews this anonymous method of mass dispersal produced.

Maybe I should have pretended to be more compliant, but my last interview ended with my leaning over the desk of the bright young interviewer to ask him if his mother knew that he wasn't at school that day. Anyway, I thought it was funny. But from the moment I had first walked into the shiny new office building, I felt doomed. No one was over twenty, they all looked like they enjoyed their work, did what they were told, worked 16-hour days, slept by their desks, and played hacky sack for entertainment. In contrast, I explained to the interviewer that I didn't work past 5 p.m. (ever!) and insisted on a six-figure income. I honestly tried, but there was just no way of disguising myself.

At the beginning of this disastrous job search, Sheila would lay out my one interview suit and an ironed shirt. She carefully cleaned off any lint, straightened my collar and waved goodbye with a confident smile as I left the house. But as the months went by, with my mood in freefall and our savings evaporating, she saw the direction things were going and encouraged me to let go our affluent life and downsize—while there still anything left to downsize. This was surprising because she had married into happier times and probably could have easily married into far better. If anything she should have been screaming at me about bait and switch and demanding that I keep her in the lifestyle she had grown accustomed to. But she didn't. And though you could never guess by looking at her, she is quite down to Earth and able to take the rough with the smooth, much like a good radial tire.

Sheila's not my first wife (the exact count is unimportant and it's not excessive for California), but, as she likes to remind me, she is my final wife. That's undoubtedly true, and, being sure in her self-confidence she also likes to remind me that she's married to a very lucky man. That's true most of the time. She's a tall athletic blond, and likes to emphasize her height by wearing high heels (just to tower over me) and then tell people, "You know he's taller than I am," finishing with perfect timing, "if he stands on his wallet."

We had met while kayaking, our paths crossing miles from shore in the middle of the San Francisco Bay. Almost immediately, from our earliest conversation, I started asking, "Have I told you about this before?" It was as if I had known Sheila my whole life and I couldn't tell when her life and mine had joined. At the time we met I was enthusiastically single, and had an ad running in the local personals that read, *"**Short, bald and English**. I like fast cars and fast women. Call me!"* It was my best attempt at self-promotion, so it was probably lucky that I'd been out kayaking on the Bay that afternoon and not waiting by the phone.

On the drive home from what was my last job interview, I listened to a talk-radio host (my usual source for life-changing advice) glibly announce that computer programmers might as well find a new line of work. His words must have rung a chord. I was a sprightly fifty-three at the time, but in computer years I'd turned to dust a long time ago, and lacking any pretence of servility I thought that he just might be right. The financial consultant's words became my excuse to throw away the past, along with a worthless present, and look around for a new future.

It would be a tough decision, though. Computing had been the only success in an otherwise useless work life, and yet I was about to walk away from it. But there was some part of me, deep down in places too murky to comprehend (where all my really big decisions seem to come from), that knew I'd been cast out. I was old and wretched.

I was already living outside the castle walls, the last six months had shown that, and in that short time a generation of anemic unpleasantly cooperative little things had filled the void behind me. All that had been missing in this bloodless expulsion was a skeletal figure in a black cloak leaning over the battlements, its outstretched arm and bony finger pointing, condemning me with the final words, "Be gone!"

This decommissioning hadn't been planned for. For years I'd been sprinkling the word "retirement" into conversations, but that was only to gain an air of avuncular seniority while talking to people half my age. It was never serious because I didn't have enough money to retire on. But after a few more months of a painful jobless malaise, it began to dawn on me that perhaps my choices were not that good, and maybe Sheila was right. The good times weren't likely to return any time soon, and we needed to downsize while we still had something left to downsize. Our cash reserves, built up during happier times and lofted by a substantial income, were evaporating. The squeeze was on. I was standing on top of a crumbling future trying to choose between the lesser of two evils: risk staying until the bitter end or go while there was still something to leave with. It was a decision that has left me debating whether it was sheer genius or the stupidest mistake in my entire mistake-ridden life.

Either way, a month later an increasingly sleepless and apprehensive part stampeded the rest of me into thinking I could sell everything, leave the madding crowd far behind and head for the hills... literally. This was odd for me because I hadn't left my pleasant, affluent Marin County in thirty-five years.

Starting a New Life

The hills were outside the tiny town of Igo (prophetically pronounced "I go") in Northern California. Actually, it's not so much a town as a stop sign and a beer bar on a small road to an even smaller town called Ono (ironically pronounced "Oh, no!"), which doesn't even boast a stop sign. Following the trail of oddly named hamlets, there's something even further out, miles past Ono, but from what I've heard about the place I would rather patiently wait in Hell for it to improve before visiting it.

Igo's spot beside this country road is a couple of miles past a local landmark known as High Bridge. It's well named, spanning a deep ravine from rim to rim, and it had replaced the original one-lane Low Bridge, which was equally well named as it barely managed to keep itself above the water at the bottom of the ravine. The deep ravine forms the boundary, a natural dividing line that marks the outer edge of what, over the years, I have come to refer to as the Zone of Civilization. On the one side of the ravine there's civilization, of a sort, and on the other side... well, there's Igo and places even stranger.

This Zone of Civilization is a narrow band of land on either side of Highway 5 with a noticeable population, malls, streetlights, subdivisions, schools, buses, businesses and essential services. But should you venture outside the Zone you will find yourself in a mountainous area of California, unpopulated except for the sparse remnants of an occasional mining town that time has passed on by. It remains largely unknown to the vast majority of Californians and by itself could easily qualify California as a fly-over state. There's no banjo music playing, but people speak with something resembling a southern drawl and often use words and phrases I hadn't thought spoken in this century.

Not believing my guesstimate of our worth, Sheila had searched far and wide and finally found a property that, by its price, was in a seriously under-appreciated part of the state. It was however, all we could afford, and on the bright side the real estate agent had optimistically told us that the property had "potential." I've since learned this is a real estate term meaning its true value was next to nothing, and over the years we have lived here I've realized that even if we had bought it for nothing, we would have still overpaid for the place.

The dilapidated A-frame and its surrounding thirty acres of land were located off a narrow county road that climbs up Buckhorn Mountain, the closest of a range of mountains that arc around the gently rolling foothills that play host to Igo. This county road was named after a bank robber, Nathaniel Woods, who had been hiding out on the mountain during the Gold Rush. With time on his hands and a mountain creek flowing by his campsite he started prospecting. Always a lucky type, he found gold and silver in the creek and after finding enough he turned legit. He found respectability, too, having his hideaway and the mountain road leading to it named after him, Woods Canyon Road. Although, at the time it was just a cart track used to haul away his spoils, the name better fits the road's current rustic nature.

This easily overlooked county road starts out innocently in the flats near Igo, passing quietly through rolling ranch land, before winding its way up the mountain in a steepening wooded canyon, crowded beside the creek and constricted between trees and looming boulders, until only one car at a time can squeeze by. It stops abruptly four miles in, beside the creek at the old mine. In a twist of history, this gold-bearing mountain stream had been given its name by the first residents of the area, ranchers, who had lived miles downstream in the flatlands. And though you will never see cows this far up a mountain, it's nonsensically called Cow Creek.

Near the far end of Woods Canyon, barely noticeable as it materializes out of a crowd of trees, there's a rough dirt road. Starting beside the creek it quickly disappears from sight, climbing up the side of the canyon and eventually reaching the ridgeline at the top before heading out into wilderness. It's called China Gulch, probably from a historical reference to the Chinese mine workers, and half a mile up this untended dirt road near the ridge was our new home. If anyone ever needed somewhere to hide out, this would be that place.

The thirty acres came with a picturesque barn, made all the more picturesque because its roof had collapsed, and a small two-room house that was last lived in a decade before. This was probably about the time that the last occupants had fled, or were arrested, and the house hadn't improved any since. But then nothing in the country with a roof over it is ever truly vacant. This uninhabitable shell of a house had become a bustling home for mice, bats, an ill-fated cat, and a bear or two. Another winter and its roof would have collapsed, just as the barn's had, its remaining windows would have probably been shot out and another wall would have finished rotting through. However, the land made up for everything that the house lacked; with waterfalls, mountain streams, stands of towering ponderosa pines, scatterings of one hundred year old oaks spreading shade and acorns all around them, and a view south, literally for a hundred miles.

This had been a classic frying-pan-into-the-fire move; begun during a time of panic, while confronted by bleak and bleaker options, and ending with a last desperate leap into the unknown. And for an aging urbanite, this was about as *unknown* as it could get. By the time the escrow closed in early summer, any delusionary boyhood images of myself as Davy Crockett had long ago faded and murky suspicions of what I had got myself had taken their place. But it was too late, there was no way to undo my signatures on the sales documents and my fate was sealed. With an increasingly shaky spirit I loaded my ancient mini-truck with the few hand tools I had accumulated during my suburban life, some cardboard boxes full of stuff that Sheila thought I might need, and a change of clothes—all the things I naively imagined I would need to start a new life.

There was a Plan, if you could call it that. It was for me to live rough on the property for a couple of weeks, while I made the house habitable again. Two weeks of spirited construction should do the job, at least that was the estimate, and then Sheila could join me. The "what" and the "how" of this Plan had never been filled out, or even started, because every time I thought about what might be involved my mind seemed to go blank, leaving nothing, which coincidentally was what I knew about construction. But early one morning, with a cheery wave and a heavy heart, leaving Sheila to finish selling our home in Marin, I headed north from our affluent lifestyle in the eternally pleasant San Francisco Bay Area, north to an abandoned house and a new life as a man of the mountains.

Feeling, and probably looking, much like Jed Clampett in my dependable old mini-truck, with assorted pieces of my former life poking out of boxes piled high and the ubiquitous mattress trying to lift off from underneath inadequate straps, I drove north along Interstate 5 as it made its way monotonously from Mexico to the Canadian border. But there was more on my mind than driving. For several weeks I'd had a sense that an overpowering ignorance was protecting me from impending realities. I had tried not to upset the situation but, ready or not, that cozy arrangement ended that afternoon. I remember clearly the moment the door to my comfortable old life slammed shut behind me and I was left standing outside in a new, very cold world.

It was at a rest stop halfway up the interstate. I had stopped, having simply run out of the will to go forward, and stood beside the mini-truck looking like any number of similar stories taking a break. A vista of rural America lay stretched out to the horizon with nothing familiar to be seen in any direction, and suddenly the emotional blinders came off. Standing there alone, vaguely aware of the impersonal din from the freeway and looking emptily around at the anonymous rest stop, a cold reality suddenly landed on me.

My house was gone. My friends were gone. My career and everything that I had built up in my former life were gone, and there was no undoing what had been done. I stood there dumbfounded, astonished at the cascading mistakes that had brought me to this point. Jumping back into the truck I hurried out of there, trying to get away from what I had seen, but the feeling of dread chased after me. My optimistic delusion had disappeared and I knew the future was going to be unrecognizable, most likely a disaster, and, even at its best, difficult in ways I wouldn't know how to deal with. I drove out of the rest stop with the past irretrievably behind, an uncertain future in front, and a Led Zeppelin CD playing as loud as I could take it on the stereo.

Two hours later, after leaving Hwy 5 behind (and apparently the rest of the known world, as I hadn't seen another car for miles) I drew up beside the thin shadow of Igo's solitary stop sign, late on what was an idyllic sunny country afternoon. There wasn't a soul to be seen. Turning onto the narrow county road and heading out towards our new home, cows were nonchalantly wandering down the middle of the road. There were green fields and tall hedgerows, peace was in the air, the birds were singing and, who knew, maybe there were even kindly strangers living in these hills. Perhaps that feeling of dread I'd had was misplaced after all. Really, how bad could things be?

Three miles of rejuvenated hope later I turned onto our decrepit driveway and bounced and banged up the quarter-mile succession of potholes, arriving outside the house followed closely by a huge cloud of dust that hovered in the air and finally settled on the truck, and then on me when I opened the door to get out. With no alternative coming to mind I decided to stay with the dusty look, and after taking my first careful look around the place, the future was looking pretty dusty as well.

I stood in front of a wreck of a house, miles from anyone or anything. There were no friends or neighbors to call. I was alone, feeling very small and dangerously unprepared on the side of an uninhabited mountain. I might as well have been standing beside a crashed spaceship on the surface of Mars, hoping for some help to arrive. I wanted to jump back into the truck and escape this alien place, before it got dark and while I still could. Drive back to Marin, and once there fall on the floor and weep, beg someone to let me undo what I had done. But I couldn't, there was nothing to go back to, and unfortunately the derelict shack in front of me was all there was.

It wasn't a time for reflection. I needed to hastily resurrect the vestigial remains of my backbone, stop whining, and, strange as it may seem, find a place to sleep for the night. The fact that I had to think about anything so obvious shows just how little planning had been done.

I had seen the property once before, briefly, after Sheila first found it. But I have never been big on details, and the exact state the house was in wasn't that important compared to getting a new place to live, any place. So, sure that I would find a place to sleep for the night, I pushed the A-frame's front door open and stood back for a second before cautiously walking into the single gloomy room that was the downstairs. Looking around, I started to wonder whom or what else had had the same idea. There was a scattering of broken furniture mixed in with an untidy layer of unrecognizable trash, and a pile of insulation that had been torn from inside the walls and made into something resembling a large nest. Bears.

I hadn't even noticed it before, but near the front door was a small windowless room—it had probably been a utility room at one time. It was so unnaturally dark that it stole what little light my flashlight had to offer. On the far side of the main room an open stairway led up to a cramped bedroom, tucked against the steeply sloped roof. There were holes in the walls I could see outside through and, between the piles of trash on the plywood floor, other holes gave views down into even more unpleasant places where beady little eyeballs stared back from the dark. I've stayed in places I wouldn't want to stay again but nothing quite like this.

Hoping for better, across the driveway was a conventional two-car garage. It might have been conventional at one time, when it still had four walls, but by the time I arrived one of the walls was missing, it was gone, there was no sign of it anywhere and there were only three walls left. This gave a certain free flowing indoor-outdoor feel but I would have still preferred a fourth wall. Still, it was in far better shape than the house, and impressed me from the start by having a solid concrete floor. There weren't even any bears' nests, and once the trash and garbage were pulled out, dragged out, and swept out, there wouldn't be any place for snakes and rodents to hide either. The bats dangling in neat rows along the bottom of the rafters didn't bother me, and, given the only alternative, the garage became my new home.

It was almost dark by the time I'd finished cleaning it out. I threw the trash on top of the stacks of the garbage already piled alongside the garage, and in the failing light I staked my claim to the place by dragging the mattress off the truck (there was no other way to move it), across the gravel driveway and into the back of the garage. The three-sided garage was mine. Then I unloaded the boxes of kitchenware, stereo equipment, and otherwise useless stuff that had no purpose on the side of a mountain, stacking them into a one-foot high and hopefully protective wall around the mattress.

Using the last of the light, increasingly aware of every sound outside, I positioned the flashlight so it would be the first thing I came across when I inevitably woke up during the night in complete darkness. There was nothing else that could be done; I flopped down on my sleeping bag and began the first night on the mountain.

Strangely, lying there, listening to an occasional bat flutter by, I couldn't be sure from moment to moment whether there was a smile on my face or a grimace. It was just a passing thought, but maybe this would be an adventure after all and not just a horrible conclusion to a string of bad decisions. Either way, that was all in the future. I drifted off into the sleep of the dead, and I'm here to tell you that nothing unpleasant came in the night to eat me.

Before this, during my former pleasant urbanite life, Sheila had used the power of repetitive requests to help me understand the need to replace a toilet seat, paint our bedroom walls, and push an electric lawnmower over our small patch of lawn on the weekends. I might have become overly impressed with how handy I was, because on waking the next morning the first rays of that early morning light wiped out that happy assessment. While walking around the house, looking at the daylight streaming through its rotted walls, it began to occur to me that I didn't have a clue how to rebuild the dilapidated structure that had cynically been described as a "house" in the sales agreement. Not a clue. My one chance at survival was that this was all a particularly bad nightmare and, not a moment too soon, I would wake up.

Though I wouldn't have believed it at the time, I was actually very lucky. (*Lucky* wasn't exactly the word that came to mind that morning, *screwed* was more like it.) This unwitting good fortune came from the fact the house still had electricity. The service was still on and there was electricity, at least to the fuse box. Without this keystone of civilization, a down-on-his-luck caveman would have collapsed laughing at my living arrangements. Still, even this stroke of luck wasn't quite that simple. All the electrical outlets in the house were missing, as was all the wiring and even the copper water pipes—they must have been ripped out of the walls and sold for their copper.

The garage had the exact opposite problem. It had outlets and outlets, outlets everywhere, and a maze of wires strung through the rafters faithfully feeding power to each and every last one of them; presumably left behind after last year's marijuana harvest. So I at least had a lucrative new career if I wanted it. Unfortunately, there was a house to rebuild before Sheila arrived in two weeks, and fun as it would have been to be grinning inanely outside a garage full of pot plants when she drove up, I could imagine feeling worse for wear at the end of that conversation. Past experience has shown me that the wife can be a little square at times.

Even to an untrained eye this was obviously where some enterprising youth had been growing dope. Looking up, there was a shiny new metal chimneystack on the garage roof, even though there was no stove in the garage and never had been. In fact, there was nothing else even remotely new on the property, yet the chimneystack was perched incongruously on top of the garage roof, shining brightly over its kingdom of decay and deferred maintenance. Its purpose must have been to fool the infrared cameras flying by on DEA helicopters. The chimneystack had been an attempt to disguise this "hot" garage roof by making it look like a cozy stove was warming the humble domicile, as opposed to a bunch of grow lights. It's a Shasta County tradition, but it's hard to imagine that this fooled anyone.

It was easy to see why the dope growers had chosen the garage, as it was by far the most solid structure on the property. But since one wall was now completely missing and I was going to be working alone and sleeping alone, with no idea what might be lurking in the mountains and far enough away from any neighbors that even the loudest screams would have gone unheard, you can imagine I found myself thinking about bears and lions during those first nights. For all I knew, the undigested parts of me could have been found some weeks later by a tobacco-chewing local in a plaid shirt, aiming a disinterested kick at my remains with the tip of his cowboy boot and mumbling to himself, "Any damn fool knows not to sleep out here."

So, well motivated and equipped with a long extension cord, a brand new $30 circular saw from Sears, a box of nails, a hammer and some sheets of plywood, I started to rebuild the missing side on the garage. It was a race to make the garage secure, before the news spread to whatever large predators lived in the area that there was an easy meal waiting for them. And while considering the appetites of things that go bump in the night, I decided to make it snake proof too. After all, this was rattler country, and I'd had visions of waking up to a rattler staring inches from my face.

So rebuilding the garage wall became my first attempt at carpentry, ever, and finishing the wall was a moment of pride. I stood back and admired my work, convinced that carpentry had become my first construction skill—one of the many skills I knew I would need. In retrospect, it was probably the worst case of wood butchery ever, and an insult to carpentry that won't be easily forgotten. This first attempt at construction consisted of banging together badly cut bits of wood, skewered at odd angles with dozens of nails, and not a straight line in sight. But being blissfully ignorant I felt encouraged, and set about tackling the next critical need, which was getting water to the house. Once again, my deepest thanks to my dope growing predecessors, because water was just as important to these guys as electricity was.

If anybody had suggested a week earlier that my job would have been to get water from Cow Creek, a third of a mile away up the side of the mountain to the house, I would have hoped that they were joking. Apart from the scale of the project, I wouldn't have had a clue how to do it. But thanks to the entrepreneurial spirit of those before me, I didn't have to do that much. All that was needed was to replace a few missing lengths of wiring and repair the breaks in the existing PVC water pipe.

This pipe began at a large pump submerged in Cow Creek, at the bottom of the property. I remember when I first saw this pump. I tried moving it, just because it was there, but decided it was fine where it was and that it hadn't been stolen (like everything else of any value on the property) because it was too heavy to walk off with. The other end of this improbably long plastic pipe emptied into the metal holding tank at the very top of the property. The tank sat on its own small rise, uphill from the house, and had an outline of what looked like John Lennon's face spray-painted on its side. Looking down from the water tank he seemed to bless all in his presence.

Simple or not, with the little I knew the repairs still took three long days and far too many hikes up and down an increasingly steep and hot mountainside, though hiking is a kindly description. Mostly, it was on hands and knees, pushing through the nearly impenetrable brush that smothered the land, and I soon learned that doing anything on the side of a hot, steep hill is a lot of work. But at the end of the third day, with the breaks in the pipe fixed and the wiring reconnected, I flipped the switch in the garage, turning on the electricity to the pump. It was going to be a while before the creek water made its way up the half-mile of empty pipe, and then, of all times, it occurred to me that the pump hadn't been stolen because it was too heavy—but because it didn't work.

I was too tired to care and walked up the few yards to the tank, sat down with my back propped up against it, and waited against all logic for the sound of creek water spilling into the tank. Ten increasingly anxious minutes later, the first gurgles were followed by a deep and importantly wet sounding burp and then by a conclusive stream of water rattling onto the bottom of the empty metal tank.

Several days of sweat and dust caked every inch of me, and I was still wearing the same clothes I had arrived in nearly two weeks earlier. But listening to the water pour into the tank, looking through the ponderosa pines, down the Sacramento Valley towards a distant hazy horizon, I felt pretty pleased with myself. I had the beginnings of a place to live, a roof over my head and creek water to the house, and that wasn't a bad streak of luck for such an ill-prepared urbanite. So much could have gone wrong, in so many ways I could have been stopped before I got started, but instead had met only problems that could be solved by a bumbling amateur.

So with this first skirmish with the mountain in the win column, the beginnings of some country skills, and maybe the first stirrings of a backbone, the evening had become a moment of triumph. I was emboldened and ready for a real challenge—it was time to come down off the mountain for a cold beer at the Igo Beer Bar.

The Igo Beer Bar

The Igo Beer Bar was frankly an intimidating place; at least I thought it was. It was old, but looked even older, and its disrepair bordered on the belligerent—a clear warning for outsiders to stay away. Out front there was an irregular row of dusty work-worn pickup trucks, done for the day, and on either side was a thin scattering of tired tin-roofed houses: some set by the road and others set back some; some of them abandoned and others still lived in, but by looking at them it was hard to see how. They're all that's left from a hundred long years ago when, for a brief time, Igo had been a booming mining town. And in places where houses might have stood once there were occasional trailers, along with some rusted-out cars and discarded appliances, apparently content to live out their final years in the tall weeds and dried grasses that had grown up around them.

Nothing was moving in the sharp heat, and scenes from a somber cowboy movie played in my mind as I walked across the parking lot to the sun-baked shack. It had a rusted corrugated roof, two small dirty windows, and what little paint remained had faded to a chalky pastel blue. Its front porch dropped down at one end where the wooden steps had collapsed, pulling the roof along with it, and there was a single narrow path worn into the boards leading up to the bar's front door. Apart from the dry twitch of the summer heat, the only sound that afternoon was a swamp cooler whirring incessantly on the bar's roof. Hesitating for a moment before walking in, I had a feeling of dread that I was about to meet some pretty genuine people, a breed I was completely unused to.

I opened the torn screen door, which had then and still has an unnecessarily noisy screech from an un-oiled hinge, then reached to open the bar's absurdly flimsy front door. As I took my first step into the dim interior the screen door slammed shut behind me and loudly announced my entrance. In the gloom I could see faces looking over towards me, but then turning away without a comment. That was a relief. Perhaps, the most I was going to contend with today was indifference. Still, each step felt stiff and awkward as I walked over to the bar.

Nothing could have changed in recorded time. The plaster walls were stained a uniform brown from decades of cigarette smoke; beer mats adorned the sagging ceiling; the bar's cheap linoleum countertop was chipped from years of dice being slammed down on it; and an unholy alliance of stale beer mixed with sweat hung in the air. Looking at the rough wooden floorboards I had the feeling I had stepped in from another place, or even another planet, or maybe another age, somewhere in some past time, but not mine.

I was sure this country bar served just the two beers, Bud and Coors, and the only real choice would be between a bottle and a can. So not really expecting anyone to have even heard of my favorite microbrewery, I leaned over the bar and asked for a bottle anyway. Without a glance in my direction or dropping a word in her conversation with a blond at the end of the bar, the bartender leaned on the oversized chrome handle to the walk-in cooler and disappeared. Still talking to the blond, she reappeared with a Sierra Nevada Pale Ale, popped the cap and set the bottle down in front of me.

This simple event was so surprising that it triggered what felt like a time warp. The bar rushed forward through time and landed back in the twenty-first century; a dusty dimly lit run-down portion of the twenty-first century, but close enough. Suddenly there were all the usual sounds of any bar and a gangly sun-baked raisin of an old man sitting beside me, holding out a sinewy hand and introducing himself as Roy Mahoney. He wasn't missing any teeth, didn't appear to need psychoactive meds, and while shaking his hand I was thinking that I might not die here after all.

Any time life doesn't go wrong beneath my low expectations I consider it a win, and by sitting on the stool next to Roy I had stumbled across an introduction into the community. For starters he introduced me to the bartender, Linda, who reached over the bar and cemented her introduction with a persuasive handshake, all the while eyeing me as if I were the latest arrival at the zoo. And, in a way, I was. Over the next few beers, which I bought with the purpose of appearing overly generous, Roy gave me a quick history of Igo and occasionally found time to talk about himself. I was learning that Roy liked to tell a story. After that I learned that there were quite a few stories to tell, which was followed shortly by the reality that Roy liked to drink beer; not compulsively but with consistency. The idea was forming that Roy might be a scoundrel, of sorts, but he was also different from what I'd expected, he seemed friendly and even welcoming.

Coincidently, we lived on the same small county road, and only a mile from each other. He described his house but I couldn't remember seeing it, and then added the unnecessary tidbit that most of the locals (who lived in the hills closer to Igo) refer to the mountain we lived on as Granola Hill—they thought it attracted fruits and nuts. "Oh, really," was the best I could do, glancing around the bar at a rough looking crew. They didn't seem much like the *fruits and nuts* types to me; in fact, they looked more like the types that made sure the fruits and nuts didn't like them. But who knew? They were probably just some locals, however rough, keeping out of the heat and finishing off another hot afternoon over some beers.

As Roy draped comfortably between his stool and the bar, and I listened to yet more of his stories, I couldn't help notice that he hadn't shaved in a week. This seemed odd because he was articulate and must have been educated at some time in his life. And why was he wearing that torn yellow-stained wife-beater T-shirt? And why tatters of what had once been a pair of jeans and a pair of worn out Jesus shoes? I felt cheated. I'd always prided myself on being the world's worse dresser, but I couldn't compete with his indifference. But by sifting through some of his many stories, the enigma that was Roy was at least partially explained.

He had finished art school and then spent a year in corporate life as an art director. Something must have happened in that year to seriously turn his mind, because that was some thirty years ago and he has been living in a goat barn ever since. And as I sat there, learning a little about Igo's past, a lot about Roy's life, and beginning to hope that maybe all the folks around these parts were artisan drop-outs, like Roy, and not just ex-cons doing their best to suppress violent urges, a piece of Igo's life played itself out as if on a stage with the bar the set.

The screen door slammed shut. Everyone looked up reflexively to see who had just walked in. It was a disheveled shiftless youth; shirtless, scratched up, covered in dust, and slinking in with that surly look of a kid who had successfully avoided achieving anything constructive in his life. Looking at this kid I just knew his favorite phrase had to be "It wasn't my fault." It was a look that I recognized from my own youth.

Walking up to the bar, and in a tone of voice that seemed to expect an immediate "No," he asked Linda if he could use the phone. Without interrupting her marathon conversation with the blond, or even giving the kid a second look, she pushed the phone toward him. Not another word was said between them. The kid sat down on a nearby stool to make his call, which was to his home. From what I heard he had been parked in his dad's car, near the top of some ravine, and with the worst luck in the world a passing truck had hit the car, knocking it into the ravine. And yes, the kid really did say, "It wasn't my fault!"

Maybe more about this rural community needs explaining before continuing on with the story. Rural, I've learned over the years, is not always happy cows grazing in grassy fields or even longhorns herded across wide-open spaces Texas style, or neat row crops in perfect lines or fruit trees and tractors and bee keepers. In other words, it's not always hardworking, industrious farmers and ranchers. Rural can be poor people who just don't happen to live in a town. There are some ups and some downs to this arrangement. One of the ups is that the community has a slow enough pace and has few enough distractions that everybody has the time to get to know everyone else. But more than that, they know each other pretty much as family, and why not? They'd attended school together, drank their first illegal beers together, roamed back roads together, and ultimately married each other; starting the entire cycle over again. They spent their entire lives with each other, looked out for each other, celebrated the small victories, and survived the great indignities life brings on us all. They're lucky enough to live in a real community that spans not just families but generations, and Igo had just such a community.

Everyone drinking in the Beer Bar already knew that the kid's car had been pushed into the ravine by a pickup truck, but they also knew it happened after a fistfight and several miles of a car chase around the back roads. In a small town news travels fast; certainly faster than the time it took for the feckless kid to scramble out of the ravine and hike overland to the only public telephone for miles around. But however interesting the kid and the crashed car in the ravine were, they are not the point to this story. They would be anywhere else but, as I was beginning to understand, this was Igo and it was some ways outside the Zone of Civilization.

The real story started when the kid put the phone down. He turned to Linda and asked the innocent enough question, "Since I'm here can I get a six-pack to go?" Without batting an eye Linda replied matter-of-factly, "You must think I'm stupid. You robbed me last year and you were only eighteen then. I can't serve you any alcohol."

"Oh yeah . . ." Busted, the kid slunk out in much the same way he arrived. Now that was community. I had never seen anything quite like it. It set me back, again, sitting in the dimly lit bar and wondering what century or what planet I was on. This slice of life reminded me just how different and how much of an outsider I was in my new home, a place where the community actually took care of itself.

With the performance over and the kid gone, Roy resumed telling stories. It was all news to me, including the surprising fact that Roy was a man of means, by local standards, being the proud owner of the Igo Inn. The Igo Inn was formerly the Welcome

Lodge, and had been the home to some ancient order of something when Igo had its brief moment in the sun as a mining town. But once the mines were played out the Inn had lost its purpose, and the rambling white clapboard building had stood essentially unchanged for a hundred years. It still had its original wood-paneled rooms and thick oak floorboards; there was a large meeting room with a stage, and an even larger room with a bar for dancing, along with a 1930's era commercial kitchen. Roy had recently tried to reopen it as a restaurant, but it was currently closed and waiting for another breath of life. Judging from the stack of empties growing in front of Roy, and the way nobody could pass by without swapping stories with him and buying another round of beers, the Inn's latest resurrection could be some time coming. Being incurably social, Roy seemed to be perfectly comfortable just where he was.

It was starting to get dark outside, so while my luck was still holding and before anything happened to make me regret coming down, I thought it best to head home. I got up to leave and waved a cursory goodbye to the rest of the crew around the bar, not expecting a reaction as I hadn't said a word to anyone except Roy the entire time I was there. But they all looked over, raised their cans of beer high and chanted in unison what I would learn later was the Beer Bar refrain, "Drive fast and reckless!" And with this simple act I felt oddly accepted. "Nice group of guys," I thought as the screen door slammed shut behind me, marking the end to the little adventure.

As I walked back across the parking lot towards my old mini-truck, I realized that it would never again be the instrument of inverse snobbery that it had been in Marin, but, for vastly different reasons, it could be perfect for Igo. I swung the truck around and headed back home on a dark and deserted road. Halfway there, still thinking about the last couple of hours, I saw a political campaign sign starkly illuminated in the headlights. It was prominently placed in front of what looked like a converted barn and read simply, "Mahoney for Mayor". What! Could that sun-dried old guy in the wife-beater T-shirt possibly be the mayor of Igo? He acted like it, and everyone treated him like he was. Now I was really worried.

Doing my best not to think about who or what else held public office, along with some other implications of Roy being the mayor, I turned onto my dirt driveway and bounced the little pickup truck up to the house and my makeshift home in the garage. Waiting for the dust cloud to settle before getting out, I was alone, in the dark, on the mountain, again.

Those First Weeks

Sheila drove up the following day with our menagerie of dogs and cats along what little remained of our former lives, packed into what had to be the oldest U-Haul still operational. And if the truck looked worse for wear, the cats looked even worse after their long journey, so I lifted their carriers into the back of the mini-truck, bounced them unceremoniously up the driveway to our derelict house and, after a few words of apology, left them locked in the bedroom. It was the only room in the house that had a door. With the cats out of the way, it was now the U-Haul's turn to get up the driveway.

I had purposely met Sheila at the barn because it was below the steepest (some would call it scary steep) part of the driveway. This near-vertical section of the driveway had been paved at some point in geologic time, a goat couldn't have made it up that slope if it hadn't been paved, but decades later the paving had deteriorated into isolated islands of blacktop with giant potholes in the spaces between. Given the state the driveway was in now, even that goat would have found another route up our hill.

A more detailed look at the U-Haul didn't raise my hopes about driving it up, either. The truck must have started its life about the time of the Great Depression, when less was expected out of a truck, and years later it was doubtful that it could pull its own weight up our driveway, let alone loaded the way it was. But I didn't care. No, I really didn't care, and had no intention of unloading everything at the barn, then piecemeal the load up the hill just to make the rental truck's life a little easier. Chances were that the U-Haul's suspension wouldn't have survived more than one trip up and down the potholes in the driveway, anyway. And since I had just spent two weeks humping heavy, often smelly, always dusty, dirty things around, I was not in the mood to add to my work. The rental truck (it's best I don't mention some of the things I've done to rental cars in my life) was going to fulfill its purpose and pull our belongings up the hill. Still, I was worried enough about my chances of getting up the driveway to unload two unnecessarily large flowerpots and their tree-sized plants. Actually, they had been loaded last and were the first things I saw when I opened the roll-up door. They were also all I was willing to take out.

After a detailed reading of the insurance clause in the rental agreement, I rounded off the discussion Sheila was having with me about the wisdom of what I was attempting, bonded my fate to the truck's fate, and pointed the truck up the driveway. I took off, my right foot pressed hard down on the floor to build up as much speed as the truck could develop. Though *speed* is an optimistic description of its lethargic start, and *forward progress* would be more accurate. The truck started up the scary steep part of our driveway, but halfway up I began to wish I'd thought of a plan "B".

I found myself staring out the front of the windshield, willing the truck to see what I could see, to use my eyes as tractor beams, transport itself to where I was looking, anything, but just keep going to the top of the driveway. Nothing worked, and in spite of literally standing on the gas pedal, there was not a thing more that could be done. Little by little the truck was losing its momentum. Then, just before it reached the top and with a long steep hill waiting behind it, the truck stopped. It hung there on the side of the hill with its engine roaring and blowing smoke.

There wasn't a choice. I kept its worn old engine at full throttle while an acrid smelling smoke started to ooze out from under the transmission cover. For what seemed like a full minute the truck hung there. Slowly, the whine coming from the transmission changed pitch, then, with what felt like a final effort (probably as the gearbox's inner workings imploded) and at a literal snail's pace, the old truck painfully crested the steepest part of our driveway and limped the remaining distance to our decrepit house. Once there, I got out, dropped onto my knees in the middle of the brown haze of oil smoke, and prayed—not to give thanks for having actually made it up the driveway, but to pray that the truck would make it back to the U-Haul store. And, if it miraculously made it there, I'd swear my sickly arthritic grandmother had driven the thing the whole time.

A few minutes later, giving me plenty of time to recover and compose myself, Sheila walked up the driveway with the two dogs. She gave me her usual lecture about taking unnecessary risks, which I always treat as a compliment and always thank her for. But this time, as a way of showing my superior judgment on all things mechanical, I added, "I don't know what you are going on about. I made it up here, didn't I?" Maybe that was a comment too far, but I would like to point out that there are times that if the words "don't" and "stupid" were removed from my wife's vocabulary, she would have nothing left to say to me.

After the first couple of minutes of whatever-she-said later, my two weeks of bachelor life might as well have never existed. Still, the truth was that I should have been eternally grateful, bowing to my wife's feet in fact, because she hadn't walked up and started screaming, not about the truck and the driveway, but about my actions and choices that had brought her to this place. Not wanting to belabor the point, with a contrived look of concern on my face and a plaintive plea of "The cats, the cats," I backed out of the discussion and headed upstairs to check on them.

I had brought the cats to Igo on the well-intentioned promise that their lives were more important than my own, and I had planned on keeping them holed up until they became accustomed to their new home. But they had always come running enthusiastically whenever I whistled for them, tails in the air, and I thought they might just do that in their new surroundings. So before unloading the U-Haul I took them out, one at a time, to look around their new home. Each cat in turn followed me around the house and then the garage, never too far away and always keeping an eye on me. This was encouraging and, with Sheila helping, we let them all outside. The nervous little herd followed us around in exactly the same way, always staying in sight and never too far away, exploring their new home. For the next hour we hovered around the cats while they hovered around us, and by lunchtime they had found places to sleep, and that was about it. They might as well have signed an agreement stating that they understood the situation, which was comforting but unlikely. So over the next few weeks I spent time with each of them, until I was sure they understood that this was their new home. The dogs looked after themselves. Their problem has always been that they don't understand the meaning of the phrases "Git," "Go away," and "Leave me alone!"

It was hard to tell whether Sheila's optimism about our move was real or she was just feigning, I couldn't tell. But her arrival with the U-Haul had brought up our last delivery from the outside world, and it was a very real reminder that, in yet one more way, we were on our own. We unloaded the U-Haul (together I can move anything), stacking yet more boxes in the garage, along with what little furniture might be useful in our new life, which wasn't much. However, the wife did upgrade my bachelor pad in the back of the garage to a full bed with a set of sheets and pillows, and then piled an even higher row of boxes around the bed.

With everything unloaded, the wife started rummaging through the still unopened boxes I'd brought up two weeks before. She magically found a change of clothes for me, and fresh out of excuses, I was forced to hose off my caked-on grime. This ignominious event marked the end of my feral life; along with two weeks of being able to hear my own thoughts and a fleeting sense of freedom that I had forgotten could even exist. But on the bright side, at least at night I wouldn't be alone on the mountain, and now that Sheila was here I could sleep more soundly. Because the secret to surviving in bear country is not to be able to outrun a bear, which is highly unlikely, but just to be a little quicker than whomever you're with.

The next morning, with a second pair of eyes to help me see, it became clear that my outstanding successes of the previous couple of weeks were not that much after all. More like negligible, at least compared to what needed to be done just to get us out of the elements, and forget about building a comfortable home. While I had been working on my own I must have had lower objectives, but by the end of our first morning together I started to get an idea of the real task in front of me. Well I thought I did, but it's hard to get good a sense of something you don't know much about, and it's even harder when you know nothing at all. In retrospect, even after that morning's radical reassessment I still didn't have a clue of what was really involved, and probably at this point in our adventure it was a far, far better thing that I didn't.

Even getting creek water up to the house, the centerpiece of the last two week's achievements, wasn't that useful. I had hoped for a different decision, but apparently we agreed that the last thing we needed to do right now was drink bacteria-ridden creek water. This was a smart move, even if I didn't think of it, as I had no idea where the nearest hospital was and we couldn't have afforded to go anyway. So, we erred on the side of caution and used creek water for washing and bottled water for drinking, at least until we could get a well drilled.

There had been a lot less erring and far less caution when I was working by myself, but in spite of Sheila's ability to make the future more complicated, for me, I was relieved when the royal *we* decided that the house was uninhabitable. For Sheila it was the rodents, though I thought they were the least of the house's problems. So we christened our derelict house the "mouse-house" and retreated, chased out by a classless chorus of squeaky little jeers. We retreated back to the garage and, as we were already there with nowhere else to go, decided to build out the back half and make it our home for the time being. The Plan, there always seemed to be a plan, was to upgrade the garage into a temporary living space and then figure out the "what" and the "how" to tackling the house. We decided the garage was to become our new home, and making this a reality became my sole responsibility.

Our first weeks working together had nothing to do with building, though. Before any construction could begin, all the junk, mess, broken things, rotten things, and abandoned things from in and around the house and garage had to be trucked off to the county dump. We had to tear down and tear off decayed and broken parts of the house. There were broken windows, broken pipes, broken doors and even broken walls. Everything was broken. If it had been left to me, I would have continued stepping over the piles of junk, as had everyone else before us, but as this was teamwork I cleaned it up instead.

Stacked high and overflowing with the accumulated products of decay and neglect, the mini-truck was perfect for its role of hauling debris to the dumps. (Meaning that it was old enough that some extra scratches or careless dings I made loading and unloading it only added to its authenticity.) And the wife and I were working as a team in a way we never had to in our former lives; when our decisions were more about command and control than anything else. Now, with our backs against the wall, making good decisions had become a matter of mutual survival. So you would think, with so much else that needed doing, that there would have been different priorities. But on the second day of this cleanup, Sheila helped me understand that a garden hose supplying cold water for a shower wasn't good enough. This was explained to me, as well as the fact that I needed to do something about it, maybe in my spare time.

I've never bothered with life's little vanities, and being European I haven't worried much about body odor either. So I did my best to point out some realities about mountain living—leaky roofs, holes in walls, bears, winter, things like that. I also tried to explain (based on my personal experience during the previous two weeks) that in the absence of the American mania for ablutions body odor reached a peak, got about as bad as it was going to get, and then seemed to dissipate some. But in one of those yin and yang moments of married life, it was explained to me that this was one of those incredibly unlikely times that I was wrong. I was made to realize that we needed hot water, a real shower and, by the way, my wife was still a female! I was stumped again.

Heat and water, I was halfway there. We had water but no means of heating it, and the only sign that water had ever been heated was a concrete pad where a propane tank once sat. There was no tank there now. The only alternative was to use electricity but, at this early stage of my evolution, electricity was just so much incomprehensible magic. No matter, it was my task to make hot water happen, and if I was to avoid appearing useless and avoid hearing the word "stupid" on an even more frequent basis, it was a case of "git'er dun".

That said, have you ever wondered why British cars are as bad they are? Well I came from the Land of Perpetual Amateurs, and after reading this you might understand better. My innovative bathroom design maintained a country charm. It consisted of a hose with a lawn sprinkler tied to an over-hanging tree branch, and the water heated using a solar setup that I'd designed myself.

Apparently there were a couple of problems with this, idiosyncrasies that I hadn't noticed while I was putting it together, but they came to my attention not long after the wife finished her first shower. First off, the water squirting out of lawn sprinkler caused the scrawny branch it was tied onto to wave around wildly, requiring some quick footwork just to keep up with it. Then, the shower's floor, which was simply the available combination of dirt and pine needles, turned to mud and splashed up slightly faster than it washed off feet and legs. I tried this for myself and it was true, there was just no way of leaving the shower without your feet and legs covered in mud, which sort of defeated the purpose of the shower in the first place. I hadn't been expecting so many problems from something so simple.

However, the worst of the negative feedback was about the temperature of the water. The shower's water was gravity-fed from the holding tank and heated by a version of the 1970 era, VW van's solar shower. I admit that these were impaired memories, but I vaguely remembered seeing a black plastic bag that had been left on the roof of a van to heat up during the day. This sketchy memory, along with the fact that anything left out in the Shasta

County sun reached a temperature that would melt lead, annealed together to give me the idea for a solar shower.

The previous day I had driven to Home Depot, determined to find something, anything, I could use to heat water. I had no idea what that might be, but wandering around lost I came across some rolls of black plastic irrigation pipe, about a half-inch in diameter. The pipe was cheap, which drew me to it immediately, and I bought a 200-foot roll of it. The idea was to spread the plastic pipe out in loose coils on the south-facing slope, between the water tank and the shower. Cold creek water from the holding tank was to be fed in one end and, two hundred feet of Shasta sun heated pipe later, hot water at a perfect shower temperature was to come out the other end. *Perfect* turned out to be an exaggeration. The failing of the system was that the first water out of the heating coils had been sitting out in the sun all day and would remove skin on contact, and once that had flushed through the water turned suddenly cold.

I tried defending the solar shower, but it was clear that its idiosyncrasies were not going to be forgiven and I needed to find a better way to heat water. Electricity was still beyond my understanding, which left me looking at propane as a last resort. This would have been fine, but the last attempted delivery of propane to the house, and that was some several years back, ended up with the propane truck in our seasonal creek.

The problem was (there's always a problem to living on the side of a mountain) that the house sits at the top of the very steep driveway. Which wouldn't matter, but propane tends to get ordered when it's needed most, normally in the middle of winter, which is also when ice tends to form on steep driveways. Years ago, a propane delivery driver, new to the area, had asked Roy to show him where the mouse-house was, and with Roy on board the two had started up the driveway in the propane truck. In case you are unfamiliar with propane delivery trucks, they're mobile versions of the propane tanks you see on the six o'clock news blowing sky high during natural disasters in the South.

In low gear, engine roaring, butt cheeks gripping vinyl seat, all was going well… until the ice patch. If there is any one thing to notice about Roy it's that he's smart, and realizing this reversal of fortunes he did what I'm sure the saner among us would do. As soon as the truck started to slide backwards he opened his door and jumped, leaving the driver to decide his own course of action.

Personally, I don't like to think what it must feel like to be sitting inside a vehicle that's effectively a giant bomb, sliding backwards at an increasing rate of speed down an icy hill before dropping into a rocky creek at the bottom. But apparently the driver was a good—no, give the man his due—a *great* company man, and rode the truck backwards all the way down the driveway, dropped over the embankment, crashed into the seasonal creek and miraculously didn't blow up. On the other hand, he didn't make any more deliveries to this address either, which in turn years later did nothing towards helping me improve the shower arrangements for my lovely wife.

By now we were both beginning to realize that, as lifestyles go, living in the country was a little more difficult than we had expected. We barely had electricity, creek water for cold showers, no drinking water, a bed at the back of the garage for a bedroom, no cooking facilities, no refrigeration, no washing facilities, no heating for the winter and no cooling for the summer. All of which would have been fine, but the house was uninhabitable and had to be completely rebuilt before winter, and on top of all this I had an extra burden. I knew that one morning the wife would wake up, sit bolt up in bed and let loose another of her blood curling screams; right after it sunk in that she really was living in the back of a garage.

These were very different problems from the ones I had been overpaid to solve in my computer career. Computing is a comforting rational world without limitations, but this world was different. There were nothing but limitations, mostly mine, and there also seemed to be a lot of very hard work involved in getting anything done, limitations aside. And it would have been nice to pretend that I was up to the task and all that was necessary was a few weeks of banging nails into bits of wood, but I knew nothing. I had essentially no tools, no experience, and we had only the thinnest of finger holds enabling us to live on the property. Then Sheila found a rough hole in the concrete floor with a large pipe staring out of the bottom of it.

She came across it while rearranging some of the boxes in our corner of the garage. Actually, this was the same hole that I had carefully placed a box over (because I didn't like the look of it) the night I moved into the garage, and then forgotten about. It was in reality an abandoned toilet drain. Hardly the answer to most people's dreams, but this crude hole in the concrete floor showed that there *should* be a septic system buried somewhere close. We didn't know how to find one if it was there, but choosing not to look in the gift horse's mouth we decided there *must* be a septic system. Suddenly, the plan to make the back half of the garage into a home finally had some reality to it. All we needed to get by for the next few months was something we could call a bedroom and something resembling a bathroom. The hole in the garage floor had changed everything.

I lied a little about my lack of skills. It was an innocent enough omission by my standards and doesn't make the slightest bit of difference anyway. In my former life I had remodeled a bathroom, in retrospect badly, but the lasting lesson from this experience was, "If a plumber can do it, I can do it." This slogan needs a happy face stuck on the end of it, but if you think about most of the plumbers you've met, you can see my point. From that remodel job I learned a little about tiling, a little about electrical, and a little about plumbing, which was the expertise I brought to the garage. And fortunately, this was before I had even heard about building inspectors.

After trying to scavenge some pieces of lumber from the piles of rubbish around the house, I made yet another of (what were to become) the near endless journeys to Home Depot to buy supplies for the mouse-house. It was the start of the time in my life when I wandered around for hours, lost in the isles of Home Depot, staring at what I had no idea, and wondering what I could have possibly done to have deserved this fate.

Still, in spite of a predictably shaky start, the interior walls for our new home got built, and I even managed to hit a nail on its head, though hardly ever squarely. With the walls up, I plumbed and wired, built a tiled shower stall, installed a sink and toilet, hung two doors, replaced the broken windows and ended up with an indoor bathroom. I repeat—this was before I had even heard of building inspectors.

While I was building, Sheila used the time to look into the future and saw that our garage home would eventually be used as a guesthouse. That would have to be in some far distant time when the mouse-house was finished. I stayed out of the visionary thing, being busy with hammering, sawing, screwing, soldering, plumbing and things like that. But with its future in mind, the shower was finished with decorative tile trim and sliding glass doors. The interior walls were finished with tongue and groove cedar boards and, once the major construction was over, the wife added unnecessarily expensive towel bars, soap dishes, flower holders, fancy mirrors and such, and of course, light fixtures. Her fetish for spending perfectly good money on expensive light fixtures started with this bathroom but continues unchecked to this day.

With Sheila adding her final flourishes I made the technological leap into the twenty-first century, became an electrician, and installed an electric water heater. I'd started to do things "to code" after hearing about building inspectors, and installed the heater with its own separate circuit and heavy-duty wiring. An electric heater was the cheapest and, more importantly, the quickest way of getting the wife hot water and a shower, and had the added benefit of putting the oft-repeated horrors of the solar shower behind us. With that we moved in some of our bedroom furniture and the back of the garage became our home. And though I didn't see the point to most of what had been done, together we had built a place to live. If I had been left to mine own devices, I would have still been wearing the same clothes I first arrived in and gone feral by now.

Talking about cleaning up (never a priority with me), we bought a washing machine and set it up in the driveway using a garden hose and a long extension cord. And though our circumstances might have looked primitive to city folk, in a little over a month we had built ourselves a place to live. We had walls, windows and doors, a bedroom and a bed, a closet to hang up our clothes, and we had retired the roll-of-toilet-paper-on-end-of-the-shovel, upgrading that arrangement with indoor plumbing and a bathroom. Though, that turned out to be just temporary.

The Mouse-House

It had taken a month to build out the back of the garage into something habitable, but it wasn't only construction that filled our time. This move hadn't been from one tidy suburb to another, we might as well have moved to a foreign country, and in a way we had. There were unfamiliar sights and sounds, a lot of unfamiliar smells, unfamiliar tasks and unfamiliar work. During those first weeks we began to understand that there was more to living in the country than just sitting around contentedly staring at the pretty scenery, and (who would have ever thought it possible?) pets were actually useful.

Since settling in to their new home, our four cats had been busy for a change. They had found a new purpose in life and had taken over the night shift—chasing down and eating their way through the rodent population in the mouse-house. In the middle of the night we could hear frantic scurrying as small paws chased even smaller paws, and in the morning I would wake up to find multiple headless and bottomless mouse carcasses scattered around the driveway. From what I saw lying around, the cats had to have two distinctly different schools of thought on how to eat a mouse. The choice was between the crunchy brain-dripping heads, or the meaty intestine-laden back ends, one or the other, but for some reason never both.

I tried not to take too much interest in these half-eaten carcasses, except to note that I didn't have to buy cat food. But early one morning, the wife got up, walked outside and stepped on a half of a mouse corpse. They were cold and wet under foot, and she announced her surprise, to me and everybody for a mile around for that matter, with a canyon-splitting scream that left the dogs frozen in place with demented looks on their faces and the cats scattering in all directions. Suddenly, dead mice had become important.

It had been an accident waiting to happen. And it would have been nice if the cats had got over this fussiness and eaten the whole mouse, or worked something out between them so both halves got eaten. But that emphatic early morning scream meant time was up, and I had to find the mouse parts in the morning before the wife did.

You probably judge me heartless about these rodents' deaths, but I wasn't. Initially, I was queasy about this nightly massacre; first thing in the morning carefully burying what remained of their little carcasses with a few kind words and an apology. However, with each passing day on the mountain, and my own circumstances getting worse by the day, there was less and less time to worry about these small deaths. The only concern I had when I scooped up the body parts with the shovel was that the untidy remains were heaved far enough away that my wife didn't tread on another one ever again.

The cats' work hadn't been in vain, though. The first room needing work in the mouse-house was the smallest, in the worst shape, and the filthiest. It was a priority because it contained all the essentials to get the mouse-house up and running, which also made it the most difficult. It was an eight-foot by eight-foot room built off to the side of the mouse-house and, at one time in its past, had been a combination bathroom and utility room. It was where the electrical power came into the house, where the abandoned propane line, the abandoned water line and the disused sewer line disappeared to who knows where. And probably because it was the darkest room with the most decay, this also seemed to have been a popular place for the rodents.

It was a claustrophobic windowless room that stank of dead animals. Its plywood floor had completely rotted away and, for that matter, so had most of the floor joists. The ceiling and walls had been ripped apart by scavengers, looking for the copper pipe and wiring to sell. It was difficult if not dangerous to move around in, and before I could try my hand at reconstruction there was one disgusting job to be done, before anything else.

The disgusting day of reckoning had arrived. There had been plenty of time to give this some thought and plan it out, so I was mentally and physically prepared. I stepped into an extra-baggy plastic-paper suit (the type used by house painters), zipped it up, taped shut the sleeves and collar, donned a facemask and goggles, and finished off the outfit with a pair of rubber gloves. Looking like an under-funded Russian spaceman, I maneuvered carefully into the semi-darkness of the utility room, balancing precariously on the remnants of the rotted floor joists, and started the cleanup.

The first task was to tear off what remained of the sheetrock from the ceiling. As each piece of sheetrock came away, years of accumulated rodent poop hiding behind it, multiple masses of unidentified feces and finally desiccated rodent bodies rained down on me. All of which added to the realization that the next time I do something like this I needed to add a hat to my protective garb. Even the dust smelt evil; and in spite of wearing a full facemask, every few minutes I would have to back out of this filthy hole, pull the mask off, and gulp some fresh air.

In one of these gulps for fresh air, dripping sweat inside my sealed painter's suit, covered in a light layer of desiccated mouse poop and itching with fiberglass insulation, I realized that there were two things I'd never needed before but were now required—gumption and backbone. And for some reason I thought back wistfully to those clever little computer days, my Camelot, when I had no idea what gumption was or that a backbone even existed.

With the sheetrock torn out and the contents of the ceiling and walls lying where they had all fallen, at the bottom of the crawl space, the worst of the cleanup was over. I wheeled in my brand new $60, industrial-strength shop vac. I had bought it for just this job. Still encased in my protective suit I gleefully, yes gleefully, sucked up the mouse poop along with the unidentified lumps, then the urine soaked wall insulation and every other piece of best-left-undefined mess, filth, and stench. (The only other time I'd seen a vacuum work this well was in a Tom and Jerry cartoon.) Each time the shop vac filled up its tank, I emptied out the contents into a plastic garbage bag, carefully tied-off the bag and threw it in the back of the mini-truck. And with the last of the bags loaded, I rushed the contagious load to the county dump. The dump is located on the far side of Igo, in the flats, and is the one convenience to living here.

Not caring much, but having been covered in the stuff all morning, I probably looked pretty much like the load I was hauling in. The effect must have been outstanding, even for the dumps, because as the nice young lady reached out her office window to take my money, she had a look on her face like someone was holding a small turd under her nose. I didn't care. I drove over to the unloading dock, threw the plastic bags of mouse poop over the edge of the pit, then peeled off the painter's suit as well as my never-to-be-worn-again clothes, down to my underwear, and threw them into the dump, too. I left still feeling incurably dirty and hurried home, bouncing the mini-truck back up the driveway, sliding to a halt outside the garage and bolting for the shower, where I stayed until it ran out of hot water. Even then the idea of being immersed in clean water seemed like a good idea, and I spent the rest of the afternoon submerged in a local swimming hole.

So this was how we started to rebuild the mouse-house. With what I know now I'm sure that it would have been far, far easier for me to have burned the mouse-house to the ground and then rebuilt a new house from the ashes up than to have rehabbed the mess I started with. During the next four years I would understand this more completely, but for now I was optimistic and looking forward to reconstructing the newly cleaned-out utility room.

Gotta Go Feed

It wasn't that important to us during our first months here, but we didn't have the time or inclination to introduce ourselves to our neighbors. They wouldn't have been that easy to find anyway, tucked away up equally remote driveways on their own equally large pieces of the mountain. Even so, there wasn't exactly a rush by our neighbors to say hello. But now that we have lived here for a few years, and qualify as being locals, of sorts, we can see that the community prefers to sit back and check out the new arrivals. And during our first few months here, our neighbors were likely going through an unhurried vetting of us. Either that or they were looking on in disbelief and waiting for the inevitable, with front row seats on some upcoming disasters.

This is a tough place to live, and gaining entry into this tight community takes years. Becoming part of the core of the community can only happen over a lifetime, and though there was nothing out-of-the-ordinary to notice about him, a great example of a lifelong local was Jim. Born here, with a family stretching back generations, he looked like this rural community had grown up around him than rather the other way around. He was one of the few old-timers remaining and authentic in a way that would be hard to reproduce today.

Jim operated heavy equipment, a risky line of work that he had been in his whole life, but it was a routine day on a routine job that finally bit Jim. He was putting in a road and had stopped to clear some branches from in front of his dozer, and while his back was turned the dozer's brake released and it started to roll forwards. A branch caught Jim's foot as he tried to get out the way, and the dozer methodically rolled over the top of him. Normally this would have been a death sentence, but there must have been a hollow spot in the ground where Jim went down. The paramedics found him lying flat on his back and miraculously still alive and conscious, but his guts were squirted twenty feet out from his side.

The first on the horrific scene was a local volunteer paramedic. With only his instincts to guide him he took off his fireman's jacket then went to the far end of Jim's guts and walked back towards Jim, picking up the guts as he went and cradling them in the jacket. Jim looked up from the ground and asked simply enough, "What do you think?" This was an old friend lying there and not someone that needed lying to. "I think you're going to die, Jim." Well, this wasn't exactly what Jim wanted to hear. "Well f%@* you then," was his defiant reply.

I've seen tough on the movies, I've heard about tough, but I've never heard about someone that tough—lying on his back in the mud with his stomach split wide open, looking up at a friend holding his disembodied guts in his jacket. How could anyone have the presence of mind to find a comeback, any comeback, with both feet in the grave? But after a medivac flight, a month's stay in the hospital, then another couple of months recuperating, Jim was back driving his dozer.

In the years after this accident, I occasionally saw Jim driving round Igo in his canary yellow Porsche 914. He always had its removable top off. The sports car was out of character with the area, but even more incongruous was the oxygen tank. It sat upright in the passenger seat, with a seatbelt around it, while Jim drove wearing a clip-on oxygen mask. But eventually, what twelve tons of dozer couldn't do to him, emphysema did. In the last few days before he died he must have known, and made a point to visit all his old friends, to say goodbye.

The community turned out for Jim's wake. It was held at the Igo Inn, filling it easily and overflowing into the parking lot. And although I didn't know the man I was invited to his wake anyway, as was the rest of Shasta County judging by the crowd that turned out.

It's customary for a wake around these parts; friends and relatives arrived in their pickup trucks, ice chests stocked with beer, planning to make an afternoon of it. Some of the guests stayed respectfully seated inside the grange, wanting to hear what others said about Jim and wait their turn to speak themselves. But mostly they sat outside and drank beer, only wandering inside for a while to stand at the back of the old hall and listen, until they needed another cold one, and then walking back outside to swap some more stories. It was a casual affair and late in the day, when the parking lot ran dry, the wake simply relocated to the Beer Bar and drank into the night. Jim would have been proud; it had been a celebration of his life and it was a closure for the community.

The fact that everybody I'd met in Igo was welcoming, always made a point to ask how I was doing, and waved when passing on the road, all made no difference. I was just unprepared for this community. It was so different from anything I had known, especially the part about being friendly to perfect strangers. My move to Igo had turned out to be far more than a drive up an Interstate, it had been a move to a culture I couldn't have dreamt existed, didn't understand, and one it was going to take some time to become a part of, if that day would ever come. Standing around during the wake, like a bump on a log, I found myself rethinking that unproven adage, "Change is good." I thought the aphoristic wisdom needed some clarification "... especially if it happens to someone else!"

Simply trying to ingratiate our way into this community would be pointless, no worse, we would look ridiculous. Acceptance here was something earned. But after a couple of socially barren months we thought that we should at least make an attempt, and offer a humble invitation to dinner. And it would a humble offering, because the best we could offer guests was sitting on a couple of splintery wooden benches and eating off the picnic table we had pulled from the trash piles behind the garage. But we did have a dining room, of sorts.

The mouse-house had something that, at one time, had been a deck. At the far end of this too-dangerous-to-walk-on and dilapidated-assemblage-of-rotten-wood, was a screen porch. (A screen porch is exactly what it sounds like, a screened-in porch to keep the bugs out.) This screen porch, although built at the same time as the deck, had survived in better shape because it had a roof over it that had protected it from the elements. Even so, it must have looked considerably better when it was built forty years ago than it did today. Today it had no screens, its inadequate wooden skeleton could hardly hold up its roof, and its spongy plywood floor sagged under each step on it. And although it was past its time, tired, and reminiscent of a long-faded movie star close to her final days, some of its charm couldn't be lost.

It still had views stretching out to a distant southern horizon, summer breezes carried the scent of the dry pine forest, and a nurturing circle of redwoods kept it comfortably sheltered from the sun. As a dinner spot, it had some plusses to it. So we carried the wooden benches and picnic table over from where we had found them two months before, and made the screen porch our open-air dining room, at least for the remainder of the summer. Now we had a place to serve the dinner, the question was who to invite?

Roy was the first person to extend a friendly hand to us (he was accepting a beer at the time, but close enough), so there was a courteous symmetry to him being the first guest to the mouse-house. He was also the only person we knew at the time, so the choice was easy, and because of his talent to sense dinner across the country mile between our two houses (about the same time that I first thought of it) he went on to become a welcome regular at our dinner table. Still, the first time Roy came to dinner was the equivalent of inviting the natives over for the first time, and we didn't know what to expect.

What little we knew about Roy was from the conversation I'd had with him at the Beer Bar. We knew he hadn't been raised in his barn and that he had been civilized at some time in his life, but had no idea how far he had devolved. I had started to turn feral in two weeks but Roy had been living that way for thirty years, so who wouldn't wonder? Sheila certainly did, and I had to spend a good part of the afternoon before the dinner apologizing for all of Roy's imagined shortcomings, my lack of judgment for inviting him in the first place, and finishing with what I intended to do when the whole thing went badly wrong. This was before Sheila had said a word to the man.

Igo's lightly employed, a good example of which would be Roy, start their evenings early. At 5 o'clock sharp, Roy's faithful old Honda strained its way up the scary steep driveway. I stared from our rotten front deck impressed, not about the car, but at the precise knowledge Roy showed coming up our driveway, without requiring a new suspension. Roy picked his route through the potholes and, blame this on a suspicious mind, I wondered once more who might have been cultivating medicinal products in my garage. But putting idle speculations aside, more importantly, he arrived wearing a clean shirt and not the yellow-stained, wife-beater T-shirt Sheila had predicted. The clean shirt was encouraging and maybe I wouldn't be spending the next few weeks apologizing for having invited him.

What about our side of this strange social event? It was probably a little early into our rebuilding to have invited anyone to dinner, especially someone as important as the mayor. But we talked about this and decided that, mayor or no mayor, Roy lived in a goat barn so we didn't get overly concerned about our hovel. Still, there was a large hole in the floor where our kitchen should have been, so Sheila had assembled a dinner from a store-bought chicken, a box of potato salad, and a couple of bottles of cheap wine.

Never one for social niceties, I started the evening by blurting out the one question that was on my mind, "So Roy, how on Earth did you come to be the mayor?" I had just assumed he was the mayor, but he wasn't. There was both relief and disappointment to this, but mostly relief. Years before, Roy had been driving through a real town with a real mayor, had seen the "Mahoney for Mayor" sign and thought of a better use for it. So he uprooted it from its manicured suburban front lawn, drove it home and staked it conspicuously outside his goat barn; giving the goat barn its current unjustified air of respectability.

I'd been imagining other town officials. The worst of which was a tobacco chewing inbred with a badge, an IQ less than half the number of his few remaining teeth, breathing halitosis directly into my face while making sure that we had an "understanding". But as Roy explained, there was nothing official to Igo and the place was essentially lawless. I wasn't sure whether to be relieved or not.

Sheila had just finished laying out the dinner on our resurrected picnic table. We were just about to sit down when Roy looked at the food and suddenly, as if an alarm bell had gone off, rushed from the porch with the inexplicable explanation, "I've gotta go feed... I'll be right back." He took off in his car, disappearing down the driveway and returning ten minutes later as if nothing had happened.

I'd never heard the phrase "Gotta go feed," but I've since learned that it's best said with a flat affect, in a slow and depressed tone, and it's the one reason for leaving any place at any time that's understood by everyone in these parts. Even if you've spent the entire day at the Beer Bar, at sometime you have to go feed your animals.

Even with this interruption our one-course dinner didn't last long, and we spent the rest of the warm evening sitting on the screen porch, finishing off the wine, and swapping stories under a mountain sky that glowed with stars. It was our first experience of just how good a country life could be. And far from being feral, Roy was entertaining. Though, this only served to remind me that I was missing, the way you might miss oxygen, all the carelessly bright friends I had left behind by moving here. And even if Roy's mind hadn't slowed in his thirty years here, he reminded me of an outpost, an outlier of civilization, and I saw my future. I started to dread that our move to this remote mountain had been a self-imposed banishment from civilization.

Out of wine and out of stories, we left Roy to sleep it off on our dusty couch while we went to bed in our garage. Still unconvinced, Sheila locked the garage door behind us, jammed a block of wood against it, and kept the dogs in for the night. I went to sleep listening to a well-organized list of all that was wrong with Roy.

When we got up the following morning Roy was still fast asleep, but we needed to clean up from the previous night. So initially we crept around, trying not to wake him, then we moved about as usual, not really caring whether we woke him or not, until finally we wondered what it would take to wake him. And while we cleaned we looked for the chicken carcass. We couldn't find the thing anywhere, and how could a chicken carcass have vanished anyway? Literally, the only place we hadn't looked, and were not about to look, was under Roy's blanket.

It was a joke (we hoped), but we were also miles from the Zone of Civilization, on the side of a mountain where banjo music would have been an innovation, staring at somebody snoring on our couch who had been living in a goat barn for a third of a century. He might have turned feral in ways we didn't want to think about and neither of us wanted to look under that blanket, and we didn't. What we didn't know was that just about any large animal living in the hills could have stolen the chicken carcass, it's the preferred take-away food of bears, and the surprise should have been that was all that had been made off with, including our sleeping guest. At the time though, it just deepened the mystery surrounding Roy, and started a tradition we've had since of blaming him for all kinds of things that have nothing to do with him.

The morning sun continued its leisurely creep across the screen porch floor until it reached the couch, with Roy still asleep on it. Finally he woke up, mumbled, "I gotta go feed", again, and with a parting "Thanks for the dinner," stumbled out to his car. He drove down the scary steep driveway with the same precision he had come up it, and I went back to my daily grind of reconstructing the mouse-house.

It wasn't a happy time. My early days of construction resembled a fruitless struggle in the tar pits of ignorance. The more

I worked on the house the worse things got, and to give you an idea of how bad things were, eventually I was forced to buy some books about construction. I didn't actually read them. But by looking at the pictures, showing how construction should be done, and seeing how it shouldn't be done while pulling the mouse-house apart, I started to get some ideas.

I also started to appreciate tools, and not just tools to get by with, as I had been doing, but tools that actually encouraged good results. My most useful tool up to this time was my universal screwdriver-chisel-pry-bar combination. Before I'd ruined it, this had been a simple screwdriver. I replaced it with a new screwdriver and a real chisel and a real pry bar, and started to accumulate real tools. I learned to use them, and after several costly replacements to even take care of them. And yes, tools were an improvement, but I still had no idea what I was doing or how long it would take to make the mouse-house habitable. Not a clue, it was a never-ending mystery that I happened to be lost in.

So every morning, not really knowing what I was doing, I got up and spent the day, head down, dealing with the one task in front of me, hoping to get done whatever simple task that was, and reduce the list of things needed doing by one. That might have been the plan, but unfortunately each new task started opened up more problems, adding even more work to be done and less time to do it in.

When I pulled apart one visibly rotted section of the house I found the whole side was rotted. None of it was worth saving or should be or could be, and a small job replacing some siding developed a life of its own. I ended up rebuilding the complete side of the house. And not being paid by the hour, with dwindling cash and winter on its way, this one step forward and several steps backwards did absolutely nothing to improve my mood.

What had I got myself into? I had no idea what I was doing and the future was looking bleaker by the day. I was lost, with bad things happening all around. However, there was one (and only one) advantage to rebuilding the side of the house. It allowed me to put in a sixteen-foot high panel of floor-to-ceiling windows where there had been only an absurdly small window looking out at the best view on the whole property.

Up to this time, I hadn't thought about making any improvements, but the idea for the picture windows was gifted to me. I had already removed the entire front wall (except for the one post I'd left in the middle to hold the roof up), and as I looked out through where the wall used to be, genius that I was, I exclaimed, "Wow, what a view." It was that simple, I had become Architect.

We put triangle windows, with their angles matched to the slope of the roof, on top of eight-foot sliding glass doors, creating a wall of glass. The view was no longer a mere peak down the valley, as it had been, but because of the window's height the view included the ponderosas standing over the house, which somehow managed to bring the outside inside. It was a great improvement, in a house that could stand some improving.

At some point in the house's unfortunate past, the interior had been painted battleship gray from top to bottom. The walls, the floor the ceiling, the stairs, every surface, everything that could have been painted battleship gray was painted battleship gray. I probably had the marijuana growers to thank for this artful upgrade, but the inspired paint scheme added an unnecessary gloom to the house, even beyond what the decay and neglect had given the place. So the new wall of windows made the place a little less depressing, and gave me hope that we might end up with something more than a badly repaired ugly little house. This could even be an opportunity to build the mouse-house into something I wouldn't mind living in.

Rebuilding the front wall also gave me one other opportunity, one I wasn't looking for. It was my first time on a ladder in decades, and although I was only sixteen feet off the ground it felt entirely new, just not in a good way. I hadn't noticed before, but since I was about twelve years old (when I climbed to the top of everything my sticky little paws could get a grip on) I've been less and less interested in climbing, and ladders were in effect a new experience. But it wasn't their newness that bothered me, it was the several opportunities they gave me to think about falling off things this late in life, when I couldn't expect to bounce as well as I once did.

I noticed that I was often standing on one leg, on the very top of my foldout ladder (normally on the exact spot where it said "NO STEP"), with the other leg waving around to help balance while reaching as far as I could trying to hammer in a nail or something. Several times I found myself suddenly dangling by one arm, with a death grip around a piece of whatever I was building at the time, and the ladder clattering down to the floor underneath me. Oddly enough, this would happen so fast I didn't know what had happened. Not a clue. But some instinct in me always found something to blindly grab onto as the ladder went away, leaving me dangling too far off the ground to jump down, and making a plaintiff call to the wife to "Get the ladder, get the ladder, get the ladder!!!!" I lie, there was nothing ever plaintive about it and it was unprintable except for the word *ladder*.

Still, trying to keep a positive view on things, I had no boss, there were only self-imposed deadlines, and my only real complaint was the unfamiliar heat of a Shasta County summer, and even that I could avoid if I wanted to. On days when the sun boiled off what little good spirits I'd started the morning with, I would stop whatever I was doing and head for Whiskeytown Lake. (Whiskeytown is a clear warm-water lake just a few miles away.) With the kayaks strapped to the top of the mini-truck, Sheila and I would drive out to the lake, paddle around the shoreline until we found a private beach, then hang out swimming and sunbathing until late in the evening, when the day's heat was finally done.

Still, as wonderful as this lake was, it hardly made up for the many downsides to my new life. I was still working through losing my job, and every day I missed the plump generous lifestyle my paycheck had allowed. At the time, there wasn't much about my new life that was plump or generous, and the move to Igo seemed more than just a step down the social ladder—it felt as if I had fallen off the thing. And while on the subject of falling, it wasn't just ladders that I was falling off. Just as painful and a lot more embarrassing, I was falling through holes.

Before starting my career in construction I would have thought it impossible to fall through a large hole in a floor. But when you spend your days carrying bulky things in front of you (blocking all forward visibility), and you're walking through a construction zone riddled with holes, then a hole becomes just one more opportunity to learn something.

The mechanics of stepping into a hole are simple but the effect is huge, and you have to picture the exact moment the mistake happens to understand it. In slow motion, the leading leg is poised over say... the center of the three-foot wide hole. The unfortunate person the leg belongs to is leaning slightly forward, in a normal walking stance, holding a sheet of plywood that's obscuring all forward vision. At this time, the back foot becomes a hinge point, staying in place as the rest of the soon-to-be-even-more-unfortunate person pitches forward. The front foot leads and the rest follows not far behind. By the time the unfortunate's torso has reached floor level it's traveling at a good rate of speed and it's remarkably horizontal. This enables the chest and face to hit the floor on the far side of the hole at exactly the same time, and I can tell you, the effect is startling.

I managed this trick twice. The first time I thought it could never ever happen again, but the second time convinced me to devote a considerable part of my waking consciousness to looking for holes, before I fall down them. To this day, if I see a hole it gets a scrap piece of plywood nailed over it. It's become one of the very few things I see no reason to put off to later.

It had to be expected. The change from leaning back in a comfortable leather chair musing how to best spend a generous paycheck to a life of real work, where I hefted heavy things around and got hurt doing it, was going to be an awkward one. And although I'm sure most of America slogs through worse on a daily basis, after a few months of working for a living I noticed it wasn't just that my previously soft hands that now looked like a workingman's hands. There were also gouges in my arms and on top of my head, strains and sprains associated with nearly every movement, and that the clear reality of my little life-adventure was becoming harder than I had imagined. Working for a living had turned out to be a minefield of unexpected unpleasantries, and it wasn't just sweat equity being wrung out of this property, there was blood involved.

Normally at the end of a day's work I would lie flat on my back in the middle of the downstairs' floor and not move for hours. I would just lie there in pain, my lower back mostly but there were always other body parts hurting, and periodically roll over to enjoy a close-up view of the rotten plywood floor, and the knowledge that this too would have to be completely replaced at some time.

Lying face down staring at the floor, at the end of a particularly bad day, it occurred to me that Life has a way of looking after us, each in our own special way. And whenever I got really fed up rebuilding the mouse-house and stormed out spluttering about how I couldn't take it anymore. Whenever I couldn't take one more frustrating broken thing in the mouse-house demanding more time and money that I didn't have—there was always an alternative. I could leave the mouse-house, leave that mess behind, and take a short walk to find that there was something else, somewhere else on the property that needed fixing. Each new thing an opportunity, if you are sickeningly optimistic, or a challenge if you are lucky enough to still have youth on your side, or just one more problem to deal with if you are unfortunate enough to be me.

There was a very dead 1985 vintage, four-wheel drive Toyota truck. I had found it behind the barn, where its last repairs had been attempted and the pieces left lying in the dirt. Sheila had named it the "Warthog" because of its good looks, and the day after Roy's dinner at the mouse-house I succeeded in getting the thing to fire up.

An hour here and there, between other fun chores, I had been putting the Warthog back together. And when the old thing spluttered back to life, and announced to the world its resurrection with a thick cloud of oil smoke, it seemed to symbolize so much about this place. Something that was probably perfectly good at one time, had been allowed to fall apart, and had finally been abandoned. It had become my unlikely role in life to restore it and get an education along the way.

The Well

Our neighbors along Woods Canyon get their drinking water straight out of Cow Creek, but then they do a lot of things I wouldn't. The water is probably fine to drink, it certainly looks clear, and I'm sure it's okay once your stomach lining has become accustomed to any twelve-tailed furry bacteria that might be swimming in it. But not wanting to experiment with the stuff, *we*, meaning the more cautious Sheila, decided that well water would be better. It was a perfectly good decision, as we already had enough problems to deal with, except for the one troublesome fact that we didn't have a well.

We needed someone to drill a well. So knowing nothing as usual, this time knowing nothing about wells, or drilling, or whatever it takes to actually get water out of the ground, we sampled our neighbor's opinions and settled on a local driller, Steve. He was the only driller in the area and we were able to reach a decision fairly quickly. Steve was our driller.

That was easy, now all we had to do was to find out where to drill, which wasn't so easy. Not commonly understood, at least by anyone that hasn't had to drill a well, is that the first step isn't finding the water. No, the first step is to find the right person who knows how to find the water. This shouldn't be a problem, but these people come from two very distinct schools of thought. There are drillers and there are diviners. This still might not be a problem, but they don't agree on where to drill, and the one thing they have in common is that they are both equally certain that only they know how to find water.

Even with the two dueling professions to choose from, this wouldn't be a large pool of people to start with anywhere, but in Igo this choice shrunk down to our driller Steve, who was already on board, and Jake, the water diviner. It was a toss up and how could we know which to choose? But considering drilling a dry hole would leave us $10,000 poorer, and still with no water, we thought it best to hedge our bets and give them both a chance, and then use our ignorance on the subject to guide us to a final choice.

Jake charged $50. This was cheap enough that even if it turned out to be so much witchcraft we wouldn't care. A phone call later and we spent a morning two-steps behind our water diviner. We wandered around the property, at least the easily accessible parts, while he told grand stories of finding water where no other could. We knew nothing. We were empty vessels toddling along like two ducklings behind our omniscient water diviner, and I soon realized that this wasn't work for him; it was a calling.

My favorite of his stories was about the water he found in the Mojave Desert. Jake had indicated the spot where the water was to be found, out there in the desert, and apparently the driller came up dry. The problem hadn't been that they were drilling in the middle of a desert or that there was no water for hundreds of miles in any direction, the problem was that the driller had misaligned his rig and hadn't drilled the hole exactly vertically. The driller had drilled down six hundred feet but had ended up three feet off from where he should have been. Three feet off, in the middle of the Mojave Desert, who would have guessed? But the story ended happily, and the day saved, when our diviner dropped a stick of dynamite down the hole. That broke up the rock at the bottom of the hole and allowed the water, those three feet away, to flow into it.

Now nothing is impossible, and I'm not intimating that his story was an exaggeration, but because of some shortcomings in my personality it was hard for me not to burst out laughing. I didn't laugh though, because this was clearly one of those occasions that if you don't believe it won't come true, and then it would have been my fault. As it was, I sported an inexplicable smile for the rest of the divining experience, and hoped I wouldn't be asked to explain what was so funny.

Three times Jake placed a small plastic marker on the ground, placing it so precisely that it gave the impression that an inch or two either way would make all the difference in the world.

Then, finally, he leaned forward deliberately and impaled a thick finger into the soil and announced, "This is where I would drill." Still grinning absurdly, I blurted out in an unnaturally loud voice "Well that's it then!" It was worth the $50, and I recommend it to anyone considering drilling a well, if just for the entertainment value.

The following day we called Steve the driller. He used a totally different method to find water, and it took under a minute. He walked behind the house, glanced around at the general lay of the land, turned to where Sheila and I stood watching, and pointed directly at a stand of ponderosas. "Over there," he announced decisively. The spot he was pointing at was, coincidently, the easiest for him to drive his rig to, get set up, and, most importantly, guaranteed him the best shade while he was drilling.

"Okay then, that's good enough for me." I replied and arranged for him to come out to drill water in a week's time. I reasoned that he wouldn't have made a career drilling in this county if all he came up with were dry holes. So convenient spot or not, I went with his choice and put my money where his mouth was.

The next week, surprisingly early one morning, the sound of heavy equipment coming up the driveway woke the wife and me. We hurried out onto the decaying front deck of the mouse-house, as usual being careful to select what deck boards we stood on and completely avoiding leaning against the railing, to watch this technological marvel. The massive drilling rig powered its way up the scary steep driveway in its compound-low multi-axle drive. (Big as it was, it looked like it would climb a wall if it had to.) It was the cavalry coming to show Nature what the humans could really do, and at the time we could do with a little rescuing.

It was obvious from my first meeting with Steve that he was a true professional. The man knew what he was doing, and watching him maneuver his massive drill rig confirmed this. Once up to the house, he steered his behemoth very precisely around our circular driveway, missing rock outcroppings with inches to spare, with tree limbs scraping down the side of the rig, and his helper out in front directing. Then he stopped the rig and jumped out. After a discussion with his helper, Steve started to very slowly and very carefully back his rig alongside the garage and out toward the drill site.

Beep, beep, beep, beep, beep… I stood back, well out of the way of such professionalism, when all of a sudden there was a *woomph* noise. The ground literally shook, followed by a loud metallic clanging and bashing of big steel things (for what seemed like a very long time), and finishing with the inevitable cloud of dust, rising slowly into the air before gently engulfing the entire garage.

I ran around the side of the garage, trying not to think what had happened, and saw that the backend of the massive drilling rig (which weighed in at some forty tons and cost a mere $450,000) had just dropped through the top of a previously unknown septic tank. Unknown up to now, that is. This had to be the septic tank that our little home in the garage had been innocently using for the last month. The rig was lying on its belly, a slight tilt to one side, with its rear wheels dangling over an unpleasant hole in the ground.

Personal responsibility was a concept that took a long time getting any traction in my life, but as way of penance, nowadays, I assume responsibility for everything, including a septic tank hiding several feet underground. And though I knew nothing about its existence (and by the way what a stupid place to leave a septic tank, and how could anybody have known one was there anyway), as Steve climbed down out of his cab I knew that could all be just so many excuses.

Considering this was his own, personal, $450,000 drilling rig parked in my septic tank, from thirty yards or so Steve's face didn't look so terrible. But as I approached, blubbering apologies, I was also braced to duck and run like hell at the first punch. I needn't have worried though, that day Steve set the gold standard for self-control. This incident convinced me that there must be some genetic factor that gives some people, like Steve, better character than me. It has to be genetics, what else could it be? Steve's father and his father before him were drillers, so probably they had become immune to their expensive rigs falling into septic tanks. I don't know, but much to my relief Steve seemed to gradually accept that I had no reason to put a septic tank there, and that it had been hiding there without my knowledge. And though he maintained a stiff attitude towards me that never encouraged me to get too close to him, an hour later, with amazingly only minor injuries to his rig, using every one of its drive axles along with its support vehicle pulling, the drill rig crawled out of the remains of my septic tank, essentially intact.

If country living was teaching me anything, it was teaching me the importance of *practicality*. Watching the rig's extraction from my septic tank I learned some more country practicality. If it had been my drilling rig that had dropped into a septic tank, I would have decided that was as much of an omen as anyone could expect to see in a lifetime, and headed directly home. But Steve became more set than ever on drilling that hole. It was almost as if he had come to do a job or something, and with the drilling rig back on its feet he started filling in the hole in the ground, so that he could finish the short drive to the drill site.

First, they filled the hole with rocks as big as they could carry, and then topped off the infill using a pile of used red bricks that were lying around in one of the nearby piles of rubbish waiting for a trip to the dumps. I on the other hand, with nothing useful to do and still working off the guilt for nearly wrecking the poor man's drilling rig, ran around like an idiot chicken throwing handfuls of small stones and dirt into the hole in a feeble attempt at a contribution. What a sight, it was splendid. With all this industrial-strength reality going on, I was still dressed in my cute running shorts and micro-fiber top that I had hurriedly put on when I heard Steve's rig coming up the driveway.

Steve fired up his rig and backed slowly over the spot where my septic tank had been. The massive rig's tires pulverized the bricks into red dust. I had never seen bricks do that before, and this caused another outburst of useless behavior. This time I ran around pointing at the cloud of red dust, talking too fast and grinning inanely like a miniature Jerry Lewis. I was such a dork! Anyway, after another thirty yards of backward beeping Steve stopped. The air brakes locked on, the rig's hydraulically operated stabilizing feet swung out, planting themselves firmly into the ground, and Steve was ready to drill.

Seeing this was my last chance, and without a clue what I might possibly gain from it, I asked Steve if this was really the best drill site. He stopped and gave me a look that clearly asked, "Are you still here?" Summoning what looked like the last of his patience, he set himself squarely over his feet then waited a second or so before starting to talk about some geological stuff that I didn't understand a word of. After another intensely exasperated look, he made a wide sweeping gesture with one hand followed by a couple of arm motions that reminded me of a baseball call of "You're out!" The explanation as to why this was the right spot to drill was over.

That convinced me, and how could anyone argue with that? And even if I was still suspicious that this was just the easiest place he could drill, I had nearly broken his rig and, after all, he did come well recommended. I was also relieved to see anything happen on this property that didn't involve me ending up covered in mouse poop, so I left him alone to do his job.

Steve positioned his rig in the middle of a large shady spot, locked its drill tower in place, and started its diesel engine. He climbed up to a metal seat, perched high on the back of the rig, and except for an occasionally fiddling with this or that lever he sat there motionless; feeling the drill shaft shaking his rig as it ground its way slowly down through the granite mountain.

His progress interested me because I was paying for this hole by the foot, and every time a new piece of pipe was added to the drill I recalculated how much more I owed Steve. But two days and $8000 later I had a 320-foot deep well delivering more then enough water for the house. He knew where to find water, and I'd guessed right in choosing him. All that was left to do was pay the man and watch in trepidation as Steve inched his way down our scary steep driveway, wondering if his brakes were really that good.

At this point, the well was now just a hole in the ground with water at the bottom. The next step was to "set" a pump. "Setting" a pump entails lowering an electric pump down to the bottom of the well. And as my ignorance extended beyond drilling wells, I thought that this was one more task that was best left to the professionals.

As he left, Steve had given me the name of the pump setter he recommended, and still feeling guilty I didn't question his choice. The two old guys who came out to set the pump were from another time and age. Long gray beards down to their chests, slow moving and slow talking, there was not a wasted movement in either of them. But they seemed to know what they were doing, and probably from quite some time back. Practical people, they didn't have any computers or cell phones, no swanky new trucks, and no hurry to rush off to the next job. Instead, they arrived in a 1950 era Chevy with just enough motor left to get it up the driveway, a set of well-worn tools from the same era, and word-of-mouth recommendations to get their next job. These two old guys might as well have stepped out of a sepia colored photograph.

At the end of an unhurried day they turned on the electricity to the pump, three hundred feet underground. Knowing nothing, as usual, I was blissfully ignorant about water in these mountains. As far as I knew water was water, and I had no idea that the area was volcanic in origin and that water can come up brown and undrinkable, or too salty to drink or stinking of sulfur, or arsenic or a host of other things best left underground. But my ignorance served me well. I stood around expecting crystal clear water and that's exactly what came burbling out of the ground. And maybe because I had just invested so much of my net worth in the well, it was the best water I had ever tasted—cool and clear on a baking hot afternoon, and all the better for coming up through hundreds of feet of solid granite.

We were almost there, and considering the only thing I had known about water was that it was wet, things had gone well, except for the septic tank. The last piece to getting water to the mouse-house was to trench a pipe from the wellhead to the house. Nowadays, I would just rent whatever type of trencher was needed and run it myself, but these were the early days and I knew nothing. So we checked through the local want ads and found a trenching machine and its operator, Dwayne.

Dwayne operated a machine called a Ditchwitch; we had no idea what it was but from what he said over the phone it sounded perfect for the job. A Ditchwitch is a small ride-on tractor with a chain-driven dirt-scooping arm trailing out the back. As the tractor drives slowly forwards, the trailing arm digs out a slit trench behind it. The Ditchwitch arrived that Saturday morning on a trailer pulled behind a well-used Chevy Suburban, which oddly enough was missing every single window except its back window. The Ditchwitch looked as if it had dug its first trench about 1930, and Dwayne looked like he had been dragged through that ditch. But we lived down a long dirt road on the side of a mountain and, as we were quickly learning, any help should be welcomed.

We made the point of meeting Dwayne at the bottom of our driveway, just to explain how steep it was. Dwayne didn't look like he was much in the mood for details. He mumbled something about how everything would be okay and started up the hill. But halfway up the driveway the Ditchwitch snapped the single rope holding it onto the trailer. It slid off the back of the trailer onto the driveway, miraculously stayed upright, and stopped where it had landed without damaging itself. I could tell the day was off to a good start.

"Some relatives came over last night," Dwayne volunteered. From the lack of any follow up, apparently this by itself was explanation enough for his current state. I have to give him credit, though. In spite of being in pain from his hangover he wrestled his trencher back onto his trailer and made it the rest of the way up the hill.

With that excitement over, Dwayne and I walked the route for the trench and a couple of hours later he had it dug. The trench he dug was fine but the hangover he was nursing couldn't have improved his day. Before Dwayne loaded his Ditchwitch back onto the trailer, he pulled a couple of beers out of the ice chest in his Suburban and downed both. "That's better," he said, throwing his empties expertly through one of the missing windows into the Suburban. He loaded his Ditchwitch onto the trailer and tied it down. I paid him the $200 and added a sincere, "Take it easy going down the hill." I was thinking that the beers, his old equipment, and the driveway were a bad combination. "Don't you worry none," and with a wave goodbye he set off down the scary steep driveway. This time the old Suburban was being helped down the slope by the combined weight of the trailer and the Ditchwitch on top.

With the place to ourselves again, Sheila and I walked back into our mouse-house, through one of the convenient holes in the walls, and sat down on our one and only couch, causing the customary cloud of dust to pop up and fill the air around us. But before the dust had started to settle, there was a series of crashes from down the hill. We ran back out through the nearest hole in the wall and down the hill toward where the noise came from. All the time I was dreading what I might find, knowing the chances were that the Ditchwitch had joined the likes of the propane truck and had landed in the seasonal creek. It had.

The Suburban was in the creek, right side up, but the trailer was upside down and the Ditchwitch had tumbled off to the side with anything that could be bent, bent. By the time we got down there Dwayne had climbed out of his old Suburban, shakier than ever, and was waving me off. "It's my own fault... I was going too fast, what with that load behind me... I should have known better." After the day he had just had, he had to be asking, "What next?"

Sheila ran back to the house to call a tow truck while I surveyed the compounded disaster, trying to figure out how one tow truck could drag all three things out of the creek. Dwayne mostly stayed down with his wrecked equipment, with the look of someone suffering from acute embarrassment and someone that didn't want any company. I hung around, but some distance off.

Finally, the yellow tow truck arrived. I was expecting the driver to be flummoxed by the mix of vehicles littering the creek and would have to call in reinforcements. But no, and at a pace apparently set by intense boredom, he fixed two sets of pulleys around a couple of nearby trees, fed his cables through the pulleys and, in a terrific example of applied geometry, separately winched each part of the wreck up onto the road without damaging anything more than it already was.

"So... this a bad one?" I asked, thinking that the question had been understated. Some time passed before I got my reply.

"Nope, it ain't nuttin." He had answered in a way that completed the conversation, and my guess was that it would have been easier to beat a conversation out of a tree stump than talk to him. So I took the few words he had said at face value and walked back to watch the operations, from a distance again. But even after the tow truck had pulled the Suburban, the trailer and the Ditchwitch back on the road (which cost Dwayne $190 out of his $200 earned that day) Dwayne wouldn't accept a penny from me towards the tow bill. He wouldn't even consider it.

This made me think a bit. The wife and I had spent most of the morning watching Dwayne digging the ditch, relentlessly confirming our superiority to him. But as I watched him drive away, I stood there wondering... if I had just gone through the day Dwayne had, would I have pushed away an offer of some money to cover the losses, whoever's fault it was? It was the start of my re-education. In the country people didn't seem to waste time blaming others, and I had a lot to learn.

With the accident cleaned up and the excitement over, the wife and I walked up the driveway to the mouse-house. The day was now shot so we took the afternoon off. Oh yes, one last thing, a small detail. As Dwayne drove away, towing the heavily dented Ditchwitch behind him, I noticed the old Suburban was now missing its back window, as well.

The First Winter

By the time we reached the house any superiority I could have felt at another's misfortunes had evaporated. The real consequence (at least from my perspective) of Steve dropping his $450,000 drill rig into the previously unknown location of the septic tank was that we no longer had one. It probably wasn't much of a septic tank in the first place and finding it the way we had been a surprise, but the one important detail, beyond all the commotion, was that we didn't have a working bathroom again. We were back to using a roll of toilet paper on the end of a shovel. And after I'd explained the new reality to Sheila she helped me understand that this situation had better not last for long. I was yet again a victim of the American fetish for bathrooms.

Like most of our recent experiences, it had been one step forward and one step back. I called Dan, a local backhoe driver, to dig a hole for a septic tank. He arrived driving, what turned out to be, a new backhoe. The scary steep driveway immediately took its toll, for a change on the way up, when Dan's new backhoe overheated and had to wait half hour until it had cooled down. Once it had stopped steaming, Dan drove it the rest of the way to the appealing mix of raw sewage lying on top of the crushed bricks.

Dan had been in this line of work for some time. With only an occasional retch, and then not a word of complaint, he and is spotless new yellow backhoe dug out the sewage, bricks and remains of the redwood box that was had once been our primitive septic tank; wheeling scoops of the still dripping mess out of the way, out of sight and, most importantly, downwind. Then he dug out the hole to my exact specifications, digging down to the depth that I had already knew the new septic tank would need. (I had ordered the tank on-line and the depth of the hole was based on the measurements given on the web site.) The excavated hole looked perfect and with his job done Dan drove away, testing the limits to his new backhoe's brakes, inching down the scary steep driveway.

Later that afternoon Sheila arrived home with the replacement plastic septic tank—dwarfing and bulging out on all sides from the back of the mini-truck. (Sheila had chosen to drive the thing home because she had the best chance of talking her way past an incredulous CHP.) Anyway, it was too late to do anything that day, but early the following morning, skipping breakfast in my enthusiasm, I dragged our new septic tank over to the hole and pushed it in. I couldn't wait. The dimensions were perfect, the hole had been dug exactly and the tank had barely enough room as it slid down into the hole. But as it stopped at the bottom of the hole my good mood became the first customer for our new septic tank. Either the tank had grown six inches or the hole had been dug six inches short, and unless our sewage could defy gravity and find a way of flowing uphill, I was in trouble.

It was just one more disastrous moment in a construction career built from disastrous moments, and I knew I was about to learn the hard way how much easier it is to drop a septic tank into a hole than it was to pull it back out. This is especially true if the hole has been dug precisely to fit the new plastic tank, without much of a gap around the sides, and there's nothing on the outside of the new plastic tank to get a grip on, which there wasn't. The two lessons learned that day were to measure before doing something irreversible, and not to believe another thing I read on the Internet.

There really are no words to describe the mix of slings and pry bars I used to get the septic tank lifted up enough so that I could slither down into the hole and, cut and scraped, get underneath it. Once there, lying on my back, I pushed it up using my feet, then turned over and used my back to push it up some more, and from there, using ropes, I finally dragged it out of the hole. The wife took pictures, and in a gallery of really, really angry faces mine would have been a stand out.

As there was no way to shorten the brand new, bright-yellow plastic septic tank, an extra six inches had to be hand dug from the bottom of the hole. Hand digging is never fun, and a lot less fun six feet down through the decomposed granite that lies under the surface soil around here. Once down six feet the decomposed granite is far less decomposed and closer to being solid granite, so the digging is better described as chipping and it wasn't a shovel I was using—it was a pickaxe. So I chipped away at the bottom of the hole for some hours, until I was sure it was deep enough to drop the tank back in, and only after I had re-measured the depth a neurotic number of times. The whole thing should have been so easy.

Fun as that had been, it was, thank goodness, the last of the major infrastructure projects for some time. For the next few months, my daily commute was the short walk from our home in the garage across the driveway to the mouse-house. The commute might have been easy but the job waiting at the other end wasn't. A primitive part of my brain seemed to understand that the decayed mouse-house had to be rebuilt into something habitable (by something other than rodents) before winter arrived, and that a race was on.

It wasn't a race I could likely win, either. I soon learned from this early work that if you can see some rot then it's highly likely that there's more rot hiding where you can't see it. Soon after that I learned that a house with rot is likely to have something else wrong with it. With the mouse-house, the "something else" was the small matter that part of the house didn't have a foundation!

Long before I made the mistake of buying the mouse-house, one of the previous owners had decided the main room downstairs needed to be larger. Not much larger but just a little larger. In fact, it's hard to believe anyone would have bothered. But instead of building a proper addition, which would have meant digging holes and pouring foundations and all that tiresome stuff, this genius thought it easier just to mark off a section of the deck, nail plywood over the deck's boards to make a floor, and build the walls up from there. Grief, the whole thing could be done in a weekend.

There was one problem with this arrangement. The problem appeared thirty years later, when the deck's inadequate pier blocks had sunk into the ground under the extra weight, dragging any parts of the house the addition was attached to along with it. To complete the disaster, the deck that the addition was built on top of, and was still a part of, had rotted. This meant that the entire weather-beaten west side of the house had to be torn off and rebuilt, from the ground up, and including a foundation for a change. My original optimistic notion that all the mouse-house needed was a simple remodel (a few gallons of paint, a couple of doorknobs and a sprinkling of decorative lights), wasn't working out as planned.

In my urban life, I had avoided cleaning up after anyone else's mistakes by pretending it would be a form of enabling. (Enabling had recently been discovered to be a bad thing.) It was a matter of principle you understand, and wasn't because helping someone would have taken precious time out of my fun life. But in a particularly vicious example of karma, and only a few months later, I was buried up to my antlers in a life where that's all I did. I cleaned up someone else's mess. Getting up every morning to do exactly what I would have threatened to slit my wrists to avoid doing a few short months before. And often during this time, I found myself staring blankly south at our hundred-mile view, towards the Bay Area and my formerly pampered life, wondering what could I have done to deserve this; though nothing ever came to mind.

It took two unplanned months to rebuild the side of the house. I dug the trenches for the foundation by hand, poured the foundation one bucket at a time, and then built up from the foundation to the roof's eves, one stick of wood at a time. But after finishing building, the strangest thing happened. I stood looking at my two-stories of new wall and windows, and felt a little pride. Actually, I must have been delirious, because instead of just enjoying what I had accomplished I came up with an idea to build an addition to the house. It seemed like a good idea at the time.

Sheila filters out most of what I have to say and it's a shock when she goes along with one of my ideas. I tend to stand there pointing at things, trying to explain some construction this or that, hoping there are enough meaningful phrases mixed in with my over-animated gesticulations to make some sense to her. But this time something I said seemed to fly with her. The idea was to move the mouse-house's only toilet from where it was currently located in the middle of the bedroom.

This is not one of my numerous exaggerations. The toilet was actually in the middle of the mouse-house's only bedroom. It was an add-on, an improvement, probably made by the same genius that built the downstairs out onto the front deck. The toilet's imaginative location had also put it directly above the kitchen, and, over some years, as it leaked through the ceiling and dripped relentlessly down onto to the same spot, it had rotted a hole through what remained of the kitchen counter. The whole situation still has me struggling for words, but you can understand why the wife would have agreed to my plan. My simple-minded insight was to move the toilet into its own room, normally referred to as a bathroom, but as this room didn't exist I had to make one.

Like most A-frames, the mouse-house had a steep roof more typical of a mountain lodge, and just by lessening the slope of the roofline along one side of the bedroom, enough new usable floor space was opened up to create a diminutive bathroom. That's the short version of what needed to be done. The reality was a lot of work and even more guessing how to do it. But my carpentry, plumbing, tiling and wiring skills had come along while building our temporary home in the garage and, one way or another, over the next few weeks the new bathroom got built.

As this bathroom was going to be the master bathroom for our one bedroom we went up-scale (that's a relative term, but it was certainly an improvement for the mouse-house), with a glass-walled shower and using imitation stone tile. By the time it was all finished it didn't look that bad, and although not saying that much, it was certainly better than anything I had mangled together before.

While I was busy building the bathroom, Sheila had been looking for a propane delivery service—one that hadn't heard about our scary steep driveway. She finally found one, and they installed an extra large tank for us (not wanting to make a deliver during the winter either), filled the tank, and then hooked it up to the existing gas line to the house. It was that simple. At last we had propane, and in a moment of giddy consumerism we bought a new stove and refrigerator, drove these two mainstays of normalcy back to the mouse-house, dragged them inside like a couple of Neanderthals, and parked them in the middle of the mouse-house's sagging plywood floor. Gleaming brightly in the filth and the gloom, they looked like an alien technology had just dropped by for a couple of laughs. They didn't belong there, but they must have inspired us or triggered memories of our former affluent lives, because we went back the next day and bought a dryer, as well. Then we dragged the washing machine from the driveway and moved it, along with our new dryer, into our newly rebuilt utility room.

We didn't have a kitchen, but we did have two disembodied kitchen appliances, which was close enough. I hooked up the stove with a flexible propane line, and plugged in the refrigerator. After months without we could finally store food and cook food, and have something other than tuna sandwiches to eat three times a day. And just in case you're thinking the addition of a couple of appliances meant that our lives were close to normalcy, let me point out that Sheila cleaned the house using the only thing that did the job—a gas-powered leaf blower.

Being busy (a decent enough excuse), I hardly ever cleaned-up after myself, and Sheila took over the task of keeping the construction site clean. This might sound like rampant sexism but it wasn't. We had a simple rule: The best person for the job does the job. And don't think that this arrangement was in my favor, it wasn't. I was always the best person to lift any big heavy things, as well as take care of the foul nasty smelly dirty things that always needed doing around the mouse-house. So Sheila volunteered for the cleaning (and most of the thinking), while I did the rest, which worked out well for the two of us.

With a rag wrapped around her head and a dust mask protecting her face, Sheila blew out the dust and accumulated construction debris, the dried up bits and pieces of rodents the cats didn't find appetizing, and all the dirt that finds its way into a house that has holes where walls should be. She blew it back out through the same holes in the walls and the broken windows it had come in. Standing downwind was to be avoided. And I remember looking at Sheila, my Nordic goddess, just visible in the middle of a swirling cloud of filth, with unidentifiable things flying around her and the leaf blower roaring, and thinking to myself, "She could have married someone with a real job, with money, maybe power and status... but she had chosen me instead." For a moment this puzzled me, and then the thought was gone.

Three months after we started rebuilding, fall was in the air. What had been done was dwarfed by what still needed to be done, and what remained of the $30k that I had naively thought it would take to rebuild the mouse-house was about to be wiped out by two more essential tasks. The driveway had to be resurfaced (rebuilt would have been a better description) and a new roof had to be put on the mouse-house before winter.

We could only get one bid on the driveway, because like so most things out here it's hard. In this case it was hard to get any contractor to come out this far, and once here, mostly we wished they hadn't bothered. But our driveway guy sounded okay on the phone and turned out to be better in person.

Our driveway was a small but difficult job. It was small compared to surfacing miles of county road but it still took most of the same equipment, and the crew spent the day shuttling equipment up and down our twisty narrow road. This cost us a lot of the little cash we had left, but it was worth it. As soon as the last of the truck drove off, I started driving up and down our new driveway enjoying the difference. And what a difference; I wasn't bouncing over ruts, hitting my head on the roof of the truck, chased by a cloud of dust, and wondering if the truck's suspension would survive.

Also, for a change, there hadn't been any equipment disasters on the scary steep driveway, but there was a coincidence. I hate coincidences because I never know what to do with them. One of our cats, the Pink Cat, disappeared that day. And though I kept telling myself that the cat-sized bump in the driveway couldn't be the missing Pink Cat (because the paving machines would have flattened it), I couldn't be sure. I should have searched more for the cat. Maybe because it was just too hot that day, or I was too tired to make the effort, I reasoned the Pink Cat hadn't gone far and would come back when he was hungry. But he didn't. And after some fruitless crawling through the almost impenetrable undergrowth looking for him, I gave up the search. He could be anywhere.

Six months later I came across his bleached bones and a little fur (a few patches of the same unusual color that gave him his name) about half a mile from the house, beside Cow Creek. It was a rescue cat that urinated on everything, a cat I could have easily forgotten, but I'm still reminded of it years later, every time I notice this unfortunately cat-sized bump in the driveway.

Our next concern was the roof. It leaked like a sieve and with winter on its way it had to be fixed. There was no choice. As usual, it was hard to get a contractor to even return a call, and it was only after many, many phone calls that our first roofers came out. They sported fresh tattoos, stayed just long enough to drop off a roofing manufacturer's spec sheet (probably picked up from a roofing supply store on their drive out here), and look around to see if there was anything worth stealing. When we tried calling a week later their phone was disconnected, and we assumed that their paroles had been jerked after they were caught doing to someone else what they rightly didn't think worthwhile doing to us.

Some more phone calls. We finally had what seemed like a real roofing contractor. He not only bothered to answer our calls but he actually drove out to give us an estimate, even after hearing where we lived. His estimate seemed high but he had actually given us an estimate. He explained that the extra expense was on account of the steep slope of the roof and its height off the ground. This meant that he would have to bring out extra safety equipment which, in itself, meant a time-intensive job and therefore expensive. It was all OSHA you know, and the insurance was astronomical.

The day of the roofing he turned up with a dozen teenagers and no safety equipment. We watched and winced as these children clambered and slipped around on the steep roof with its thirty-foot drop-offs. At the end of an eight-hour day, the roof finished, we gave him the $6,000 for the day's work.

I wish I could write about how wonderful every moment of our new country experience was. I wish I could but I can't. Every time we went through one of these no-bid contracts, I stood there gumming the air like a half-dead guppy, looking into a penniless future with no way to improve it. I had stopped noticing the natural beauty that brought me here in the first place; much closer to my thinking and adding to the sense of doom was the hole in the bottom of my pocket. With the well, the driveway, the roof, and the money spent rebuilding so far, the $30k cash we had started with was gone. And if we wanted to continue living here, let alone finish rebuilding the house, we had to take out an equity line of credit just to finish making the mouse-house livable. It meant going against everything I knew was important to our financial survival—we were about to spend money we didn't have. And that's never a good idea.

We had investments in the Bay Area but these were still euphemistically "maturing". A lifetime before, while being interviewed by the biotech start-up, I had been offered stock options in lieu of a higher salary. I wasn't new to the game and had had stock options offered me many times before. My response wasn't the gratitude any employer would have expected, instead, I sneered at him and scornfully asked that they be printed on rolls of soft paper—at least that way I could do something useful with them. The stock options were forced on me anyway, along with another roll or two of them just in case, but however many there were I took no notice and forgot about them. Then in March of 2000, at the peak of the Tech Bubble, the *lab rats* became excited about the stock price.

It's always better to be lucky than good. I knew nothing about stocks and thought the stock price had to be a mistake. But a few seconds of simple math later I realized that I could be worth a lot more than I deserved to be, so I called my stockbroker with the one-word instruction: "SELL!!!" That was the day the stock price peaked, and it never got that high again.

Waiting for the enormous check to arrive in the mail, there were two days (I can close my eyes and still remember every delicious moment), when the world became enchanted and I was someone special. I didn't feel lucky beyond anyone's wildest dreams, as I should have, instead I felt newly entitled. It was wonderful, I was going to invest it all and be rich! This was just the start. But the day the check arrived the wife grabbed it out of my hand, before I could give it to a smart young man in an Armani suit (never to be seen again), and bought apartments instead. And far from being rich, the reality was that every dollar I made was diverted into supporting them (at least while I still had an income), and years later they were still only breaking even. But they were a good investment (not speedy but good) and if we ate air for a few more years, then maybe, our apartments would come to our financial corpses' rescue.

So we justified a small equity line on the house, if it allowed our investments to mature, us to live hand-to-mouth for another year or so, and the sweat equity earned rebuilding the mouse-house could be seen as a form of income. With that reasoning, the equity line would merely be a loan to our makeshift family business. This rationalization sounded reasonable, and coincidently was the only thing left for us to do. But I had run out of more than money.

By now I was sure that this move to the mountains had to be the dumbest decision in a lifetime of dumb decisions, an embarrassment to stupidity. I couldn't have fallen any lower. I had traded in a successful career in the Bay Area for isolation, squalor and making-do on a shoestring, and then tried to pin the title of "retirement" on the disaster. At least, that's the way I saw it then. If I could have changed my name to Dorothy, clicked my heels together and disappeared, I would have. If I could have just closed my eyes and ceased to exist I might have done that too, but there was just no easy way out. Sure, it had been my own actions that had caused me to become a manual laborer, but it just wasn't the best time of life to start that line of work.

Summer turned into autumn, which made it more pleasant to work. The days of triple-digit heat were over, my brain didn't boil so quickly, and I could remember my name for more than an hour after the sun came up. But improving conditions or not, there was still far too much construction to get done before winter arrived, living on thirty acres was turning out to be a job in itself, and then there were the animals.

Animals, especially needy hungry animals, seem to seek you out in the country, and in spite of our efforts to avoid them we still ended up accumulating them. We were driving through the flats outside of Igo when Sheila saw this severely neglected and obviously starving horse by the road. I tried to ignore it. Neither of us knew a thing about horses, and as we drove home we did our best to rationalize why we should just forget about the horse, but we couldn't. So knowing nothing as usual, this time about horses, we decided to rescue it instead. Brilliant.

You would think that the horse's owner would have been glad to get rid of this nearly lame bag of bones. It had no shelter, was left out in all weathers, and being beside the road it was a 24-hour advertisement to the owner's indifference. But he held firm to his principles, and threatened to keep starving the horse unless we paid the ransom he demanded. We had no choice, and with a lot of the little money we had left, we paid the $500. The dark gray horse, with his aged-white coat around his eyes and extending down over his muzzle, was named Thunder.

Some of Woods Canyon's equestrians must have heard what we were doing and magically drove up with a trailer at the same moment we handed over the ransom. Without a second's delay they led Thunder out of his prison, into their trailer, and took the poor horse home for us.

Up to then, the only thing I knew about horses was to say in a slow-talking countrified voice to anyone who owned one, and then only to be irritating, "Where there's stock there's trouble." But now I was the one doing the owning. Now the wonky-walled, collapsed-roofed, should-have-been-used-as-a-bonfire pile of plywood that some decades ago had been called a barn, had to be rebuilt and rebuilt into something useful, so the old horse had a comfortable place to stay for the winter. We didn't have much of a roof over our own heads at the time, but what did that matter?

The consensus from the equestrians was that Thunder was somewhere between twenty-five and thirty-five years old. And he might have been a thundering kind of a horse in some prior time but, with the way he looked now, I thought the past tense of his name suited him better. We expected him to be long dead before spring, but the tough old horse didn't die. He went on to take full advantage of the situation, living years longer than anyone could have guessed, and making his ransom seem like a minimal down payment on his food bill. Still, unexpectedly, this simple act of kindness turned out to be about the only time that karma has actually benefited me. During the years of caring for Thunder, the old horse somehow helped me see both the land we owned and to some extent the nature of life itself.

Not that things were getting out of hand. We now had four cats, two dogs and a horse, thirty acres of land that needed clearing, and a mouse-poop shell of a building we were attempting to have reclassified as a house, when another cat walked into our garage-bedroom. This far out in the wilderness, a domestic cat had better be a special kind of a cat. Every predator except coyotes lives in these mountains, and the only reason there are no coyotes is because the mountain lions eat them. So a domestic cat is a long way down towards the bottom of the food chain, a light snack, and sharing a place on the menu with squirrels.

I was pretty sure I had seen this cat the day before, even though at the time I wasn't sure what it was. I saw a black blur about the size of a cat, but it went up the side of a hill faster than I had ever seen a cat move. Yet it was a cat, just not an ordinary cat.

It was a "Shasta Cat", a genetically superior cat made superior by the evolutionary pressure of generation after generation being starved, neglected and generally maltreated by the least well-informed of Shasta County. This one was eighteen pounds of solid muscle and it had walked into our garage home, by our other four cats and two dogs, none of who had picked a fight with it or even voiced a complaint. They must have known better. Instead they had shown it to where Sheila and I were sleeping and told it to jump on the bed. "You go right ahead... it's okay."

The cat had arrived during my darkest hour and I couldn't take care of one more thing, not even another cat. So a few days later (over Sheila's repeated warnings that I wouldn't be happy if I did it), I packed the hefty cat in to a crate and drove him two hundred and fifty miles to the Humane Society in Marin County. They have a no-kill policy. With a couple of white lies about where he had come from, I left him for adoption thinking he would be on his way to a new home by the afternoon. Every bad decision has a good idea buried in it somewhere.

As soon as I drove away the regret set in and the first thing I did on getting home was to call the Humane Society, to ask for my cat back. No such luck. Once dropped off the "real" owner has to be given a chance to contact the humane society. I tried to think of another lie to counter my first lie, but nothing came to mind, and so the cat was in for the duration. The cat had to be inspected, evaluated, vaccinated, and finally neutered. "And how long does this all take?' I asked. "About two weeks," was the reply.

So for those two weeks I badgered my Marin friends to stop in and see the cat on their lunchtimes, and after work, and any other time they didn't really have, to help assuage my guilt. On the much anticipated release date from his kitty jail I called to arrange a pickup. Things were going from bad to worse; now the cat had developed a kennel cough. After another two weeks, which I used to repeatedly accuse the Humane Society of preferring to kill the poor cat rather than give it back, I was able to drive to Marin to rescue my very, very unhappy walk-in Shasta cat. In the end this "free" cat had cost $450, at a time I really didn't have $450 to spare, but it turned out to be money well spent. This event proved to a metaphysical certitude, something that I already knew, that Sheila had married me for the sole purpose of having someone close at hand to laugh at. The beast of a cat was solid black and we ended up naming it "The Evil Cat"; not for anything he actually did, but just because he looked like he might do it at any moment.

By mid-December the mouse-house's exterior walls were mostly finished and all the windows and doors were in. The utility room was rebuilt, the new bathroom completed, and we had the beginnings of a kitchen. Many of a home's essentials were now in the house. And as the garage didn't have any heat and we didn't want to put any more money into the garage, it was time to abandon it and move in to the mouse-house.

The "one-step-at-a-time" approach had finally paid off. Six months after arriving on the property we moved into the house, though barely. We had a couple of clip-on lights on the end of extension cords for lighting, the house still had no heat, there was very little wiring, no interior work had been done, and the remaining cracks and gaps in the exterior walls allowed any breeze that felt like it to blow through the house. Still, we were living in the house, and thanks to the cats we were also the dominant species.

Three days later it snowed. The day had that soft threat of snow to it, but I'd heard that when it does snow in these parts it's usually light. So I planned to drive into town and stock up with some extra supplies after I had got some work done. I also left it till late in the day so I could make the most of the minor thrill of driving in the snow.

The drive into town was fine. I started to hurry through the shopping because the snow was getting thicker and on the way back home it started to dump. There were only a few cars on the road and with each mile there were fewer, until there were none. In fact, I hadn't seen a car coming from the direction of Igo for some time. It wasn't a good sign and then, about halfway home, I came to the first grade that could pretend to be a hill.

It wasn't much of a grade, but the mini-truck was two-wheel drive and each time I tried to get it up the first hill I nearly ended up in the ditch. Getting stuck in a ditch wouldn't have been so bad but the idea of my neighbors driving by snickering would have, so I called it quits and parked the mini-truck off the side of the road. Then, after sorting through what I really, really, really needed, I left the rest of the groceries in the soon to become a refrigerator-on-wheels and started to walk the remaining few miles home.

By this time it was dusk, and the hills on either side of the road were disappearing under an endless supply of snow that was slowly burying everything in sight. I walked the rest of the way home, a grocery bag in each hand, without seeing another soul. I was marooned in a world of fluffy white, and with only the muffled crunch of snow underfoot, each step of the walk home was magical.

During the night three feet of snow fell, the most snow seen in the area for thirty years. Sheila and I woke up to that unusually bright light you get after a snow and the skies have cleared. Peeking out from underneath our stack of comforters, we looked over the snow piled against the windows at a wonderland of white. And after months of a sweaty struggle with dust and dirt, and then later with cold and mud, it felt like a holiday. So we got up, quickly added some more layers over the several layers we had gone to bed in, and took off walking; first down our driveway and then our narrow county road, down the hill toward the little town of Igo.

We had Woods Canyon to ourselves. Our neighbors knew better, they stayed indoors and waited for the snowplow, but we were newly arrived rubes from the city. It was breathtaking. We had the place to ourselves. Our only company was the creek following along beside us: burbling, bitter with cold between its snow-topped boulders. The one-room miner's shack, tucked back from the road, had always looked decrepit and forlorn, but now looked picturesque and even cozy. The split rail fencing, with snow stacked high, completed a scene from the eighteenth century.

And it could have been a scene from the eighteenth century, if for no other reason than by the time we made our way back home from our walk there was no electricity and no phone. We had been looking forward to warming up and get something to eat, neither of which happened. What we couldn't know was that the electricity was going to be off for the next two weeks.

That day, we learned yet another lesson about living in the country—it's best to have one heat source that doesn't require any electricity to operate. The same snow that had blocked the roads with drifts and turned the house into an icebox, had also pulled trees down onto the power lines and knocked out the electrical grid throughout the county. And with no electricity, we were left with our kitchen's propane gas range as the only source of heat in the house.

So, huddled in multiple layers of clothing, we lit all the burners on the range. This raised the temperature inside the house above the freezing mark it had reached during the night, and made the inside of the house marginally warmer than the outside. But with refreshing drafts of cold air coming through the holes in the walls, and the occasional snowflake drifting in as well, it never did get much above freezing. We needed more heat than the stovetop could give us, and the only other way of heating the house was the fireplace.

The question was could the fireplace help heat the house? We had used the fireplace off and on in the weeks before, but it never seemed to do much more than suck the warmth out the house and shoot it up the chimney, and now that we really needed the fireplace to work there was just one problem. How were we going to find firewood buried under three feet of snow?

Before the snowfall, not wanting to waste money buying it, we'd been scavenging firewood from the land, and then only when we needed it. So we hadn't stacked a tidy cord of wood under some convenient eve beside the house. Before this, and only in moments of complete desperation, the two of us stumbled around just before it got totally dark, pushing and pulling our wheelbarrow over rock-pocked slopes around the house, picking up whatever looked like it would fit in the fireplace. But this freezing morning, when we needed the firewood the most, whatever wood was out there lay underneath three feet of snow. And even though it wouldn't have been the first thing either of us would have thought of even a day before, some straightforward country thinking came to our rescue.

It was a Shasta County emergency measure. I fired up the chainsaw and started cutting up the front deck for firewood, and for a change we had an advantage: the deck was as old as it was rotten and needed cutting up anyway; there was a lot of it; it was conveniently close to the door; and forty years of baking under the sun had done a great job of preparing it for its selfless last act. By the afternoon the interior of our experiment-in-prolonged-draughtiness-that-could-at-some-future-point-become-a-house was up to a toasty fifty degrees, and this was how we existed, huddled in the dark around our fireplace.

It could have been worse, but after a week of sitting in the cold, isolated and immobilized in our drafty box of misery, we ran out of food. We suddenly realized we had important business in the Bay Area and hiked down off the mountain, dug the mini-truck out of the snow bank, and fled. We didn't come back until we knew it was safe—after the power had been turned back on.

A Glimmer of Hope

During this less-than-enjoyable first year, neither of us had much of an inclination to explore the area, if for no other reason than survival trumped sightseeing. But the few times we did drive beyond Igo, further west into the outlying mountainous areas of Shasta County, it was revealing. And if I ever wrung my hands about living too far out, beyond any last trappings of civilization, then these road trips showed me just how much further there was to go.

It hadn't been a good year, every fear I had about living here had become a reality; I'd begun to whine. I would have fallen to the ground and wailed, but sniveling noises were limited by the strict two-week rule the wife and I had about making each other miserable. Actually, this two-week rule was only about *me* making *her* miserable, and after all, it had been my actions that had caused us to be living here in the first place—a fact the wife wasn't shy about reminding me.

As a way of avoiding the inevitable row (a row I would have started out on the wrong end of and had no way of winning) I decided to get out of the mouse-house for a few hours and take a drive west through Shasta County. It was an area I had been told that made Igo look cosmopolitan, and though that was hard to believe this road trip did convince me that things could have been worse, far worse. I should have been celebrating my good fortune instead of whining.

I also had another reason to take a drive. Since we first moved here, Sheila had been trying to breathe some life into the small garden behind the garage, but as fast as she put a plant in the ground the deer ate it. They were walking into the garden through a hole in the fence where a section of stakes was missing, and *we* decided that *I* should find replacement stakes. The problem (there's always a problem) was that they were a type I'd never seen before; they were hand-hewn redwood. I had called around looking for them locally, without any luck, but was told about a lumberyard that probably stocked them. As this lumberyard was in western Shasta County, and as I was already headed that way, I thought I might as well look for it, and the little town it was in.

At least it was identified as being a town on the map. The town, if you can call it that, was thirty miles down a winding road, hanging onto the sides of forested mountains in what was once logging country. I could have easily driven right by it. Apart from a couple of boarded-up buildings the lumberyard seemed to be pretty much all there was left of the town, and whoever worked there must have melted back into the hills at the end of the day.

Still, this had to be the lumberyard I had been told about. So I pulled in and parked in front of a likely looking tin shack, the one that looked the most like it could be the office, and found it locked. Not surprising really since it was lunchtime, and with no one else in the yard I walked around looking for the stakes. There were piles of them and exactly what I had been looking for, stacked outside and exposed to the weather, next to some huge sections of redwood tree trunks. So I walked back to the pickup, opened the tailgate and sat on it, swinging my legs like a bored teenager, waiting for someone to get back from lunch. I didn't have to wait long. An older man, older than me for sure, hobbled across the yard heading toward the redwood tree trunks. Everyone I'd met at the Beer Bar who had worked in the logging industry seemed to have a debilitating injury of some kind, so his limp didn't surprise me.

While I'd been waiting I'd been wondering, idly, how the stakes were made. I could see the massive sections of trunk and the piles of finished stakes, but had no idea how one extremely large thing could end up as stacks of perfectly formed stakes. And as there was nothing else happening in the under-employed yard, I ran after him to ask if he knew anything about the stakes and ask how they were made. As usual I knew nothing, this time I knew nothing about hand-hewn stakes, and it had never occurred to me that hand-hewn actually could mean hand-hewn.

I'd found the right man. He'd been making the stakes for years and didn't seem to mind wasting part of his lunch break to explain how it was done; though I had a feeling he didn't have too many people to talk to during the day. Matter-of-factly he explained to me that he first debarks a "round" (a length of trunk), a task I would have baulked at in my twenties. Next he splits the round through the center and down its entire length, how I couldn't imagine. Then he splits the halves into quarters, then splits and splits again, until the wood was hewed into four by four inch posts, and finally into the two-inch wide stakes I was there to buy. By the end of his explanation I was looking at the old man in astonishment—so that's what *hand-hewn* meant!

His tools were lined up against a bench. There were sledgehammers and wedges laid-out on top of the bench, several axes stuck in the side of it and a few other tools lying around, but I had no idea what they did. With nothing better to do I hung around to watch him work for a bit. As he walked away towards his bench he turned back to add, "My stroke slowed me down some." What? While he had been talking I had noticed that his left arm seemed to be hanging, and I began wondering how could this man, who was not only older than me but also disabled, possibly manage this type of work?

Thinking that a good day for him would be equivalent to my worst day ever, I didn't want to waste anymore of his time asking questions. But there was an incongruous pile of sawdust, at least three feet high and just to the left of where he was setting up to split a round. I didn't understand why he would have chosen to leave a pile of sawdust in the middle of his work area, especially since the rest of the area was kept tidy.

He had to do everything one-handed, even wielding his cumbersome sledgehammer. I watched as he positioned himself carefully before each stroke, first stooping to look closely at the grain of the wood, and then lining himself up by swinging his left leg around, repositioning it like a post underneath him to steady himself. I watched him work for a few minutes and occasionally he got off balance. Then one time he fell over, and not gracefully. He spun as he fell, with one arm outstretched into the pile of sawdust, which was why it was there.

I jumped up to help but he waved me off, struggling on the ground until he got into a position he could push himself up using his one good arm. Without bothering to dust himself off he continued just where he had left off, splitting the wood as if nothing has happened. I thought this old man must fall several times a day, every few minutes for all I knew, but nothing stopped him. And judging by the man's dogged perseverance, I would bet that he arrived for work every morning, day after day, month after month and year after year; five days a week and church on Sundays.

His stakes were all perfectly made, split exactly down the grain so they wouldn't warp or twist and, being redwood they would last for decades. This humble man became a life lesson for me. And since then, whenever I've found myself thinking that my self-inflicted inconveniences were the worst problems in the world, I remember this simple wood-splitter's unassuming determination.

A week later, in the middle of a prolonged wet spell, with nothing more than cabin fever and sour thoughts for company, I went for a walkabout on the property—just to get out of the house again. The mountain had been made even more remote by the winter weather, stuck in the middle of a cloud for over a week, and this was just another day in a long series of dreary days. Even the trees seemed to take part in making my life a little more miserable by accurately targeting purposely large raindrops down my neck, and it really couldn't be called a walkabout because the land hadn't been cleared yet. The *walk* consisted mostly of my crawling on hands and knees, with soggy boots and even soggier jeans, pushing through thick manzanita brush with nowhere really in mind, and nothing much to see except for the bottom of the next bush.

It was while pushing blindly through the brush, not even sure where I was exactly, that I emerged from the undergrowth at a waterfall on the seasonal creek that topples down our property. This particular waterfall must have been made by something catastrophic a long time ago, because nothing in my experience of weather and rain could have caused boulders this large to end up where they were. But as I stood there, dripping, and thinking without conviction about what must have roared down the creek and rolled the truck-sized boulders to their current resting places, it occurred to me that the creek's route around these huge boulders could stand some improving.

Soaked through I was one with the water anyway, and never having fully grown up I've kept the need to play with water. The stream wound round the base of these giant boulders, pouring into gaps and then slipping shyly away, out of sight into a deep crevice on the far side of the fall's granite face. Then I noticed that there were some heavily silted channels the stream had made and abandoned, maybe decades ago, and as they were headed towards the face of the waterfall I decided to restore them.

First, I rolled a boulder into the creek, mostly blocking it and forcing the water to follow a shallow channel I kicked with the heel of my boot. That gave the water a new direction and the water did the rest. With very little help from me the stream washed out its old channels, and within minutes there were several cascades of water dropping over the face and down the thirty feet onto the boulders at the bottom.

In spite of what I felt about them, my thirty acres weren't completely useless. They had spectacular features, but they hadn't been cared for, and over decades of neglect they'd become buried under a smothering blanket of manzanita. This was not an occasional ornamental manzanita bush, but a continuous impenetrable thicket of living and dead manzanita—some small, some large, and some the size of trees. This scourge had succeeded at the expense of every other scrap of vegetation, and now stood shoulder-to-shoulder topping small trees and then pushing them down until they too died. Clearing this thick mass of obstinately difficult brush from such a large area seemed remorselessly out of scale with anything I could do, and standing beside the waterfall in the rain and winter drear, I remembered happier times when I wrote computer code. I thought how stupid I had been not to hang in there, whatever it took, and not finish out my work-life comfortably staring at a computer screen, merely discontented.

Maybe I had reached the bottom. Maybe I was finally fed up with wallowing in despair, but for some reason my small improvement to a waterfall marked a turning point. I felt a glimmer of hope that maybe I could do something useful with my land. And it was from this insignificant success at an obscure waterfall, a meaningless milestone on an otherwise dreary day, something changed in me and for the better. I didn't think about it, but somehow it just became a fact. It was possible to remake the land, and it didn't matter how or how long it would take, it was going to happen. I could have just as easily ignored the land, left it the way it was and lived perfectly well, but for some reason I couldn't. It must have been seeping into my soul, because it wasn't the house I dreamt about when I went to sleep at night, it was the land.

By now it was getting late in the afternoon (country life has a simple schedule to it), and as I was walking up China Gulch's dirt road, back towards the mouse-house, a car drove up, a rarity, and stopped, even rarer. The driver got out and introduced himself as Igo's new pastor. He was on his rounds introducing himself to his congregation, or at least the few he could find in the hills. He was a nice enough, well-meaning young man, so I disguised my leaden disbelief in the whole god subject, and having thanked him for stopping by continued my uphill slog to the house. Just a couple of minutes later, though, there was a gunshot from further up the hill. It was close and came from the direction the pastor had driven off to.

On the lookout for anything that might add some interest to the day, and with nothing better to do, I thought I'd find out who had shot whom. I was pretty sure that the gunshot had something to do with a grumpy old neighbor who lives further up China Gulch, Dale. For years he's had everybody for miles around convinced that a step onto his land would be their last one. It's all bark, I think, but as I was on my way up the road to Dale's the pastor came flying back down. I waved as he went by but he didn't seem to notice, he seemed to be intensely focused on his driving, and I had a suspicion that however strong our new pastor's belief in heaven was, he had just come a little too close to finding out if his belief was well founded. "Welcome to the neighborhood," I called out as the pastor drove by.

This was intriguing. Five minutes later I knocked on Dale's front door, it was the safer door to approach, and my grumpy old neighbor opened the door, without his shotgun. Apparently, the pastor had made the mistake of arriving at Dale's back gate, and not the front door that "anyone with a brain" would have used. Before an explanation could be made, a warning shot had been put over the pastor's head, and not surprisingly the pastor had fled.

"You're going to hell for that, Dale." I find lasting joy in telling devout Christians that they are going to hell, but the funniest part was that Dale attended the pastor's church. And, as an aside: "No!" My almost spiritual revelation about my thirty acres and the coincidental appearance of the pastor were not related. But on the subject of spiritual, walking back from Dale's house I had what has to be the most magical experience of my life. (That's except for one night in a bedroom in Los Angeles.) I was walking down the gravel road, head down, buried in an unimportant thought and completely unaware of my surroundings, when I was suddenly startled back into the here and now.

I had nearly walked into a baby deer standing motionless in the middle of the road. I was so surprised that it took a couple of seconds of adrenalin to even recognize what it was. The fawn was facing me, completely unafraid and looking up at me with huge trusting eyes. It was the most perfect creature I had ever seen. I was drawn to it and wanted to touch it. I was in the presence of perfection. Expecting it to run away I slowly reached out to it anyway, and instead of running off it took a step closer to me.

The situation was beginning to take on a surreal quality. I love animals but I couldn't see how this little deer knew that, for all it knew I was imagining it between two slices of bread. Then I looked up and saw at least another dozen baby deer, standing about thirty feet away, huddled together in a tight group and facing me, just standing there and staring, as if they were waiting to see what happened to their friend. For the first time in my life I was speechless. It made not the slightest sense. I must have been whisked off to heaven in the last few minutes, somehow not noticing the event, and was enjoying the first few moments of that eternal happy holiday where only good things happen. Probably that pastor again. He must have run me over in his hurry and I had been awarded some utterly undue compensation. It made no sense.

The metaphysical moment seemed to have no end. I started stroking the top of the fawn's head and found that even its coat was the softest I had ever felt. Then, as if on cue, the whole group of baby deer walked forward, each with their trusting brown eyes staring they surrounded me, pushing at me as they nuzzled with their warm noses, all of them looking for attention. Dropping into a crouch, I did my best to pet a dozen needy fawns with just two hands.

I might as well have been in heaven. I was cloaked in cloud, feeling totally at peace, surrounded by these beautiful trusting creatures asking for love. It didn't matter what the explanation was, I wanted the moment to last forever, and the only reason it ended at all was because the fawns got bored and wandered off. "Come back, don't leave..." my empty hands pleaded. But off into the mist they went, like so many lost children into the forest.

Unfortunately there was a simple explanation to this, and the explanation was about as much use to me as finding out what causes rainbows—no, less use. Weeks later, I learned from Jill, the wife of my famously grumpy old neighbor, that she had taken delivery of the fawns from a deer rescue group. The mothers had been killed in accidents and by hunters, and the babies had been bottle-fed at the rescue center. Now they needed to be transitioned back to a wild life.

They had been dropped at our neighbor's, where they could be weaned off their human intervention and allowed to return to the wild. As with a lot of explanations, I preferred the magic to the facts, but I will never forget the brief time I spent with those fawns.

Manly Activities

When I was naively thinking about buying the mouse-house, the previous owner had pointed at the almost solid wall of twenty-foot high manzanita bushes laying siege to the house and warned, "You won't believe how hard it is to clear that stuff. Ten feet into it and you'll be done for the day. It's exhausting." The man never impressed me much so I didn't pay attention to anything he said.

Supposedly, the indigenous Indians called manzanita "Iron Wood". The Indians didn't use iron at the time, so it's hard to see why they would have called it Iron Wood, but that's another story. It's about as evil as vegetable life can get, and owes its success to a combination of factors: It has no known use; it's miserable to get rid of; it's mean, hard and unforgiving; if left to its own devices it will proliferate and choke out everything around it; and by far the worst of shortcomings—it burns with an intense heat. As our land was covered from property line to property line with the stuff, if a fire had come through with this much manzanita for fuel, it would have nuked everything. The dense brush would have sent flames shooting up into the trees, turning them into torches, and left behind a moonscape of charred toothpicks standing over thirty acres of ash. And even though I would have been ecstatic if any excuse for a fire—seemingly spontaneous combustion, a carelessly tossed cigarette, a dubiously intentioned match, or even a well-aimed flamethrower for that matter—had burned the mouse-house to the ground, trees like these take hundreds of years to grow, and I wanted to protect them.

So in spite of owning an expansive acreage, our land was less than useful and the manzanita had me penned into a small cleared area around the mouse-house. Pushing back this wall of brush became a priority. But unfortunately, apart from the admonition about it being hard work, there was nothing I knew about clearing, nothing except that I would need a chainsaw. So, on one of my enumerable trips into town to pick up building supplies, I made a detour to the chainsaw store.

This store catered to loggers, professionals, not an amateurish wannabe like me, and imagining loggers were a tough group I wondered if I had the right stuff. And although during my short time working as a manual laborer I had developed an authentic look, with scrapes, cuts, and gouges in all stages of healing, I still had the same old problem. As usual, I knew nothing. This time it was nothing about chainsaws, but I walked in anyway.

I'm still not convinced the salesman told me the whole story when he said that I would find the extra power useful, but I took his advice, anyway. I ended up buying a chainsaw that was big enough to fell a small forest in an afternoon and drag me off my feet doing it. But what became obvious as soon as I started to use this beast was the extra size and extra weight added to an already hard job. I should have bought something more suited to a syphilitic seventy-year old, and would have got just as much work done with a tenth the effort. However, on the bright side, I strode out of the store with the giant chainsaw balanced on my shoulder, and didn't see any obvious smirks or snickering. So at least I got something for my money.

It was a new toy and, weather permitting, I started nibbling away, clawing back some usable space from the manzanita thicket surrounding the mouse-house. Puffed up and pretending to be a Mountain Man (but without the ugly plaid jacket), I would fire-up the oversized chainsaw and head out on a mission to drop as many of the Enemy Manzanita as I could get done in a day, dogs in tow. They find everything I do fascinating.

These manly days were not just about cutting down the manzanita; they were also about burning what was cut. However, between the cutting, the dragging, and the burning, there was a lot of work in ridding the land of these tree-sized bushes. The ten to twenty-foot gangly branches had to be cut off, the trunks cut into pieces that could barely be lifted, and everything dragged back to and heaved into the fire, which never seemed quite close enough. I soon found the previous owner's description of the work an understatement that bordered on a lie.

Towards the end of a long day, the dull ache at the bottom of my back started giving way to violent spasms. I should have noticed the stupidity of it all but I was driven, and instead of rationalizing that there was always tomorrow, I imagined what a real mountain man would do and kept going. So only when my back wouldn't let me move another inch and I was practically immobile, and certainly not able to hold the giant chainsaw out in front of me or bend to pick up that one last branch, only then did I inch my way back to the fire, painfully lower myself onto the ground and lay, stiff as a board, staring at the bed of coals as it died down.

After an hour or so, leaving everything, especially my giant chainsaw where it was, I would slowly shuffle back to the house with the dogs following along behind; holding my lower back, reeking of wood smoke and occasionally groaning from the pain. And in the cold night air, hot from lying by the fire and still damp with the day's sweat, steam rose from all over my clothes, leaving wispy contrails in the air behind me. I must have looked like a tormented ghoul emerging from the dark.

Fun as this was, the previous owner had been right. It was exhausting work and thirty acres was looking like too much work for one old man. So when I heard of a bulldozer for sale, an antiquated bulldozer that was in my price range, I decided it was all the difference the situation needed. I rationalized that I could use the dozer for a year, get done what was needed and then sell it for about the same price I had bought it for. That was the plan, but one more time I was jumping into something that I knew absolutely nothing about. This time it was nothing about dozers.

My famously grumpy old neighbor volunteered his maxi-sized pickup truck to get the dozer and, after stopping in town to rent a trailer, we drove the short distance across town to buy the thing. With my now practiced Shasta handshake I introduced myself to the dozer's owner, and then set about giving his dozer a comprehensive, and comprehensively phony, inspection.

I knelt down in the mud and peered underneath things, climbed up and pulled on things, walked around some and stood back and assessed some, and always with a very serious look. The dozer's owner had worked heavy equipment his whole life, and just stared at me. He waited for the pantomime to end before asking, "Well, do you want to buy it or not?" Show no fear I thought. "There doesn't appear to be anything wrong... but do you mind going over a few things for me first?" It was all I could think of saying without giving the game away, and letting him know that I knew absolutely nothing. I needed some way of getting him to show me how to drive the thing. He did, but in a way that only a heavy equipment veteran would. He assumed I already knew what he was talking about.

My driver's education course consisted of him walking around the dozer, once, at different times pointing in the general direction of its cab full of levers, and rattling off which lever did what. I followed behind with my arms awkwardly crossed on my chest, and not wanting to look like I was stupid or something, making positive sounding grunting noises, nodding occasionally, and, of course, not asking any questions. With that everything that needed saying had been said. I paid the man and the scratched up, dented and gouged, big yellow and rust thing was officially mine.

I stood back in carefully concealed awe as he started the dozer and drove it up onto our rented trailer. Then he tied it down with some strange unfamiliar things that were designed to keep tons of metal from falling off the back, and with that we were ready to leave. I gave a cherry wave but the dozer guy just kept staring at me. The whole thing had had a dream-like quality to it. We drove slowly away, with the weight of the dozer a constant reminder as it alternatively pushed then pulled on the truck from behind.

It had snowed again while we were gone, but the county had just finished clearing Woods Canyon when we drove up, so we were able to trailer the dozer to the bottom of China Gulch, which was close enough. China Gulch is a dirt road and I could drive the dozer the rest of the way home on the dirt, at least to the barn. But first I had to unload it from the trailer, and this was to be my first time operating a dozer.

Drawing on my prior experiences of running heavy equipment (pushing an electric lawn mower on a weekend); I climbed up into the cab. I was wondering how I had gotten myself into another fine mess and prayed that this wasn't going to turn out the way most did. But ready or not, I was about to start operating some heavy iron; it just happened to be parked on top of a trailer at the time.

I tried to remember which knobs and levers did what, and in what order, to start the thing. But the truth was that I had only remembered the first couple of things the dozer guy had said and after that it was just a confused blur of jumbled words. I pressed the worn "Start" button, anyway.

The motor started with that soon-to-be-familiar rumble of its diesel engine. I waited for the motor to warm up, which also gave my courage time to get up to temperature as well. With plan 'B' in mind, the jump for my life plan, I pressed my left foot as hard as I could on (what I hoped) was the foot brake, and pulled on (what I hoped) was the gear shift lever, putting it into (what I hoped) was reverse.

Sometimes I get lucky. The transmission shifted into gear, giving a little telltale jerk on the tracks, and telling me the dozer should at least be headed in the right direction. Before my foot went completely numb, I slowly released its death grip on the foot brake. Nothing went wrong; in fact nothing happened at all. I gave it a little gas and the tons of iron started to squeak and creak slowly toward the back of the trailer. I couldn't believe I was actually operating a bulldozer!

The tricky part to unloading from this type of trailer was that at some point the trailer bed was going to teeter-totter backwards, as the dozer moved its weight from where it was parked, over the trailer's wheels, and towards the back of the trailer. And sure enough, there was this moment when I could feel the trailer bed, along with the dozer and me perched on top of it, start to lurch backward. I reached up and grabbed the roll cage with one hand and eased on the brake, slowing the dozer's progress until it was just inching back, and greatly impressed by just how precise such a dumb lump of iron could be.

Slowly, almost as if somebody who knew what they were doing was in charge, the trailer's bed leaned back and hit the ground with a clang only tons of steel could make. The dozer, with me attached, pitched back, and seemingly oblivious to the steep slope it was now on, crawled methodically off the back of the trailer and onto solid ground. I didn't relax though, it was all too new, and I was far too busy absorbing the creaking screeching metallic noises and just the physical presence of big iron. I had made it off the trailer okay, but what I really needed was a sign glued to my forehead that asked people to stop me from doing stupid stuff before I did it.

With a "Thank you" to Dale, shouted over the noise of the diesel, and leaving him to return the trailer, I pressed on the throttle, pulled on the steering levers, spun the dozer around in the brown slush of mud and snow, and started to trundle up China Gulch.

The first thing I noticed was that a little snow doesn't slow this many tons of iron down and, soon after, driving a dozer in a straight line was boring. I wanted to find out what my new toy could do. Through one part trial and a lot of errors, I figured out which levers did what to the six-way blade hanging in front of the dozer. I was beginning to understand what a "six-way blade" was, and with hands flying between levers (half the time causing the exact opposite of what I hoped would happen), dipping and lifting, angling and slanting the blade to the road, I drove up China Gulch pushing the three feet thick snow off to the side, along with an occasional piece of the road. After couple of passes, the dozer had China Gulch's dirt road open for traffic again, and lined the sides of the road with a high bank of jumbled blocks of dirty snow. My driving was still a flurry of misdirected hands randomly pushing and pulling on control levers, but since there was nobody around to see it I congratulated myself on a job well done. With the last drop of adrenalin in me used up, and slowly freezing on the dozer's open-air metal seat, I called it quits for the day. While I was still ahead and before I did something really stupid that a neighbor happened to see.

I swung the dozer off China Gulch, parked it beside Thunder's barn, pulled on the kill switch and climbed down out of the cab. I had become a heavy equipment operator. Probably not quite the best yet, but better than a couple of hours before when a former computer geek had flailed in a one-sided argument with a piece of heavy machinery. And you would have thought that this large loud metal thing intruding into his quiet world would have impressed Thunder, but it didn't. He looked over once, and then went back to snuffling around in the bottom of his bowl for some leftover oats.

With the dozer shut down for the day, I stood in the lightly falling snow with my body still buzzing from the engine's vibrations, the sounds of large pieces of iron creaking and banging still echoing in my ears, the smells of diesel in my nose. I wished there was a way to let everyone know how great it felt, but there wasn't, and this was a private celebration. So I christened the big rust and yellow metal thing "Sting" (because manzanita would soon be trembling at its sight), turned my back on the afternoon's excitement and walked back up the hill to the mouse-house, using exaggerated steps to help climb through the three feet of snow.

A couple of weeks later the snow had cleared and the ground had a chance to dry out. For some reason, I wanted to drive Sting up to the mouse-house. There were plenty of other places, easier places, I could have chosen to get more time driving the dozer, but for some reason I was determined to make this my first test. I started to scout a route from the barn. Our newly resurfaced driveway couldn't be used because the dozer's metal tracks would have torn it up, so I had to find an overland route. It was going to be steep and it was going to be rugged. I scrambled around the slopes, over and under the manzanita, until I was certain I had found the *easiest* route (there were no easy routes). At the end of the day I wasn't scared, but I'll admit to some feelings of trepidation.

With the scouting complete, the weather cooperating, and wearing what became the essential gear for the dozer—the feed store leather jacket, oiled stained Levis, gloves and boots—it was a barely confident hillbilly tank commander that swung up into the cab. With a quick glance up the hill, just to remind myself of what I was about to attempt, I started the diesel. The first part of the route up was easy, actually following the footpath paralleling the seasonal creek, down to the spot that gave the best route up the mountain. Trundling the dozer down the path I reached my turn and pivoted Sting around, with a last look up the slope, I opened the throttle and started up the side of the mountain.

Driving a dozer is an unnatural experience. It moves utterly methodically, pulverizing the ground underneath. It has no suspension, it lurches and screeches and squeals and bangs, and it sets a course as if it had destiny in its pocket. With all the power under my control I was feeling like a supreme being riding a force of nature. I was master of the world. Of course, any local watching my performance would have turned away in disgust, spat deliberatively, and then offered the opinion, "That's the *stupidest* @#**# thing I've ever seen."

Maybe I need to explain some facts about manzanita, to help explain why it is the enemy. It is a very, very hard wood. It's also mean, it likes to kill or maim if it gets the opportunity. It will bend, but only under tremendous pressure, and then only so it can fly back and smash anything in its path, especially if that happens to be a small-boned old man. If it lands on your head, it hurts. If it gets the opportunity to poke you, it hurts. It prefers to spear you, which hurts even worse. It is heavy when you want to drag it and gets even heavier when you drag it uphill. It has lots of small branches that love to catch on everything, and even the smallest of its branches is determined enough to grab hold and stop any human-powered forward progress, with ease.

It even has strategies for dozers. If you make the rookie mistake of simply running over manzanita it lies down under the dozer and turns itself into skid plates, causing the tracks to spin helplessly and the dozer to be stuck. If you drive over a large enough piece of it you end up high-centered with the tracks spinning in the air, and again stuck. If you fail to notice it poking around the tracks, it gets pulled through the tracks and pops them off the rollers, and stuck again. Over time, I learned each of these things the hard way.

The dozer powered its way up the mountain, dodging the biggest boulders and crushing the rest. As usual, my hands and feet were flying from one control to another, wrong exactly half the time, while I repeatedly stopped and backed up, using Sting's blade to pop each manzanita bush out of the ground and then push the bush out of the way. It didn't take long to blast a path up the hill. With the diesel roaring at full throttle, I burst out of the undergrowth near the mouse-house pushing a thicket of manzanita in front of me, oblivious to the fact I'd just snagged the guy-wire supporting the utility pole by the house. This had caused the forty-foot pole to shudder and sent the 12,000-volt lines thrashing around in the air over my head. Oblivious, Sting and I came to a stop, parked in the middle of the front lawn outside the mouse-house.

I was expecting a hero's greeting from my loving wife, who was standing outside the front door motionless, staring at the power lines. It was my fault. I had left her earlier with the misinformation that I was going to find somebody experienced to drive Sting up the hill. In a way I had, but instead of a hero's greeting my eager ears heard, "You … &*@@?%*##@#%." It went on for some time, but being the larger person I overlooked her narrow take on the situation (along with her obsession with the power lines) and interpreted her outburst as merely misphrased praise. Then, just to show just how responsible I was, I put Sting's rusty coffee can over its exhaust (to keep the snow out), and maintaining a decent perception of myself, strode inside and out of the cold.

The Day the Wheels Fell Off

To be precise it was my second day driving the dozer, and it wasn't a wheel that came off, it was one of its tracks. Being new to the job, all my attention was inside the cab (trying to figure out which lever did what), and the little attention that was left over was outside the cab. But what was needed was 100% attention outside the cab at all times.

I was in the middle of an uncoordinated attempt to push a large tangle of brush sideways across the face of a slope, and as I was pivoting Sting around a boulder my tentative dozer driving came to a halt. I looked down in astonishment at the right-hand track slowly peeling away from the side of the dozer. There wasn't a warning bell, there wasn't a loud noise or a grinding sound, there wasn't any give-away that something was going wrong, but it had. I couldn't have been more astonished if I had looked down and seen my right leg had just fallen off!

At this point I knew nothing more about dozers than where the start button was, and my first thought was that I was sitting on a piece of expensive *yard art*. Yard art, for you city folks, is an old piece of farm equipment, mostly rust and a patch or two of paint, often seen in an encampment of weeds at the far end of a field where it had last stopped working and was left. It might look picturesque when driving by, but I was thinking that I was sitting on one. A $10,000 piece of junk, paid for by a fool who knew nothing, out of a dwindling home equity line and, if there could be worse, I could just hear my new best friends at the Beer Bar, "I told you he don't know s%*t."

So there I was, sitting on an immobile six-ton piece of iron, leaning over on the side of a steep soft and muddy hill. The downhill track, with most of the dozer's weight on it, was buried in a foot of mud, and the uphill track was lying disjointed, half on and half off. I shut the diesel down, climbed glumly down from the cab, then bent over, straddled the errant track, and reached down with both hands trying to move it. It wouldn't budge, and with that experiment over there was nothing else worth trying. I trudged back up to the house, my spirits dragging in the mud behind me. I expected this to be the end to a very, very short dozer-driving career, convinced I had broken the thing.

In what I was certain would just be a pointless Hail Mary, I made one phone call. Picking up the local phone book I searched the yellow pages and chose the likeliest looking quarter-page ad. I already had the conversation planned out before I placed the call to the parts department of a local heavy equipment dealer. I gave the parts guy the dozer's make and model and then dropped in the innocent question. It was carefully worded so I wouldn't sound like I was an imbecile who knew nothing about dozers but owned one anyway. "Is there anything different I need to know about putting the track back on this model dozer?"

"No, I don't think so. Just release the pressure on the ram and slide the track back on the idler wheels, then pump the ram back up. There's nothing different about that model, there's no problem with it." I tried to take the high-pitched glee out of my voice before answering.

"Yep, that's just what I thought, but it's always best to ask." And after another small pause to again restrain the glee, "Oh, before I let you go, do you have one of those pumps in stock?"

"Sure."

"I'll be right down, then."

Before driving into town to get one of those pump things, whatever it was, I ran back to the dozer to match the words on the phone against what I saw. I found the thing that possibly could be called a *ram*. After looking all over the ram, I found the only anything that could possible be used to put in or get out whatever it was that was inside the ram. It was just a grease fitting. So I loosened it, very tentatively, arms outstretched and head turned away, expecting an explosive release of whatever was in the ram, but out oozed grease. It was ordinary grease and the mystery was solved. Just to prove it though I used a six-foot pry bar to force the ram back some more, it took a six-foot pry bar to move it, and out oozed more grease. I could move the ram and the ram was full of grease. I now knew the 'what' and the 'how' to remount the wayward track.

It turned out the "pump" was just an oversized grease gun, and this apparently catastrophic event is an everyday occurrence driving a dozer. It's dealt with nothing more than a giant crowbar (or two), healthy wads of spit and some swearing helps, and a dozer-sized grease gun. The oversized grease gun surprisingly moves great masses of large metal mechanical things with ease. It was all news to me, and though the parts guy's "No problem" was a bit of an under-statement, it was maybe looking doable.

Everything on a dozer is heavy because it's made of over-sized lumps of iron. This should have caused me to get some advice but, as usual, to avoid looking like I was ignorant or something, I had skipped asking the guy at the equipment store something sensible such as, "No, really, how do you get 500 lbs of impossibly heavy track back on a dozer?" Instead, I trusted my Druid heritage and figured that as long as it only meant moving something immensely heavy, the answer would come to me eventually. That would be after many hours of inevitable missteps and with great difficulty, but at least I wouldn't look ignorant to the parts guy. So you see my point.

I have no idea what I'd do without luck on my side. The dozer was equipped with a six-way blade and rear drag bars. This probably means nothing to city folks, but it meant a lot to one old man on the side of a muddy hill, whose impossible task it was to slide a 500-lbs steel track under six tons of dozer—by hand. It meant I could start Sting's engine and, with no more effort than pushing a couple of the control levers (hopefully in the right direction for a change), lift the dozer clean off the ground and suspend its great bulk between its blade in the front and its drag bars in the back. Well, that's the rough idea. Again the hill, the slope, and the mud came into it, but with carefully placed logs pushed underneath, to give the blade and rear bar something solid to push off, I soon had the uphill drive-wheels lifted clear of the ground with enough space underneath to let me slide the track back under them.

Considering that I'm just a little old man, I'm not weak, but this dozer track was more than I would normally ever want to move, even in the best of circumstances. In the current circumstances, working alone, sitting in the mud, with my legs and arms (and sometimes my head) extended underneath six tons of machinery, balanced over me in a best-as-I-could-do-under-the-circumstances kind of a way, on the side of a steep slope, I was having doubts about the wisdom of attempting this repair. So often it's a toss up which has the upper hand with me—luck or stupidity—but only once did a crowbar come flying back and knock me senseless into the mud.

Even with my best thinking on the subject, gravity conspired to work against me. Nothing got accomplished without a lot of heaving and pushing and cursing. But after several failed strategies, I finally figured out the right combination of pushing, shoving, cursing and crowbars to finally get the track back on the dozer's wheels. The success should have been enough to stop me from cursing, but seems there was still a bit more that needed saying on the subject.

So still cursing, covered in mud, cold and soaked through, of course, I climbed into Sting's cab, started it and drove the big diesel back up the hill. And with some mixed feelings, I parked the rescued machine by the garage, thankful for my Druid heritage, but wondering one more time, what the %^#** was I doing here? I called it quits for the day and trudged in the house to take a shower and get warm. It had been a hell 'a day.

The following morning I was back on the slopes. Sting no longer seemed invincible, but it had let me know where the cliff was. There's always seems to be a cliff there, somewhere, when trying out new stuff and you know absolutely nothing about what you're doing. But this time I had found the edge before plunging into an unforeseen catastrophe. And even though it wasn't a pleasant experience, and I'll admit to having a few moments of distress, this first exposure to a dozer's mechanics had turned out to be a great success for a near disaster.

The wheels fell off several times after that, but each time the repair got easier and quicker, though never exactly easy or quick. Mostly what improved was that I learned to drive a dozer so the tracks didn't fall off, which simply meant using some common sense and slowing down, easing round rocks rather than crashing into them for the fun of it. Still, apart from the occasional repairs, I was having a great time playing the part of a hillbilly tank commander, sitting up high in the cab and looking the part in my feed store leather jacket, heavy gloves, and work boots.

Every time I plowed down a slope, taking out a six-foot wide swatch of manzanita, I remembered just how hard it would have been to do it by hand. I was clearing brush on an industrial scale and building giant piles of manzanita along the way. But this wasn't an exercise in logic or reason; it was a noisy, calamitous, and dangerous mayhem. Beside the racket of the diesel roaring and metal parts screeching and banging around, there were branches, some as thick as a thigh, cracking like rifle shots when they snapped. Jagged branches whipped into the cab and smashed into the roll cage, and sheared off branches speared into the open cab from every angle. In places hard to see, there were branches working into the tracks, rocks to avoid, holes not to fall down and slopes not to slide down, and way worse, not to tumble down. And in the middle of all of this confusion I was ducking and swiveling around, trying to see what was next, what was beside me, what was left in my wake, and all the while working the controls. Between the adrenalin, the controls, and being thrown around inside the cab, towards the end of the day I got tired, lazy, and made mistakes.

While backing up I didn't always bother to look behind me. Instead, I relied on memory for what was I was backing into, as well as an overly broad notion that the dozer would crush whatever it was. I was using this faith-based method to blindly back up, content to listen to the noise of things being pulverized behind me while absent-mindedly staring out the front of the dozer, when I had a thought that just the right-sized broken manzanita branch could be waiting back there, perfectly placed, and come through the one inch gaps in the steel brush cage and spear me. Whatever the source for this premonition, I turned round just in time to dodge out of the way of exactly what I had thought of. A split second later and a one-inch thick spear of jagged manzanita would have impaled my neck, driven into me with all the weight of the dozer, and through me as easily as a knife. That was the very last time I backed up without turning around to see where I was going, but the race between experience and disaster was probably pretty close.

Luckily, my great ignorance seemed to attract safety tips like flies to road kill. I was talking to a CalTrans crew boss at the Beer Bar, a Norwegian and the sort of guy you want on your side—he was the size of a large bear. Between listening to his stories about blowing up mountains and building bridges and viaducts and tunnels and all kinds of neat things, I was nattering on about my antiquated dozer and my amateurish adventures on the mountain. I just happened to mention that I preferred not to wear its seatbelt; explaining that I wanted to keep the option to jump clear if something went wrong. Actually, the real reason was that the seatbelt was dirty, but I didn't want to admit to something that stupid.

The giant Norwegian didn't show any change of expression, and kept staring into his glass of beer, which I assumed was there but couldn't be sure because it was completely hidden from sight by his two giant paws. He asked me patiently, "Do you notice which way you're going when your dozer pitches you out of your seat?"

"Well yes, of course, it's downhill. But I never get turfed out because I grab the roll bar." Even as I was saying these words, I was sensing that some plain country logic was about to be applied to my way of thinking.

"And what happens if you miss that roll bar, where do you go?"

"If I miss it? Oh... I suppose down, down in front, or off to the side and down... depending, of course."

"And what's coming right behind you... depending... as you go down in front or down and off to the side?" The big Norwegian made what I considered an unnecessary emphasis on the word *depending*, and I was regretting trying to finesse my answer.

"The dozer?" I asked.

It helps to have driven a dozer and felt its sheer mass to imagine the effects of something this heavy tumbling down a hill after you. The sheer weight and the unforgiving nature of one of these things are completely alien to thin-skinned squiggy bags of biological material. And the smallest mistake is not just likely to be fatal; chances are it will kill you several times over and then for a very long time.

After this conversation, I retired my over-rated reflexes in favor of a dirty seatbelt, but I can still remember his closing statement on the matter. "You might lose an ear or some fingers... maybe more... but at least you won't be dead."

A Semblance of Normalcy

In spite of the facts, in spite of the daily realities we had to deal with, Sheila stubbornly insisted that our move to Igo had been a good idea. She kept the Faith. She stayed optimistic and said that our move was an opportunity; calling it an adventure. What to call this move we didn't agree on, but she was right about one thing— her optimism. Someone had to remain optimistic, and living as rough as we were it was lucky I had a wife willing to be a part of whatever it was that we were doing here. What's astonishing is that my whining and sour moods didn't pull our marriage down faster than the house went up, and during that first winter I privately sainted Sheila for her tireless work supporting me. Without her strength I'm sure we would have spiraled down through diminishing affection, weeklong silences and screaming rows, ending up with a half-built mouse-house on the side of what would have become Mount f^%%# Despair. Our first winter was rough, very rough, but Sheila kept the Faith and kept it for the two of us.

Even after the December snow had melted, we continued to feed the front deck into the fireplace, and only when there was nothing left to burn did we break down and buy a propane gas heater. But with the wind still blowing freely through the house, and broke as we were, we didn't dare waste the gas and the house stayed frozen. In fact, it was colder than ever.

Adding to the depression, the interior was still painted the same battleship gray it had always been, and, being mid-winter, it was also getting dark by four-thirty in the afternoon. Between the gloom and isolation I could see us chasing each other around wielding meat axes and chainsaws in the middle of the night. So Sheila insisted and I wired up some new sockets, then we splurged on some $5 clip-on lights. Which lifted the gloom some, but our evenings were still spent wrapped around each other under several blankets on the couch, watching television, until that was too much fun. Then we went to bed dressed just as we were, apart from our boots, and happy to have the dogs piled on top for the extra warmth. As I'm sure they were, too.

In the month after the Christmas snowstorm the weather warmed up to a more usual winter temperature for these parts, with just an occasional snow. And motivated by the previous month's misery I used any breaks in the weather to repair more of the exterior walls; replacing the rotted siding on the outside and the insulation and sheetrock on the inside. The north wind had to finally blow around, as opposed to through, the I-should-have-burnt-it-to-the-ground-when-I-had-the-chance   assemblage   of building materials that had been erroneously identified as a house in the sales agreement. But there was still a lot to get done. My time was spread among other must-do chores, and it was late spring before I finally had the mouse-house sealed up—for all the good it did us then.

With the exterior walls doing something useful for a change, the next challenge was what to do with the downstairs floor. All I had done up to then was nail scraps of plywood over the holes, after falling through them a couple of times. I hadn't thought about the floor since, partly because I didn't want to be reminded of about it, but mostly because I didn't have a clue what to do with it.

During the decade the mouse-house had been left abandoned, the roof had leaked and soaked the floor for several months each winter. This had left some areas rotted through and obviously needing replacing, but other parts, even though they hadn't rotted completely, were so weakened that they had sagged. So apart from the holes, the floor also had built-in dips and hollows. I thought about tearing the whole thing out and starting over, but that seemed like a lot of work, I didn't know how to do it, and I couldn't have afforded to do it anyway. The solution that eventually came to me seemed off the wall at the time, but actually worked. It was to use a layer of mortar to level out the dips and hollows, and then lay concrete backer boards on top of that to construct what would essentially be a concrete floor over the original plywood.

Most construction details I skip over because I'm sure that reading about them would be as tedious as doing them. But to give a sense of how much work was involved in rehabbing the mouse-house (at least at the rate I got things accomplished), we were into our second summer here before I started on the floors. I can fix this in time because while I was mixing the buckets of the mortar and humping them into the house, sweat was flying off me like a lawn-sprinkler and simultaneously washing away fresh splatterings of mortar along with the last stubborn remnants of my self-worth. I was scurrying around, mixing, carrying, pouring and leveling, trying to stay in front of the materials before they dried out, doing something better done by a whole crew half my age. But nothing could have bothered me by this point, I was just grateful that this was the last of the grunt work and the floor was ready to be tiled.

We had chosen tile because of all the animals. Our new floor had to be vomit proof, carcass proof, and occasionally poop proof, it also needed to be durable, washable and cheap, and no other flooring could have qualified. After this first year in the country, I would have also liked flooring we could have hosed off once a month, but that would have been asking for too much. We had to tile the entire floor area of the mouse-house (the animals would have found any spot we didn't tile), and with almost 1000 sq ft of floor, this meant 1000 tiles and several runs to and from Home Depot in an overloaded mini-truck, just to get all the materials.

Judging by mass of material stacked in the driveway, it was going to be a big job. But each tile took only a few minutes to lie, and by the end of the week the complete downstairs floor had been tiled, grouted, and even the mess I'd made doing it cleaned up. Finally, we had a floor we could walk on (without falling through it or getting splinters in the bottom of our feet), and we could look forward to next winter without watching in stunned amazement as the occasional snowflake blew up through it. One by one, the holes in places there shouldn't have been holes, were being sealed up.

By the middle of this second summer all the walls had been rebuilt. The new energy efficient windows kept the weather out, we had interior walls, and now a floor. Sheila trimmed around the doors and windows and painted over the battleship gray styling of the marijuana growers. All that was left to do was to clean up the rough-cut wood beams that spanned the downstairs. These beams were the only architectural feature in the whole house worth keeping, but the battleship gray paint had to be sanded off first. It was the last truly dirty job, and two days later, still covered in a mix of finely powdered gray paint and wood dust, I was able to stand in the middle of the mouse-house, look around, and feel unusually good about what had been accomplished so far.

The mouse-house was livable, not finished but maybe livable, and although months of finish-work lay ahead, we didn't care, we wanted to move in. We moved the tools and the last of the construction debris out of the house, and then thoroughly cleaned the whole place. It was even safe enough to find our one oriental carpet, stored for the last year in the back of the garage, and roll it out with the reverence it deserved.

It's a small detail, but the only leftover from the Great Construction was our couch. It had been in the house the whole time and survived. It had seen a year's construction around it and on top of it, used as tool bench, a short ladder, and a platform, it had never once been cleaned but it had proved itself indestructible, and earned itself a place in our lives.

Together we carried this remarkable couch onto the deck; I set up our Sears 5-hp compressor and unleashed the deep cleansing power of a high-pressure air nozzle on it. For an hour, accumulated dust and filth flew out of the couch and drifted down the valley. It was a stain in the sky but, as it drifted away, it seemed to take a year of primitive living and a lot of bad juju along with it. By the time we were finished it was still possible to pound a new dust cloud out of the couch, but at least the cloud didn't come with its own shadow. And since it was now a hundred pounds lighter, we easily pushed the couch back inside the house, along with a promise to treat it better this time.

The mouse-house was livable at last. There were plenty of exceptions to this I could bore you with, but we could sit in one spot, stare straight in front, and pretend our lives were more or less normal. The unlikely day had finally arrived. We had the first glimmerings of what a finished mouse-house would feel like, and the days and months of wondering if this point could ever be reached were behind us. For a moment, giddy optimism filled the air.

The next tasks, on a still unending list of projects, were building a kitchen and rewiring the entire house. Again, I won't bore you with the details, but just one small part of the rewiring meant I spent days on my back in the dirt, dragging wires through a spider-filled crawlspace with muck raining down on me. You can figure it out from there, but I can guarantee that there is far more work involved in rewiring a house than there ever was wiring it.

However, the main problem I had with rebuilding was that it was costing far more than I'd thought possible, and we were nowhere near done. The cash we had arrived with was gone, along with all of the modest home equity line we took out, and we were once again out of money. No matter how low we ducked, our everyday living expenses came to a lot more than the slowly increasing income from our apartments. We were in another financial crisis.

I couldn't return to my computer career, which was already two years (centuries) out of date, and even if I could have doddered to an interview and feigned interest in writing software for some newer and even more useless gadget, my old skill set was probably on display in a technology museum with school children walking by and snickering at it. Plus, a small point, in the two years since I had worked for a living the smartest thing in my life had been a hammer, and that formerly clever computing part of my brain had rusted solid. The only thing we could do was to increase our equity line and, if we had to, build out the property for sale. Once sold, we could then start on some another dilapidated wreck, and probably on and on, further into old age until I mercifully died in the harness. It wasn't exactly a happy prospect but seemed quite likely.

Fortunately for us, this was at a time that the banks were still eagerly throwing money out their doors at anyone that had recently fogged a mirror. So we asked for a larger equity line, one to get us through the rebuilding, and our Wall Street bank gave us more. Flush with cash, finishing the kitchen didn't seem half the problem it had been two weeks before, but we had been chastened by a year's hard living and had developed a habit of scrimping. We chose to make inexpensive tile counter tops, use a basic line of stock pine cabinets from Home Depot, and buy only the occasional stainless steel thing. Two short weeks later we had a kitchen and the downstairs was finished, or close enough for the time being.

The upstairs of the mouse-house consisted of the bathroom that we had built-out a year before, and the still untouched bedroom. Its floor was not in as bad a shape as the downstairs floors but I leveled it anyway, using my now proven method, and since I was getting pretty good at it, we tiled that too. After some finish work and painting, we moved in our bedroom furniture and the two-room mouse-house had become a home. The big lumps were finally done and the pressure to rebuild was off. I could finally relax.

So the next week, looking out at the view from our newly finished bedroom, and a little bored, I had an idea to remove a couple of trees. They had always bothered me but I'd never had the time to do anything about them. These were not ponderosas but scraggily gray pines (hardly trees at all, more like giant weeds), and they were plum in the middle of the hundred-mile view that had enticed me into buying this property in the first place. With a new purpose in life, but not wanting to listen to a half-hour of warnings about the real and imagined dangers of doing such things, I waited for the wife to drive into town before dropping the two trees.

The tricky part about dropping these trees was that they were easily a hundred feet tall but only fifty feet from the power lines running up to the mouse-house. The downside to one of these trees falling on the power lines was substantial. Listing them, and not necessarily in order of importance: There would be no power to the house, the downed power lines could start a fire and burn the place down, and lastly it would be an embarrassment that the wife would never let me forget. Most people would have stopped right there, but I've always felt that there's more to life than being prudent.

So encouraged by the timeless wisdom from the seventies—"Don't buy into bad until you have to!"—I pulled the giant chainsaw out of the garage and walked the fifty yards to the doomed trees. I had cut down a lot of large manzanita during the previous winter, though I had never dropped a tree and certainly nothing as tall as these two trees. I decided that was a mere detail and this was just a matter of scaling up some.

It was all in the cut. I'd overheard how to drop a tree at the Beer Bar, and the idea, if I understood what had been said, was to cut a wedge out of one side of the tree (out of the side it was meant to fall), and a steep back-cut on the other side, which was to meet the wedge cut halfway through the tree. The downward angle of the back-cut should leave enough wood to make sure the tree couldn't fall backwards, in this case fall backwards into the power lines. So with a great deal of trepidation, and maybe not enough, I fired up the chainsaw and stood beside the first tree; glancing up at the tree—dwarfing me—just to remind myself how much *scaling up* I was getting into. About to make the first cut I carefully lined up the saw, trying hard to reason that this should go as planned, but feeling the same way I have so many other times just before something went terribly wrong. Sometimes I wish that there really were an omniscient deity whose job it was to help out intentionally stupid people.

Amazingly, it went as planned. I cut out the wedge on the side it needed to fall, and then with the last of the back-cut done the tree began to slowly tilt, away from the power lines thank goodness. It leant, ever so slowly at first, then decidedly, falling exactly where I had hoped it would drop and hitting the ground with a satisfying cloud of dust. I was ecstatic, but also half done. After sitting for a few minutes, hoping that what was left of my courage hadn't taken the rest of the afternoon off, I stood ready to drop the remaining tree. I still wasn't feeling confident but I restarted the chainsaw anyway and cut the wedge out of the second tree. That went well, and now all that was left to do was the back cut. This final cut would sever the tree from its stump and allow it to fall.

When using a chainsaw to cut through a large tree, one eye nervously watches the tree in case it decides to fall on you (out of ill will, or a gust of wind, or something you hadn't thought of yet), while the other eye is carefully watching the gap left behind by the chainsaw blade as it cuts through the wood. This gap tells you which way the tree wants to lean, and the minute changes in the gap as it opens or closes behind the blade let you know if you are doing the right thing, or not, by continuing to cut through what's left of the trunk.

As I was making the back cut, I was surprised to see the tree seemed to be neutral about the gap. It didn't care, it wasn't opening and it wasn't closing. With the chainsaw chewing through the tree at full-throttle, my attention was split between the tree wanting to land on me and the chainsaw wanting to amputate a leg or some other body part. The meaning of the gap neither opening nor closing wasn't exactly my top priority, when it should have been. Just as the chainsaw finished cutting the last of the back cut I understood what the meaning of that neutral gap was.

The tree didn't fall and made no attempt to fall. It just dropped the quarter of an inch into the space the chainsaw had left, trapping my chainsaw's blade under the full weight of the now amputated tree. Which was bad enough, but not as bad as what was about to happen. The tree stood absolutely still for a few seconds, improbably balancing on the stump, before leaning ever so slightly back towards the power lines. The only thing stopping it from falling into the power lines were the few short inches of wood left by the back-cut. About this time, it occurred to me that the increasingly inadequate looking back-cut could only encourage the tree not to fall on the power lines, not actually prevent it, and did nothing to make the tree fall the right way. Then I noticed the small wafts of occasional afternoon breezes. As I looked up at the now severed tree towering above me, leaning its weight against those few inches of back-cut, I saw that even slightest wind was moving the tree. I realized that my fate hung on which chance waft of summer breeze came along first.

I tried pushing on the tree, but it didn't have the slightest effect. I tried my hardest, with my shoulder pressed against the tree and my boots scrambling like mad for some traction in the dirt, but it hadn't the slightest effect. Things were looking really bad. Fueled by adrenalin, the situation called for some quick thinking followed by some decisive action. I skipped the thinking and went straight to the action. Leaving the chainsaw trapped by the tree I ran back up the hill, pulled a pile of cargo straps out of the garage and fired up the dozer. If an old man couldn't move that tree, Sting sure could.

Not waiting for its customary warm up, Sting covered the ground back to the tree as fast as it could rumble, which was never that fast and at best a walking pace. All the while I was glancing furtively up at the tree, still teetering towards the power lines, and whimpering to myself, "Don't fall, please don't fall." Nearly at the tree I pivoted the dozer, turning it around so it could back up and tie the cargo straps to the tree. I was busy driving the dozer and thinking about wrapping the straps around the tree to pull it over, but I hadn't actually thought this plan through, at least not through to the end. With the advantage of hindsight it's obvious that if it had gone as planned I would have pulled the tree down on myself. Which might seem obvious now but at the time I was in a hurry.

Just as I started to back up the dozer, and I didn't see or hear it coming, the tree crashed to the ground. It landed right beside the dozer with the usual extended ground shaking thud that large trees make, missing one of the tracks by a foot, and close enough that the dozer ran into the still-bouncing tree before I could find the foot brake in the confusion. Any other time, I wouldn't have been able to resist a facetious "Oops", but another second and the dozer would have been right under the tree. And much as Sting's roll cage looked tough, I'm not sure what a hundred-foot tree would have done to the roll cage and me inside of it. Unimportant. The tree hadn't dropped through the power lines and had actually landed right where I wanted it to, exactly beside the first tree.

There was no attempt at self-congratulation. For the rest of the afternoon, and the next few days, I came up with new and wonderful ways of linking my name to the word *stupid*, ways that even my loving wife couldn't have imagined. But that was a private scolding, and under no circumstances could I allow what had happened to go public. When Sheila came home later in the afternoon, I nonchalantly mentioned I had taken the two trees down, and when asked how it went I answered, "Oh fine," and continued eating my sandwich, staring vacantly out the kitchen window.

A couple of months later I sold Sting. The cash squeeze was getting tighter and looking around at what the dozer had done the previous winter and what was left to do, the money talked louder. I was really sorry to see it leave, and the day it went I continued to look down China Gulch until it was out of sight. I had had a bond with the old piece of machinery. The day before, Sting and I had driven out across the property, by all its great accomplishments at a slow idle so we could take our time remembering. It was my last ride on Sting: the last metallic creaks and groans, the last noises and smells of its diesel motor, and the last memories of being a part of the world of heavy metal.

I still felt I had betrayed the old thing. The morning after it left I was driving into town, and as I sped along I spotted out of the corner of my eye the rusty coffee can that I had used to keep the rain out of its exhaust stack. It was lying in the ditch beside the road and must have blown off while Sting was being towed. I have no idea how I spotted it, but after screeching to a halt I ran back and have kept it as a memento. I suspect it was the dozer's way of giving me something to remember it by, though it needn't have bothered, I would have kept the memories anyway.

Burn Piles

The thing that always puzzled me about the Mayor is that could have done well wherever he had chosen to live, and risen to the top of whatever he had chosen to work at. And of all the opportunities he could have pursued and places he could have made his home, why he had chosen a goat barn in Igo I never quite understood. But he always seemed happy to have lived in the woods for literally decades, which is unusual, and without a job, which is remarkable.

For thirty years Roy had successfully avoided work. He still managed to put food on his table (for that matter even had a table), under a roof (long in need of repairs but still, a roof), survived in a modest style and achieved an elevated status in the community. He's one of those rare and fortunate people that are always at ease, and that glide effortlessly over the trials and tribulations that mere mortals have to endure. He lives in a permanent state of grace.

There's no ideology involved, he's not materialistic and he's not exactly a minimalist either, but his charmed life had to be underwritten by something, and of course it was. He survived through bartering, and being that he's probably smarter than most of his trading partners, bartering turned out to be good for Roy, and oddly, for his trading partners, too. It was as if Roy found value in places that it had been overlooked and then unlocked the hidden potential to the benefit of both sides of the bargain. Not that I'm referring to huge sums, but enough for him to get by for a third of a century, which was good enough. And it took me some time to realize this aspect of Roy, because it was seamlessly inter-woven with an always-amusing personality and his soothing laissez-faire manner that charmed everyone around him. But by far his greatest gift was his unerring ability to see the best in people, whoever that was.

So I was always glad to have him sit down for dinner, a couple of times a week, and I was equally glad to lend him the mini-truck or tools, last seen with an enthusiastic smile and a careless wave. The wife remained skeptical, then that's her nature, and it wasn't her job to rebuild a house for little or no money. In Roy, I had a world expert in getting by on practically nothing sitting across our tired picnic table, and I felt extremely lucky to have become a part of Roy's invisible, yet very busy, economy. However, I did find that there was one inconsiderate truth to the arrangement, one that I didn't waste time dwelling on. Whatever I loaned Roy came back either empty or dented, or both, or broken, or all three, that's if it came back at all. It wasn't a big thing and it would have been pointless to mention it anyway, as I would have just come away from the conversation confirming how lucky I was to know him. So I didn't waste my time.

His locally infamous goat barn had been built decades ago in, what was, true Roy style, and whenever my visitors stared in disbelief at the mouse-house, I would take them by Roy's goat barn to stare some more. He had started thirty years ago with a goat barn that had been built a century before, and to help distinguish himself from the previous tenants Roy had poured a concrete floor. Then, paced by his casual lifestyle, he built an interior to the barn. He kept the original beam structure, put in a kitchen and a bathroom, and improved it until it could reasonably be described as a house. Its name never changed though, and everyone still refers to it as the "goat barn". The other thing of note about the goat barn is that everything used to build it was donated, recycled or found. (That's using the larger sense of the word *found*, but nothing had been bought for sure.) And looking around the barn at his collection of artifacts, it appeared not much of value got thrown away in Shasta County without Roy making sure he couldn't use it first.

His country home had developed a unique look. Its castle-like front door was built from solid wood with iron fittings. The original hand-carved beams more than held up the roof, the walls had been built from reused planks of solid redwood, artfully laid at an angle, and reclaimed oak floors dating back a century or more, also artfully laid at an angle. In the middle of the great room stood a wildly ornate wood-burning stove, that could just as easily have been on display in the Guggenheim, and the full length of one side had been extended out into an arboretum stocked with tropical ferns. As finishing touches, hanging imposingly on the walls above the front door, were a stuffed moose head, a rhino head and a buffalo head, scrounged or donated from goodness knows where. It might have been built for next to nothing, but there was a purpose to it, and the end result had an oppressively male presence. There wasn't a sign of a woman's touch anywhere, and hanging above the front door Roy might as well have had a sign, "Leave all hope outside and please remove your panties before entering." It was an artist's version of an unrepentant bachelor's house that had been built to provide dinner, a night's stay, and a slow breakfast. Checkout was at noon.

The one thing missing from Roy's carefree life, surprising really, was a pickup truck. Well, that's not exactly true; he was also missing any and every type of tool that might have enabled him to do any work of any kind. Which was probably not by accident, but even so, you would have thought that a pickup truck would have been a necessity, a requirement really for Roy's underground economy to operate effectively. Something to make sure this or that got delivered here or there to complete some transaction or another. And having clearly seen this, I should have remembered that Nature abhors a vacuum and not been surprised as the mini-truck became absorbed into Roy's invisible economy.

I wasn't fully awake one morning when I drove by the Inn and stopped in to see Roy. He was cleaning the place prior to yet another grand opening. And although I was only half-awake at the time, I should have known that the mini-truck would shortly be busy hauling trash to the county dump. There might be some kind of a deal involved but the certainty that morning was that I was taking a load to the dumps.

Experience counts, especially at times like this, and Roy was a half step in front of me. He was on top of a ladder replacing a fluorescent light at the time, and, without loosing focus on what he was doing, he baited the trap. "There's a slab of redwood out back... I've been saving it for you... have a look... I thought you might like it." What a guy, I thought, even though he was obviously busy and with so much going on, he was still thinking of my welfare.

"A slab of redwood? Wow, thanks, Roy." Still not firing on all cylinders I hadn't noticed that there was a deal here and, by the way, I had already accepted it.

"Good. See if there's anything else you could use back there... while you're there, would you mind taking the trash to the dumps?"

Things were improving—at least now it took a substantial bride to get me to drive to the dumps. But looking at the slab of whatever-it-was that Roy had just bribed me with I thought this was just going to be a repeat of a table saw he had generously given me a week before, just before I hauled another load of accumulated junk to the dumps. The table saw consisted of a homemade plywood box with an electric motor bolted inside and a blade poking menacingly out the top. It didn't work, which was fortunate, because its only possible purpose was dismemberment. And after wasting time and money trying to repair the lethal device, it went where it should have gone in the first place—the dumps—before it killed or maimed somebody. With the way this slab of wood looked I started to feel cheated before I got within twenty feet of it.

I completed my half of the deal, the drive to the dumps, and swung back by the Inn. The two of us lifted the slab of wood into the bed of the pickup, strapped it down, and I drove it morosely back to the house where I set it on a couple of sawhorses by the garage. It looked awful. I couldn't go near the thing without feeling despair and didn't have a clue what to do with the thing. I looked at it again and again over the next few days, trying to figure out what could be done with it, and finally an idea took hold. There was no reason to rush. There could be only one attempt at resurrecting it into something, useful other than firewood, and there were some problems to be worked around. It had a slight curl down its entire length, it was rotted at the corners and the first inch of its soft, powdery surface could have belonged to just about any other material, but not wood.

Because of its size and shape it might make a table, but with so many defects and flaws was that even possible? After looking at it for a week, an image from medieval history came to mind. A living piece of wood, celebrating its flaws, unashamedly hand-finished, a surface worn smooth from use and corners rounded through the years. That was the "what" my imagination saw under the powdery surface of this warped and weathered slab of wood. The "how" became an excuse to buy a large and extremely capable belt sander.

Wearing a mask and goggles for protection, the dried out exterior of the slab literally blew away under the sander, burying everything downwind in an inch of fine brown powder. In a couple more minutes some healthy wood started to emerge, and two hours later the outside layer of wood had been sanded off and the curled dish shape had been sanded flat. It was a stunning slab of old-growth redwood.

Over the next few days, and by using finer and finer sandpaper on my new and extremely capable belt sander, the table's final look emerged. I left the rough sides and the rotted corners for authenticity and finished the top with layers of furniture wax. Sheila had a couple of marble stands, left over from an arty glass-topped table that had met a construction accident of mine. The glass top hadn't survived the accident, but the artily tapered stands matched the slab's tree-trunk taper and the marble's texture perfectly complemented the redwood's grain. And though it started life as the other half of a barter for a dump run, the table has become a piece of family furniture—something our relatives are sure to write their names on and fight over during probate.

It was a first for me—making something useful and artful from discarded items and, more importantly, for practically nothing. And I'm sure Roy knew the potential in that slab of wood when he gave it to me, but he never mentions where it came from or how I ended up with it, though he does make a point of running his hand over its polished surface, appreciatively, whenever he stops by for dinner.

What I hadn't seen at the time, and what took me several more years to understand, was that Roy's very busy but invisible economy was often as not organized to someone else's benefit. If you were to look behind the scene of any charity event in Igo, you would find Roy working with a core of other locals to selflessly put it on. It was probably why he appeared to be the mayor of this small community, without him ever asking for the job, which had never existed anyway.

During my first winter on the mountain the Mayor often drove over to help with my burn piles, and the first time he helped he saved the day. I was attempting my first large burn. It was a cold drizzly morning and I had been pouring diesel fuel on mud and rain-soaked branches, trying to get something to start burning, but I was having a problem.

Growing up in the middle of a city, my only experiences of fires were the bonfires made in the backyard of the family's row house. I remember the smoke had hardly left the low flames before it disappeared, blending seamlessly into the smog that smothered London for entire winters before the Clean Air act. Those bonfires could hardly be called a fire, as they were more a pile of smoldering leaves than anything else. And the closest thing I experienced to burning while living in the Bay Area, was dutifully packing the offending leaves and twigs into a garbage can to be hauled off to the landfill. But in the country, there's always stuff that needs burning, and the more land the more stuff.

It's required really, especially if you were smart enough to have paid what little money you had for thirty acres covered by a dense blanket of thick undergrowth. And it shouldn't be described as undergrowth: after forty years of uncontrolled growth it had escalated into more of an overgrowth. It reached over the top of smaller trees, causing the trees to grow parallel to the ground instead of the more usual up. And the only way to get rid of this infestation and reclaim the land was to cut the brush down to the ground and burn it. Luckily, this was also a truly satisfying method.

My first burn was a small grass fire. I had in mind an experiment, one of those "controlled burns" I'd heard about. But even this first small step showed that there's seldom such a thing as a controlled burn. And on an increasingly long list, getting longer with every day here, a burn was just one more thing that I knew nothing about. For a change my ignorance aroused suspicions, and I chose a grassy area just down slope from our driveway. I was pretty sure the driveway wouldn't burn, which was fortunate because within seconds of starting this "controlled burn", my running around in tennis shoes trying to stomp it out wasn't proving that effective. The fire effortlessly took off along a rapidly expanding front, burning out to the sides and then up the slope, and was only stopped by the driveway, which it tried to jump, starting spot fires on the far side. Sheila put those out with a hose, after she came running out of the house to see what all the yelling was about. Without her help there would have been fire trucks and fire bombers, a lingering and unspeakable embarrassment, and made this my first, my only and last attempt at a burn.

The next attempt at a burn, months later, was a step up in size. It was my first large pile of manzanita, pushed together using the dozer. But I didn't have a clue what I was doing and, taking into account how well my first burn had gone, I'd waited until it was raining before trying to set light to the mix of mud and wet wood. After two hours of soggy frustration, Roy happened by and had my burn pile blazing in a few minutes.

He started with a couple of handfuls of dry grass, then some twigs, then small branches then larger branches until it was roaring, and that's how my first burn pile was started. The Mayor spent the rest of the day running into the heart of the fire with logs and unwieldy branches over his head, heaving them as hard as he could and rushing back out before his clothes caught fire. It looked like fun so I joined in, and by the end of the day we had cooked our skin, ending up looking like a couple of well-done turkeys.

In spite of these troubled beginnings, I went on to create burn piles on a previously unimaginable scale, using the dozer to push the manzanita into industrial-sized burn piles fifty feet across, and sometimes more, but with a lot less dirt and mud than that first time. And the best time to start a burn was not to wait for it to be actually raining, as I had, but to get an early start on a winter's morning, with cold damp air and no wind. Of course, if anything can change, the weather can.

There was always a tinge of apprehension to starting a large burn, and several barely survivable errors in judgment taught me that it only takes a small change in the humidity, or the sun peaking out from behind the clouds, or even a simple gust of wind, and one small ember later I could have easily gone down in local history as the fool that burnt out the entire valley. So when considering whether to start a burn, I tried hard to remember that the words *fire* and *control* don't go well together, and especially since a burn pile is surrounded by acres of the same fuel it's made of. And no matter how many precautions I took, there was a sense of foreboding whenever I walked up to one of these enormous piles of dried out wood with a propane torch.

One click of the igniter, a harmless blue flame into some dry leaves, and a few seconds later the fire had caught the twigs. I would stand back to watch the slow-moving white smoke change into a fast rising column of heat, and after that there was nothing to do, or could be done, except ride it to the end. Whatever that might be.

I remember one large pile in particular, actually the first monster-sized pile I put together. It measured sixty-feet across and was piled ten-feet high in places, essentially covering the face of a hill that had a good thirty degree slope to it. I had put the burn pile together using the dozer, pushing in the manzanita from acres around to make the pile, and it was going to be a big burn.

The pile had been sitting for a month while I waited for the right weather before lighting it. It was winter but it hadn't rained, so it wasn't summer dry but it had dried out some. With this in mind I lit the burn pile from the top. The idea was that the flame front would grow more slowly working its way downhill. Far slower than if I lit it from the bottom, where it would have shot up through the pile and guaranteed that the whole thing would have gone up in one giant ball of flame. I had a feeling that might not be a good idea.

On lighting the burn pile I found, once again, that a fire does what it wants. And even though I nervously, the nervousness should have counted for something, lit just a couple of leaves at the top far corner of the pile, five short minutes later the entire giant pile of wood was engulfed into one screaming tower of flame.

In those five minutes my mood turned from a common garden-variety trepidation into a to-the-bone fear. I was running around the fire whimpering, "What have I done, what have I done?" The flames, really one giant flame, was a hundred feet high, and not just a friendly cherry red or even an angry dark red, but at its core a demonic black that only became a conventional red colored flame about fifty feet up in the air. It sounded like a jet engine at full throttle, and acted like one too, shooting smoke and heat hundreds of feet into the air, along with burning chunks of things that came down trailing smoke and landing with small thuds. The giant flame had quickly engulfed the entire burn pile, and with every second it got hotter and hotter, which in turn consumed the wood faster and faster, which got it hotter and hotter... you get the picture.

I backed off to get away from the heat. I didn't have the slightest idea flames could get this angry, and then, to my amazement, it got worse. The fire started to breath. It started to gulp great masses of the surrounding air. I could feel the air surge past me and hear the fire pulsing with each breath. And I can tell you from this intensely personal experience that times like this can be unnerving, especially when you are standing there holding a garden rake—the tool most recommended for containing a fire. I was standing so far back that even if I had tried to throw the rake at the fire, I couldn't have even reached it. That's how much use the rake was.

But as I stood there, the fire at its worst, head cranked back, slack jawed, staring up at this monster flame, convinced that I had set the planet on fire and that the flame's next escalation would be the end of me, the two inches of snow covering the ground finally made it into in my consciousness and I had this reassuring realization, "Nah, not today." Even so, I thought the fire was going to reach out and snatch the rake out of my hand, just for spite, and the memory of that fire can still jerk me from a sound sleep.

I learned during the following burn seasons that even after all the best preparations, it's changes in the weather that can bite you the hardest. Just once, and once was plenty, the solid overcast cleared, the sun came out and a wind came up, of course, just after I had started a burn. It all happened at once. In a few minutes the small (by my standards) burn pile had changed into a disaster.

The sun dried out the leaf litter lying around on the ground and I saw *creepers* moving out from around the burn. Creepers are small, ground level flames, that use the leaves and dried grass as fuel, and creep around until they can find a better fuel and then take off. It doesn't take much to start a creeper, a single spark will do it, and by themselves creepers aren't that bad, as long as you have the time to cut them off before they can reach any serious fuel.

Then burning pinecones started to roll out of the bottom of the fire down the hill. These are called *rollers*. They leave a sputtering trail of burning grass behind them as they roll down a hill, which in this case was steep, and these rollers often made it a hundred feet before stopping on a bush or something, and then catching that alight. Then the wind picked up, blowing burning embers upwind, up hill from the burn pile into the now-dry brush.

Within minutes the burn pile had morphed into a nightmare. I had spot fires running downhill from the burn pile, other spot fires were starting on the hill above it, and creeper fires were coming out from all around it.

It was a mad triage. I spent one of the longest hours of my life running all over that hill. Up and down, left and right, heading off whatever flame front seemed to be gaining the most, or whatever flame front was headed towards even more fuel, or a steeper slope, or picking up speed or caught by the wind and was generally getting away from me. All the while, I was scared to death that the right combination of wind, fuel and slope would combine and I wouldn't be able to scramble under the smoke and heat and get close enough to slow it down before it got even worse—let alone stop it. I would have lost everything if that had happened. There would have been fire trucks, bombers, the embarrassment, the neighbors, their lawyers and finally the financial ruin. It was all enough to keep an old man motivated well beyond his advanced years.

Not that I was actually able to put out a spot fire, and certainly not on the first pass. I had to run up to the flames, drop onto all fours just before getting there, to get under the heat and smoke, and then use both hands and feet to frantically claw, kick and scrape away at the dirt to shower the flames with dirt and at the same time clear the area of the grass and sticks the fire needed to burn. This formed a rudimentary firebreak, which slowed the flames down, but it was still just a matter of who moved the fastest, the flames or me. And if the wind had picked up just a little more, I wouldn't have stood a chance.

Over that long hour, my frantic scrapings established more and better fire breaks around the spot fires. Gradually the breakouts slowed and I was able to surround each spot fire with a ring of cleaned fireproof dirt. Finally, and looking quite mad by now, covered in sweat, dust, leaf parts, brambles and grass sticking out of what little hair I have, I collapsed on the ground, as exhausted as I have ever been in my entire life. It had been a do or die effort.

Burns weren't meant to generate this much excitement. Ordinarily, a burn was just an excuse to spend a winter's day outside. A manly day, in the rain or the snow, it didn't make any difference. Bundled up in several layers that were topped off with my ubiquitous feed-store leather jacket, sitting on a comfortable log staring at the fire with my legs stretched out, drying soaking wet boots as they steamed in the cold air. Occasionally getting up to fold-in the pile, throwing in any branches, logs or even small tree trunks that were left half-burned on the edge of the fire as it burned down.

It was at one of these times, towards the end of one large burn, at the end of a long day and I was getting tired, too tired. There were some large piles of heavily inter-twangled branches that were just too big and awkward to try muscling into the fire. I could have cut them up with the chainsaw but I was too tired, so I decided to use the dozer.

The problem was that I had built the fire in the bottom of a steep draw, and to push these outlying piles into the fire I had to drive the dozer down into the draw. Which I did, carefully, checking that I could back out again without the tracks spinning helplessly on buried branches and mud covered rocks. That is until the last snaggle of branches, when I tried to back out and couldn't.

This was the perfect example of my not having enough sense to stop doing something risky while I still could and before it was too late. And before the wiser among you start the lectures (I've heard them all before), I've wasted a perfectly good life finding the limits to things, and I'm perfectly aware (better than most) of the downside to this. This was just one more time I wished I hadn't done what I just did.

There wasn't the "almost stuck" warning that I had been hoping for. There was no warning—the dozer was stuck! I had driven the dozer into a burn pile, while it was burning, and now it was stuck. I would have spent some time congratulating myself but the intense radiant heat of the fire was already warming the exposed hydraulic lines and the flames were almost touching the blade. The flames were headed this way.

I jumped down from the dozer and frantically tried to find what was under the tracks causing them to spin. Panic. There were branches buried in mud, but nothing I pulled or pushed on wanted to move an inch. I had perhaps two minutes before the dozer went up in flames. So I jumped back on and tried full power this way, full power the other way, but both tracks were spinning. It wouldn't even lurch a turn so I could try another angle and back out of the hole it was sitting in. Nothing. If anything, my efforts had caused the dozer to slide further into the fire.

I jumped off again and ran around to the front of the dozer, looking for something to use, and then I saw it. I swear to whatever imaginary-super-power-in-the-sky you might or might not believe in, but there was a still un-burnt (with the fire raging underneath it) foot-thick layer of full-sized branches and logs spanning the fire to the other side of the draw. It made an admittedly burning bridge, but a bridge anyway, across the fire.

So with nothing to lose and a pointless plea of, "Feet don't fail me now," I drove the dozer out over the top of the fire, sparks and flames all around, made it to the other side and just kept on going; full power up the far side of the draw and clear. It was a blur of adrenalin. I stopped at the top of the draw and jumped down to see if anything on the dozer had caught fire, without a clue what I could have done about it if it had been.

Sting and I had made it, though. The bridge had held, the tracks had found enough to bite on, the slope up the far side of the draw wasn't too steep, and nothing on the dozer had caught fire. And I wish I could pretend to be wiser from the experience, but that's always been a hard call for me. After all, in the end nothing actually went wrong, so it's hard to know what the lesson could actually have been.

Not all burns turned into life or death, do or die, moments. These few, but memorable, moments of terror were more than balanced by relaxed days spent outdoors. Mostly, burn days were just good grunt work folding-in the pile as it burned down, with the smell of wood smoke hanging in the air and the warmth from the fire, then finishing the day off watching the fire settle down into a bed of softly glowing red coals, and all making for a wonderful outdoor experience.

If it wasn't raining I liked to stay late into the evening, lying on the ground on my back with my hands behind my head, watching the sparks shooting up into the night sky. It was a simple pleasure in an uncomplicated world. By the way, a word of advice, these beds of coals were often a foot thick. Innocent looking things with their cool gray surface of powdery ash, they would continue to burn for days. Never walk on one, at least not more than once, even in thick boots. Trust me.

Pol Pot

"Hard work never killed anyone." Whether that's true or not, during my time working this land I often wished it would. And I'm able to understand why, for centuries, people have fled the country in favor of noise, traffic, muggings, pollution, pestilence, plague, and overcrowding. In fact, there were plenty of times I was nostalgic for some pollution and overcrowding myself. No matter how good it's meant to be for you, dragging a worn-out old body up and down steep slopes, with mud to sink into and rocks to slip on, and awkward heavy things to drag around in all weathers, and pretty soon that utopian notion of working the land loses some of its appeal. The romance is gone for sure, and I would never have worked this hard if I hadn't been volunteered by an empty bank account.

Sure, now I'm able to stroll carefree through acres and acres of grass and wild flowers, shaded by tall trees, where an impenetrable high wall of manzanita and blackened dead brush used to cover the land, where even the trees were invisible, except to a bird. It was just a lot of work to get here from there. And even though about half the property was cleared using the dozer, which paradoxically made as much work as it saved, the rest was cleared using a chainsaw, one gammy old man's spindly muscles, and a lower back that wanted nothing to do with any of it.

That overly capable chainsaw I'd been sold hadn't become any lighter, and the thirty acres of tree-sized vegetation (deceptively described as *bushes*) weren't conveniently laid out to be cut down. Instead, they were locked together by entwangled limbs, forcing me down on hands and knees and sliding under out-stretched branches, holding the dead-weight chainsaw at arms length, just to get into a position to cut one down. This might be fun for a bit, but after a few hours of wrestling with bushes the size of small trees, there's not much fun left. In fact, I was constantly reminded of that premeditated nonsense, "Pain is just weakness leaving your body." To tell the truth, at my age, I couldn't have cared less if it had stayed just where it was.

Before I'd started this new life of working the land, I hadn't been the typical computer geek—a fragile, sickly looking thing with butt-white skin from years of staring at a computer screen in semi-darkness. I should have been, but most days I snuck out early to spend an hour running or kayaking, and always outdoors sucking air. This hour or so of exercise helped, but years of sitting for a living had been the worse thing possible for my back.

It was a hand-me-down back, inherited from an irresponsible youth who had used it for anything promising an adrenalin rush and a small chance of survival—always searching for that sweet spot between fun and danger. So it came with constant pain in my lower back and numbness in my legs, which only got worse with the years. By the time I was fifty, picking up a one gallon lavender plant early one Saturday morning put me in bed for six weeks.

So although probably in better shape than the average aging urbanite, I still had my problems. And before moving to Igo I had expected all the usual old man aches and pains, along with feeble attempts at getting things done. I tried not to even think about my back because what could I have done about it anyway? But in a stunning surprise, the country life turned out to be healthy—good for a bad back and just about everything else for that matter.

There are ranchers around here that are still working in their eighties and even nineties, wizened men who are neither young nor old, timeless really. They're all sinews and grit, moving slower than they used to, but the one thing they have in common is that they haven't let go their grip on life, not for a second. They are my heroes; but attempting to tread (however lightly) in their footsteps has been tough. I would have preferred a temperature-controlled gym with my personal trainer handing me sensibly sized weights, then, after standing politely to the side, congratulating me on my progress this week. Instead, I was struggling alone with malevolent manzanita bushes gouging at me, on rocky slopes in a winter rain. It didn't seem fair at the time.

I'll admit that the dozer got a lot done, but if it was busy pushing and stacking piles of manzanita, it was just as busy churning the dirt into chaotic ridges of mud and rocks that made the land look like it had just been bombed. The original idea had been to beautify the land. Add to this mess the thousands of broken branches the dozer had missed or scattered while pushing piles of brush around, or worse, crushed into the ground while driving over the top of them, and some cleanup was required.

So in the days after the work-saving dozer had done its worst, I stomped around in the mess it had left behind. First dragging away the larger pieces of trees and bushes, then picking up armfuls of smaller branches, one crumby stick at a time, and stumbling the awkward bundle over to a burn pile. As I had to use the few sunny days during the winter for dozing, this normally meant the cleanup was on a rainy day, and I was stomping around in thick mud, of course, on a steep slope. I used the opportunity to kick down the ridges of mud the dozer had left behind, using heavy sweeps of my soggy boots to smooth out the worst of the mess, and hoping nature would take it from there. I hoped, but had no real idea, that the ground would recover from the mayhem and not stay the mess I'd made it.

Whether the land would recover, or not, this was work; and though it was very manly work it wasn't exactly making the best use of my years in college. It was on one of these long muddy days of cold, sticks, and dirt that I started to suspect that I had been secretly relocated, spirited-off to a place even further out from civilization than Igo, and was now actually interred in a Pol Pot retraining camp undergoing indoctrination. And I know I shouldn't make comparisons between my minor inconveniences and one of history's worst atrocities, but convincing proof that I had been shipped to Cambodia came just days later.

After the clearing the land it needed reseeding, so the soil had something to hold it together through the rest of the rainy season, and also gave something for the native grass seeds to catch onto when those seeds were blown in during the following years. This entailed me heaving a fifty-pound bag of seed over my shoulder, walking it to whatever acre of mud I was working on, and then spending the day casting seed by hand, neurotically obsessed in making sure that they landed in an near-even pattern. The next day I did the same thing but with hundred-pound bales of straw. The seeds wouldn't germinate without the cover of straw, I have no idea why but it's a fact. So starting at the top of the property, always at the top, I rolled the straw bales down hill to where they were needed, then pull them apart in handfuls and spread the straw over the seeds until they were covered in a bed of straw.

The thing to know about bales of straw, apart from their weight, is, although squared, they will actually roll given a steep enough slope. Though "rolling" doesn't accurately describe their motion because half the time they were careening through the air about head height. And once a bale started down a hill it took some running just to keep up with it, turning it was next to impossible, trying to stop it was suicidal, and letting it overshoot any distance had a nasty uphill penalty phase attached to it. The only sure method for stopping a speeding bale of hay was to nudge it in mid-flight so it hit a tree and stopped that way.

The images that came to mind were originally from any number of dreary Thomas Hardy novels I had been forced to read as a child, but later my situation felt far more like Pol Pot's vision of an agrarian society. During the winters of my internment, I carried and scattered a ton of seed over my thirty acres, one small handful at a time, and the same, but more so, for twenty tons of straw. If anything was a reversal of fortune, this was. And as I mindlessly trudged up and down these sprawling fields of dirt and devastation, casting seeds and covering them laboriously with straw, the irony of the situation failed to amuse me.

It did manage to generate some other emotions. With the thoughts I had in my head I could have easily spontaneously exploded right there and then on the side of the hill. In fact, I wished I would have, leaving behind a pair of muddy boots and a thin curl of smoke rising up to join the leaden clouds drifting slowly by just out of reach. I was a long way from a climate-controlled office, a comfortable chair, clever thoughts, and interesting little places to lunch.

But Nature must have been feeling kindly toward me, or more likely been saving me for some further misery. After a few days' mix of showers and late winter sun, up came millions of green shoots. The first I noticed was while walking back to the house from feeding Thunder. Never having planted a seed in my life, I had no idea what to expect or what to look for. Nothing seemed to have happened in the week since I had planted the seeds, but kneeling down for a better view and looking out across the acres of straw; there was the slightest green hue. I couldn't actually see any shoots but there seemed to be a green hue.

A few days later, the whole area had turned an unnaturally intense green, and by the end of spring the grass stood three-feet tall. My blighted property had morphed into the grassy hills under towering ponderosas and spreading oaks, at least the few acres that had been cleared. And there was an added benefit, one that I couldn't have imagined; the hard work had built a bond with the land. The land had become a part of me.

Now when I'm on one of my walkabouts, I find myself thinking about how the varieties of grasses have changed with each year, or how the latest volunteer ponderosas will look in ten or twenty years from now, or how the balance of trees will change over the next forty or fifty years, and what I can do to improve it. I do this in spite of the disquieting reality that I'll never live long enough to see any of it.

Don't Play with Snakes

We mostly hid from our neighbors for the first year, that's apart from the Mayor, and he lived in a goat barn. We didn't want anyone to see our pathetic lives. But after a year or so, things had improved sufficiently that we invited our neighbors over for dinner without too much shame. Coincidentally, as our lives improved, during our first year here the Beer Bar went through its own transformation. Linda sold the tired stalwart to Tom.

Throughout this book, I've treated the Igo Beer Bar with a deference normally reserved for a holy site, and for good reason. The bar's purpose goes beyond serving vast amounts of domestic beer through long hot summers, it's the nearest thing to a community center that Igo has. And when things go wrong, or go right for that matter, it's where the community meets.

Linda had run the bar for almost ten years, long enough to make the bar hers. She could out drink her patrons and probably out-fight them if she had to, but normally her personality was enough to keep whatever little order she wanted in the bar. She was born in Igo, and had grown up knowing everyone of her customers, dating some of them, and had made the bar, well, the place it was. It was hers. But when Linda fell in love and, in a questionable decision, believed her latest boyfriend when he said that he would always look after her, she sold the bar to an old friend of hers, Tom.

Tom quit his job with a package delivery company, sold his house in Chico, which is the only town to have any sophistication in the entire northern end of California, and along with his partner, Raymond, moved to Igo, which has no sophistication and doesn't have any plans for any, either. The bar came with an acre of land along with three trailers, in various stages of decay. One trailer could no longer support human habitation, one came with Big Ed living in it, and the third became Tom and Raymond's new home.

It's hard to imagine what that package delivery company did to Tom, but he still says that he would much rather be doing what he is now than his old job. Looking at the endless hours he has to put in at the Beer Bar, I think they must have had him strapped to a rack for eight hours a day. And buying the bar had been a risk. Apart from all the work the two were taking on, they were coming to the community as outsiders, buying an institution pickled in a culture that stretched back through generations and was populated to a large extent by scofflaws. But the two of them stood their ground, took the bar that Linda handed-off to them and made it their own—including the community's acceptance.

With all the pickup trucks, cowboy hats, and abstinence of education in the area you might have thought that a gay couple running a beer bar would have been the ingredients for a disaster. Yet there wasn't a culture clash, maybe a little, but none really. It showed that the locals weren't the evil archetypes that outsiders (such as me) might have suspected. The only change I noticed when Tom and Raymond took over the bar was that it gets cleaned, and the only change to catch anyone else's attention was the nickel increase in the price of a beer. And yes, the bar did lose some of its lawlessness with the introduction of cleaning products, along with and a new coat of paint, but it still functions as the community's meeting place, just the same, and things happen there that are very unlikely to happen anywhere else, just the same.

I had been having problems replacing the head gasket on the mini-truck. This was the only problem the little truck had given me in a quarter-million miles, and as the old thing spluttered to a steaming stop, I realized just how much I had grown used to a vehicle that cost me nothing to run. My impoverished state meant things needed to be kept that way and I had to fix the thing myself. I had faint memories of pulling engines apart during my misspent youth, but this was my first attempt in a long time, and I had been picking away at it, resting my mind between each step. I didn't want to make things any worse than they already were.

I'd learned from our well driller and parked the mini-truck in the shade of a large oak. It was a scene that could probably have been found in a hundred backyards across Shasta County, where other shade-tree mechanics were spending their afternoons underneath broken pickup trucks. But by the third day of this, my AADD had got the better of me, and I pulled my bicycle from the garage. There were plenty of other things that needing doing, but I didn't want to find them either, and without a thought about how to get back up the hill I took off down Woods Canyon—tucked down over the handlebars, with dirty hands and a dirty face, flying headlong down the twisty narrow road towards Igo. I had left my mountain retreat to waste the rest of the afternoon at the Beer Bar; and with gravity helping on the way down, a swamp cooler and a cold beer waiting at the bottom, it had been such an easy decision.

It might seem like a mere technicality to some, but even in Igo it's the law—smoking isn't allowed in the bar. However, there is a covered patio out back for anyone that wants to smoke, and when I walked into the bar it was empty and everyone was out back.

Tom had just set a beer in front of me when one of the smokers poked his head round the backdoor, keeping his cigarette behind his back, of course, to let us know that there was a baby rattler out there. This I had to see. The baby snake was only six inches long, shading itself up against the wooden fence, and for a poisonous snake it did look cute. It was coiled up making occasional mock strikes, a frightening three inches into the air, before ineffectively recoiling itself for its next clumsy lunge. In case you don't know this one small detail, a baby rattler is just as venomous as the largest rattler.

Out back that day were the regular regulars of the Beer Bar, the afternoon crowd. One of them was Aaron, whose father had raised rattlers to milk their venom, and Aaron had grown up handling them. He stepped forward and gently picked the baby snake up, dropping into the palm of his hand. Calmly, Aaron guided the snake as it slithered across the back of one hand and onto the other, making Aaron a celebrity and the snake feel, apparently, right at home. But, as with most bad endings, this innocent start was going far too well.

Everybody crowded round for a better look, and very soon clumsy hands started to poke and wave in front of the snake. Being the new guy in town and knowing nothing about snakes, I watched from the back of the crowd, jumping up and down to see over people's shoulders but without the need to get much closer. This brings me to the question that needed answering that afternoon. How do you know when you have handled a rattlesnake for too long?

Maybe in his happy haze Aaron thought the snake was his friend, a pet maybe. But whatever Aaron thought the snake didn't seem to care, ending the afternoon for everybody by sinking its fangs into the tip of Aaron's index finger and, for a while, hanging there like a worm on a fishing lure.

Time stopped with a gasp and then silence. Aaron and his buddies stared at the new reality and began to comprehend (in the nearest thing to slow motion I've ever seen) what had just happened. It was most likely the pain that finally made it through Aaron's alcoholic haze, but then panic took over. He started running around the patio area, his drinking buddies scattering out of his way, suddenly wanting nothing to do with this; first shaking his hand trying to get rid of the snake and finally resorting to yanking on it. This ensured that the snake drained every last drop of venom into Aaron's finger, delivering more than enough to kill him and, come to think of it, most of his buddies running around the yard along with him. Anywhere else that would have been the story, but this was Igo and, as with so many other events in Igo, the real story had only just started.

I had no idea until then, but it's common knowledge in Igo that copper is the actual poison in snake venom. And, as any idiot knows, the way to cure snakebite is to neutralize the copper with electricity. Copper neutralized by electricity. Simple.

So armed with this most powerful knowledge, it was just a matter for a dozen drunks to find a source of electricity and the afternoon would be saved. I tried to voice some doubts about this course of treatment but my accent makes me sound like I've marbles in my mouth and this was mob rule anyway. Fortunately Tom had already called 911.

Apparently, any electricity will do. Conveniently parked out back of the Beer Bar was a 1980 Dodge K-car, and like most cars this old and unreliable it came equipped with a large, nearly new battery and a pair of jumper cables. So with his arm starting to swell and his finger turn black, Aaron was ushered back by a concerned group of drunken caregivers and leant against the front fender of the 1980 Dodge K-car. Eager hands opened the K-car's hood and propped it up with the 2 by 4 lying on the top of the engine. (It was there for just that purpose.) One end of a jumper cable was attached to the #1 plug wire and the other clamped onto the end of Aaron's finger.

Unless you skipped adolescence you probably know what it feels like to get shocked by a car's plug wire. It's unpleasant. Whichever arm is stupid enough to be involved flies up violently, normally injuring itself on the corner of the hood but willing to settle for any sharp metal corner. Then you jump back as if you have just seen the Devil and stand where you've landed, cursing the car, yourself, and anything else that comes to mind.

Aaron didn't get a single shock and leap out of the way— he was in therapy. He just stood there, his arm held straight out in front of him with a jumper cable clamped to his finger, his whole body spasmodically jerking as the starter motor cranked over, delivering 12,000 volts to his snake-bit finger several times a second. His caregivers stopped the treatment every minute or so for a brief rest and another round of beers, then back to it until the battery finally went flat.

This was the scene the paramedics of the volunteer Fire Department walked into behind the Beer Bar. So did the Sheriff, the CHP and finally an ambulance, which had driven out all the way from Redding. Even then it still took some convincing for Aaron and his caregivers to give up the electrical shock treatment and allow conventional medicine a try. But obviously unappreciated, and the presence of the Sheriff spoiling their afternoon buzz, they drifted back inside the bar, leaving Aaron alone and defenseless against the combined emergency services of Shasta County. Reluctantly, Aaron allowed himself to be loaded into the ambulance and taken to the hospital in Redding. The miracle buried in this story is that someone had called 911.

The motorcade took off, sirens wailing, with a sheriff's car clearing the way for somebody who could die at any moment. Again, anywhere else, this would have been the end of the story. But the hospital admissions made the mistake of not letting Aaron smoke, even after Aaron had emphatically stated: "The guy in the ambulance let me smoke. Why can't you?"

Aaron is not an unreasonable man. He thought hard about the imposition and, as soon as the nurse turned her back, he took off for a cigarette. He walked round the corner, down the corridor, out of the hospital, and once out of the hospital he decided to keep on going. But Aaron had neglected to factor in to his escape plan the single most important fact—he wasn't in Igo but deep in the Zone of Civilization. He was among people who respected laws and regulations, surrounded by people who had finished high school and even gone to college, who considered it their job to find him before he died, and, to make matters really difficult, hadn't spent the afternoon drinking.

After first searching the hospital, the full breath of the caring community leapt into action and very soon it became a police priority. Find Aaron! The town's police swarmed into the area, and the impressive response included a police helicopter. It was the helicopter that eventually spotted Aaron, passed out behind some bushes only a block from the hospital. Redding has the advantage of having some large convincing corn-fed boys on its police force, so there wasn't much discussion and Aaron was delivered back to the hospital where he stayed.

A month later Aaron was released from the hospital. He had almost died; he was in intensive care for two weeks, very nearly lost his entire arm and, in spite of the hospital's best efforts, not everything survived intact. As permanent evidence of that afternoon's events, to this day, a dry white bone sticks out through the shriveled skin where the tip of Aaron's finger once was. This makes it very hard for him to hold a cigarette, but not impossible, as he still proves thirty or forty times a day. Aaron lives on, unchanged in any noticeable way, his adventure now a part of Igo folk lore, but still remains unconvinced about the need for that trip to the hospital.

My adventures with rattlers are tame in comparison, but then I do my best to keep them that way. My first encounter with a rattler was on a hot summer's evening; it was in the early days, about a month after we had moved into the garage. What sounded like the world's loudest lawn-sprinkler started up from under the decayed front deck of the mouse-house. This was odd because we didn't have any sprinklers. Slipping on a pair of tennis shoes I ran round to the front of the house, ducked down under the deck and crawled on hands and knees looking for the source of the noise. The idea that it could be a snake never crossed my mind, but there in the shadows was our citified cat, BuggerHead, calmly facing off against a large coiled and emphatically angry rattler. The general rule of thumb is the louder the rattle the angrier the rattler.

I had the sense to be born in a city and spent my entire life without ever seeing a snake of any kind, so I hadn't the slightest idea of what to do with one. The cat didn't seem to have a problem though, sitting calmly three feet away from the snake. I was drawing a blank. I couldn't yell at BuggerHead to get out of the way because that would probably have caused her to move and the snake to strike, and I couldn't get at the snake because the cat was in the way. Surprisingly, in spite of my world class talent to make a bad situation worse, I stopped.

Not for long, though. I might not know what to do, but I couldn't simply do nothing. So I did the next thing to nothing and moved very slowly towards the two combatants. Who knows why? But creeping forwards, I got into a position where the snake started to focus on me and not the cat. I didn't want to stir the snake up even more than it already was and cause exactly what I was trying to avoid.

As usual, not knowing what I was doing was working perfectly. By moving closer I must have become its target, because the snake turned to face me with its lawn-sprinkler still at full volume. I clapped my hands and simultaneously yelled at BuggerHead, who jumped out of the way with that off-handed way a cat has of pretending it was about to do that exact same thing anyway, leaving me crouched in the cat's place. I was buzzing with adrenalin and every nerve in me was focused on the snake, as it focused on me.

I didn't know what a snake could do. This one was only about four feet long, which is full grown for a rattler, but I was pretty sure that snakes couldn't run very fast or leap up in the air. So how could it possibly reach me (guessing here) if I stayed four feet away? Anyway, that was my reasoning, but it was only a best guess. And normally I would go out of my way not to harm an animal, any animal, but in the heat of the situation and the fear of the unknown, I turned into something primeval. I backed out carefully, only to fetch a shovel and return to kill the snake.

With an instinct that had to be resurrected from ancient genes, I became focused in a quiet icy still that I'd never felt before. I knocked the snake out with the flat of the shovel and then beheaded it with a downward chop. What I didn't know, no ancient genes to help here, was how easy it would have been to move it. There was nothing to be afraid of, rattlers don't give chase and normally only bite after they're trodden on, sat on, or (on rare and hard to explain occasions) picked up and handled. Once it had been allowed to calm down, this poor snake could easily have been moved using a stick and a bucket, but at the time I didn't know. There were cats and dogs to worry about, too.

Adrenalin ruled the day. Nowadays, if I come across a snake near the house it's an opportunity, a gift really. I carefully pick up the snake with a stick, drop it into a five gallon plastic bucket, plop a lid on the bucket, drive the snake to the house of whatever neighbor last irritated me the most, and drop it off. That's the eco-sensitive thing to do, and while on the subject, here's another observation. Snakebites always seem to be called accidents, but that implies something unforeseen, and from my observation of these accidents they were inevitable. And having said that I'll probably step on one tomorrow.

The North Wing

One cold wintry day, while we were first looking for a place to live in Shasta County, a particularly sour local had stood in the rain, glowering from under the hood of his slicker, to spread a little wisdom our way. "I don't know why you want to live up here, there's nothing to do in the winter and it's too hot to do it in the summer." He had the look of someone that had been rained on once too often and at the time I didn't pay much attention to his pithy little insight, but after living here through several seasons here I can see his point. Coming from the Bay Area's perennially pleasant climate and moving to an area where the winter can give you frostbite and the summer a heatstroke, it has been an education.

The mouse-house was less than a 1000 sq ft, and although grateful for anything at first, the more time we spent living in it, the smaller it became. This was especially true during the winter when the weather kept us stuck indoors. So, along with all the other ideas we had for making the mouse-house more livable, we thought about building an addition; consisting of a second bedroom along with its own master bathroom. It was also an opportunity for a dream I'd had since first lifting a hammer here— *architectural significance*. It was an opportunity I deserved after spending two years fixing other people's rotted-out mistakes.

The mouse-house has a circular driveway behind it. It's unusual to find a circular driveway on the side of a mountain, there's normally not enough flat ground to waste on what is essentially a luxury, and our cramped location forced the driveway to tightly circle a small granite outcropping at the back of the house. This outcropping is a miniature of the land around it, a mix of mature ponderosas and the granite boulders they'd pushed effortlessly aside as they grew up.

Near the top of this outcropping was a wide notch in the rocks, coincidently at about same height and across from the second story of the mouse-house. And I'd often thought about building an addition from the second floor of the mouse-house, spanning over the driveway to this conveniently situated notch. Why I couldn't have just built something on the ground I don't know, but this intentionally different idea became the plan, though without a clue actually how to do it.

It would be a narrow twelve feet wide, the width of the top half of the mouse-house's A-frame, and thirty-foot long because that's all the room there was between the house and the island. Its relatively long narrow shape, with its steeply sloped roof resembled a covered bridge spanning the driveway. And we named it the North Wing, in deference to the grand wings found in other great country houses throughout the ages, and also to the fact it pointed north.

It had to be engineered, though. By the time the engineer, the architect, and the county had made sure that it would stand an earthquake, a tornado, and a few other even more unlikely catastrophes, there was a lot of steel and several times more concrete in this small addition's foundation than the entire rest of the house. But pleased to have the unusual plans signed off we started construction, which first entailed digging the holes for the foundation.

I'd hand dug the hole for a foundation, just the once, and wasn't about to do it a second time. So I called Dan again, and happy not be digging up my old septic tanks he spent an hour digging the holes for the foundation, at least the part of the foundation that was going to be buried under the driveway. All I had to do was sweep up. There were no accidents, no problems, and no pain. It was so unexpectedly easy.

The next step in the construction was laying out the steel reinforcement rods for the concrete foundation—it's called *rebar*. The county seemed to want a lot of this rebar for such a small project (there were those improbable catastrophes to consider), and I spent a day cutting, bending, and laying out the rebar in the foundation's hole. At the end of the day, a three-dimensional grid of rebar was wired together; hanging suspended in the foundation's hole by wires tied to 2 by 4's laid across the top of the hole. Everything was ready for the concrete to be poured in the morning. There was nothing else to be done.

I woke up at first light the next day to the silly sheepdog barking. He wouldn't stop, and seemed even more confused than normal, if that were possible. It's a nice enough dog, not the smartest, and lives in a near permanent state of confusion. (I'm sure that's because the breed's been rewired to protect little things that any normal dog would eat.) When I went outside to see what the ruckus was, the sheepdog ran around the foundation hole and barked and barked and barked. It's his job and he does it very well. The two other players in this little morality play were the Evil Cat, who was calmly sitting on the rim of the hole preening himself and planning, and a baby rabbit. The rabbit was at the bottom of the hole, running around under and through the newly assembled, precisely positioned and delicately balanced rebar. The Evil Cat had probably stashed the baby bunny in the hole for later, but it wasn't saying, and the sheepdog had sensed that the baby bunny was in danger, and hence his agitation. The problem was how to get the bunny out of the hole without disturbing the three-dimensional grids of carefully positioned rebar, because there was a concrete truck arriving in an hour.

The answer is, of course, you cannot. A small bunny can run around and under and through three-dimensional grids of steel reinforcement and you can't. That's not quite true, you can, it's just that you destroy everything in the process, which is what happened. Only after most of the previous day's work had been wrecked did I manage a one-handed grab of the baby bunny by its little bunny ears; it must have weighed an ounce. I put it in a shoebox and drove the bug-eyed bunny to a shady spot by our seasonal creek, somewhere far enough away that the Evil cat couldn't re-find it. After wishing it a long and happy life, I rushed back to repair the rebar—the concrete truck was arriving in an hour. I repaired it, approximately, but it wasn't precisely positioned or delicately balanced anymore.

Whenever heavy equipment arrives on the property, I make a point of meeting whoever it is at the bottom of the driveway and have them walk up, so they can get an idea of what they face before they drive up. Today was no different, except that the driver who climbed down from his cab could have been from Central Casting. I hadn't asked for a celebrity driver, but it was Calamity Sam himself. Sam had a shock of flowing white hair, ending with a flip that rested on his shoulders, an exaggerated off-white curling moustache, along with a line of non-stop chatter. Yes, Sam was a talker. Walking up the driveway I heard a lot about Sam's childhood, happy days spent hunting deer with his dad in the hills around here, but I had no idea if Sam heard the few words I snuck in about the driveway. Near the top of the driveway he interrupted himself with, "I got it." So I presumed he had.

I watched as this top-heavy contraption snaked its way up the side of our hill in compound low, crawling up the impossible angle with its engine roaring, flat out, at no more than five mph. And making the sight truly bizarre, Calamity Sam was driving apparently without a worry in the world.

This was going to be my first "pour". As usual, I knew nothing, and this time it was nothing about pouring cement. Who does what, what does what, who should be where when, and what to look out for—it helps to have done it a few times. So I was glad to have Erin as my "concrete guy". Erin is a hard working, honest as the day is long, and sometimes under-employed local I knew from my infrequent stops to the Beer Bar. He had been in construction most of his life and had seen and done just about everything there was to do on a construction site, and more importantly he had also been at a pour or two. He knew where to have the concrete truck park, so it could swing its extending chute over the foundation hole and pump the mix where it was needed, which I didn't. And as this was new construction, with the county inspectors looking over my shoulder, I needed things to be done right the first time.

So Erin worked while Calamity Sam and I talked, Sam mostly. With the pour complete, the truck washed down, and Erin still working the concrete, Calamity Sam and I drove down the scary steep driveway. The driveway seemed even steeper than ever from the cab of his top-heavy cement truck, but Sam didn't skip a syllable on the way down and kept on talking at the bottom of the driveway. After what felt like a week, I finally extracted myself from the conversation and walked back up to the house, where I found that Erin had finished the concrete work and even cleaned up for me.

I was feeling pretty good about having somebody else (who actually knew what they are doing) do the work while I did nothing; it was a shame I couldn't afford it. I had limited means, and signing the checks for the day's work had left me feeling weak; similar I imagine to a mild case of malaria. So my madcap spending spree came to an end, and I was forced back to work.

The first consequence of this was that I had to pour the other part of the foundation (the one on top of the outcropping), myself. It was out of character, but by using some hard to find commonsense, I first cut in some narrow steps into the side of the island. Then, using my electric cement mixer to make a batch of concrete, I waddled up the steps with a five-gallon bucket of wet concrete dangling at the end of each arm. I don't know how many times I made the pilgrimage up these steps, but too many tons of heavy wet concrete later made for a long day, and with the last bucket poured into the forms I wearily cleaned up after myself and called it quits.

There really is no peace for the wicked. My lower back was as stiff as a board and I had just flopped onto the dusty couch when our famously grumpy old neighbor called. He had been monitoring the local emergency frequencies and had just heard there was an accident on Woods Canyon Road, and as I was the closest he called me. As any accident is likely to involve a neighbor we always hurry to see if we can help, but this accident wasn't, it was just a re-discovered wreck of a truck in Cow Creek.

Whenever there's a new helicopter pilot in the area, various wrecks get re-discovered. The helicopter pilot flies over, sees what looks like a fresh accident, and calls it in. This wreck was five years old, and this was its second re-discovery that I knew of. The pilot had spotted one of the four pickup trucks located permanently off Woods Canyon Road, down one of the steepest parts of the canyon where it was simpler to just leave them. They are a legacy of Igo's past, when the Beer Bar's refrain was still "Drive fast and reckless!" and you weren't trying unless one of your vehicles was a hundred feet down the canyon. People must have sobered up some since then, because there hasn't been another wreck on the road while we've lived here.

The helicopter was still hovering overhead when I drove up. So I climbed down the ravine, to make sure there wasn't a new wreck, and had just made it back up to the road when the fire truck arrived. It happened to be driven a local volunteer firefighter, Andy. I doubt if he's the greatest fire fighter west of some river somewhere, but he has to be the funniest.

My favorite story of his was set in a particularly heavy freeze one winter. Andy's truck had been called out to respond to sprinkler alarms going off. The winter freeze had triggered the alarms, but there was nothing much for the fire department to do, and after a morning of routinely responding to these calls, with his supervisor in the passenger seat, Andy headed back to the firehouse.

This was during a brief experiment when the fire department used inmates from the county jail to help out around the firehouses, giving the inmates an opportunity to do something useful for a change. That morning, while he had the station to himself, the fire-house's little criminal thought it would be a good idea to hose down the station's equipment yard. The yard might have been a little cleaner, at least that's what the little criminal said he was trying to do, but it also covered the yard in a sheet of water; which quickly froze and turned the entire yard into an ice rink.

The first Andy knew about this was when he drove back into the yard (at a speed you'd expect from someone hoping to find a warm lunch waiting for him) and tried to turn the 50,000-lbs fire truck, which didn't happen, and then brake, which didn't happen either. The big truck glided effortlessly across the middle of the yard, and as Andy described the event in his practiced deadpan voice, "You'd be surprised just how easily a 50,000-lbs fire truck can mow down a fueling island." The fire truck did finally stop, but not until it was halfway through a parked car on the far side of the yard. The supervisor hurriedly climbed down from the fire truck, fell flat on his face, picked himself up, and inspected his crumpled car.

There wasn't a supervisor on Woods Canyon. After Andy had used his radio to explain the situation to the helicopter pilot, and with an ease of command that can only be developed from years of high-level decision making, he climbed back in his truck and announced: "Okay boys, our job here is done. Let's get some lunch!" And as quickly as they could back their truck into the nearest driveway and turn around, they were gone. They left behind the sound of squealing brakes, long after the fire truck had disappeared from sight, as it squeezed its bulk back down our narrow canyon road.

The North Wing was to be elevated above the driveway by four substantial steel posts, two on either side of the driveway. On top of these four posts, two large beams were to be bolted. These were to span from the side of the mouse-house, across the driveway, and onto the foundation on top of the outcropping. After allowing the concrete to cure for a week I dropped the ten-foot steel posts onto the mounting bolts protruding out of the foundation. This was a warm up for the beams, as I was determined to do all the heavy lifting myself. Not just to prove that sensibly sized people can accomplish something (even if it is something more than three feet off the ground), but also to avoid shouting frantic directions to helpers while very heavy objects are precariously balanced over their heads. It's just better to do things dangerous yourself, whenever possible.

The steel posts had been easy, but my first attempt at lifting the beams was a mistake. I tend to think of "first attempts" as throwaways and don't expect much from them, but I should have expected more. I'd built a just-strong-enough plywood platform on top of the mini-truck's lumber rack, to stand on, and was going to lift the beam into place from there. I drove the truck under where the beam needed to be lifted, crab-walked the beam beside the truck and barely managed to lift one end up on to the just-strong-enough plywood platform. Halfway there and everything in place, I climbed up onto the plywood platform to lift the beam onto the posts.

It had gone pretty much to plan, so far. But straining with everything I had, trying to get one end of the beam on the top of a post, with the beam pushed as high as I could get it over my head; the more it, me, and my plywood platform all started to wobble uncontrollably. It dawned on me that being underneath something that heavy, unwieldy and ill-willed was not a good idea, and I realized, probably just in time, that it was about to land on top of me with the effect of a pile driver. Even after putting a beam-sized dent in my head it would have kept on going, found other parts of me to crush on the way down, then my makeshift platform and finally the mini-truck. So I lowered the beam back onto my inadequate plywood platform, and opted to use a block and tackle to lift the beam instead. This placed me safely off to the side and not underneath the giant beams, which probably increased my life expectancy.

With both beams in place and bolted to the steel posts, I called Erin to help me with the carpentry. It's a fact, on a construction site two people can accomplish several times what one person can, and this is especially true when the other person knows a lot more than you do. In a couple of days we had built the floor, spanning from the island over the top of the driveway to the side of the mouse-house. We tied the floor into the side of the mouse-house and not only were we "out of the ground"—we were also up ten feet in the air.

The following day we raised the walls. Building each wall in one piece on the newly built floor, then standing it up and nailing it into place. I rented a hoist lift for a week, and two days later we had the rafters up, another day and the plywood skin to the roof was on. Then the windows, the doors, and the plywood siding was hung, and with that the addition was sealed up.

It really helps if you work with someone who knows what they're doing, and it took just two weeks for a completed shell to be sitting on its steel posts; spanning the driveway where nothing but air had existed before. Somehow we were able to satisfy the building inspector (an admittedly kind-hearted inspector who seemed to respect our good faith efforts), and two months later the county signed off the North Wing. It had only taken three months from beginning to end, but what I learned from this project, and it surprised me, was that I don't climb on roofs.

I had climbed most of my life. I started when I was three years old, and the London fire department thought they were rescuing me when they pulled me off the steep slate roof of a three-story building. Most of my childhood was spent swaying in the tops of trees, the higher the better. Later, during my immortal period, I'd discovered mountains and climbed them too. So while planning the addition, it never occurred to me that working twenty feet off the ground would be a problem, but it was.

Maybe if I had taken some time to acclimate to heights again it would have made a difference, but that first look down stopped me in my tracks, even my palms were sweating. And I'm sure I could have re-acclimated to heights, but this was a construction site, the clock was running, and this was a fear I didn't have time to deal with. Erin took over and tied-off with a rope around his waist. This crude safety equipment might have stopped a headlong fall to his death, but a sudden stop on the end of the rope wouldn't have felt much better. He didn't hesitate though, working in and around the rafters, balancing precariously and extending out into thin air to get my roof built. I stayed safe, his "gofer", cutting the lumber to length and handing it up to him. It revised my self-image some.

It was a reality about getting older that I hadn't noticed before. And maybe it's better not to get too far off the ground when you are nearly sixty. If I had slipped my tired reflexes would have resembled government intervention, and there definitely would have been no chance of twisting cat-like in an amazing save. No, I would have plunged headfirst towards the ground with a look of horror frozen on my face. Still, it wasn't just me getting old and developing a dislike of heights. I remembered our roofer, an older gentleman about my age, had his teenagers clambering around our roof, he never set foot on a ladder, or even laid hands on one if I remember correctly.

On a sad note, as this construction wound down so did life in the country for my sweet BuggerHead. She went missing. It was a reminder that life here can be raw. She had been the best cat, falling asleep on my lap every time I sat down for a minute, and had always come whenever I whistled for her; her tail enthusiastically in the air, running to be picked up so she could wipe a cat kiss on the side of my cheek. But one morning she didn't. I spent days searching for her in case she was injured and holed up the way cats do, but there was nothing, not a trace of her.

Before moving here I had promised the cats I would make sure they were safe. And even though there was only so much I could have ever done to make that promise a reality, I still felt guilty about her death, and think about her years later.

Dirty Burt

Not surprisingly, my thoughts about living in the country have changed considerably over the years, along with that so has the way I see many of our neighbors. Not all of them, but there is one that I see very differently. He's Dirty Burt, and he's someone an out-of-towner would think a character even from a distance, which is coincidently a good place to view him from.

His nickname sounds judgmental, but for anyone standing near to him it's observational. Even Burt agrees he's dirty; and not just a conventionally dirty from having been out in the fields working all day, or from getting in late and missing a shower last night, but from not having bathed in literally years. And between the aroma pervading the air around him, his clothes, and his physical appearance, he was an assault on my refined senses.

He might not have looked it but he's just a harmless old man—unforgivably filthy but, from what I heard, harmless. He's lived with his dog three miles down, what is now, a footpath off Woods Canyon Road. He lives in the back of a Dodge van that, years ago, had been taken on a joy ride down a ravine and abandoned. And since he's in his late seventy's, I'm sure he will end up dying there. Not from neglect but from natural causes, after a long life with little influence from the civilized world busily whirring along not too many miles away. He might not be the only strange old man living out in these hills, it's possible there could be someone else even further out, but Burt's appearance is sufficient in itself to can cause some earnest anthropologist to want to follow him around taking notes.

He's old, and not just from his many years but also from the life he led, living most of it outdoors, rain or shine. He's snaggle-toothed, stooped, and bowlegged. His arthritic fingers look like the roots of a tree, and although there are only the remnants of the man to see this trait in, there can't be a better example of how the male of the species goes feral if left to his own devices. Given the opportunity most men go feral to some degree, but Burt hasn't had to compromise and has gone as far as he could.

When I first met him, about a week after moving here, I remember being fascinated, among other things. His face looked black, but black wasn't the right word, and I couldn't think of the exact word to describe the color. The word needed to imply something more than just a color, but I didn't know a word for a rancid color, and I wasn't sure if I wanted to find one either. Or, for that matter, a word for the stench that hung in the air around him. It's gotten worse over the years, it's like nothing else I've ever smelled; and there's the rub.

Originally out of pity, whenever I saw Burt walking along Woods Canyon Road I stopped and gave him a ride. I clearly remember the first time I gave him a ride, I was still an innocent. It was a leap of faith, and within seconds of letting him in the truck I realized my mistake. I cranked my window all the way down. Shortly after that I added to the airflow by turning the fan to full blast. Then I regretted not opening the passenger-side window before he got in, as I wasn't about to lean over and open it. In the end, I pinned myself against my door and drove with my head out the window, which got me through this act of kindness, though barely.

Burt comes with the territory, and with his daily ritual of walking to the Beer Bar to buy a hamburger for his dog and a bag of Cheetos and soda for himself, it was inevitable we would meet again. And at the pace he walks, or hobbles, depending on what piece of himself he's damaged recently, he's a presence on Woods Canyon for a good two hours a day. That's more than enough time to catch me on a regular basis as I drive in and out picking up building supplies for the mouse-house. So the novelty of helping Burt had the chance to fade early, and over the years my humanitarian ways have thinned some. Now I have him ride in the bed of the pickup and not in the cab.

If I see him on the road I stop, get out, lower the tailgate, and politely help load him into the bed of the truck. I say "politely help" as my help doesn't extend to actually touching him, which I don't, but I do close the tailgate after him once he's in. Then I drive him wherever he wants to go. He spends the whole time talking about stuff I can't hear, even with the window down, and have no idea about what. But he always seemed happy enough, and I'm sure he was, because there's really not much to complain about when you are riding in the back of a pickup—propped up against the cab, immersed in the sights, scents, and sounds of the hedgerows and fields passing by.

During my first years here, this arrangement of having him ride in the bed of the truck applied to the summer months only. I took pity on him during the winter. But nowadays, in spite of the fact that I've got to know him better, I don't care. It doesn't matter if it's winter and it doesn't matter if it's raining, he still rides in the bed. He has to hunker down behind the cab, which keeps him remarkably dry, and if it's pouring I'll throw a blue tarp over him. And my thinking has been that there wouldn't be a raindrop that could land on him that wouldn't have landed on him in sheets if he had been walking. So the Lord's work has still been done, or at least as far as I'm willing to go along with it.

He's living the remainder of his life tucked away in the hills, the last of a tribe, completely out of touch with our modern society and its caring community, which wouldn't have a clue what to do with him anyway. He's finishing out his allotted time with his only possessions the clothes on his back: the same clothes he wears everyday, the same clothes he never washes and are literally the only possessions he has in this world.

I sometimes wonder what his life would have been like if he had lived in a city. He'd probably be huddled over a heating grate outside a high-rise; being stepped over, stepped on, and despised. So even if he is missing some of the creature comforts we all take for granted, he's avoided far worse, and I don't see a better alternative for him. Anyway, he's too old to change. He has his dog and his daily rituals, his neighbors on the road look out for him, and probably one winter morning he won't show up and that will be end of it.

During our first winter here, Burt sold us some firewood. At the time, that was how he supported himself, cutting and delivering firewood. The morning of the delivery, we heard Burt's ancient pickup truck start up the scary steep driveway. He got halfway up, stalled the truck on the steep grade, and tried to back down. We came running down and found a very confused Burt about to back off the side of the hill. He had stalled his truck because he didn't know how to put it into a low enough gear to get up our driveway, and he wasn't coordinated enough to back down, either. It took some convincing, but eventually Burt climbed out and I climbed in. I found the low gear he couldn't find in his confusion, and drove his truck the rest of the way up the hill.

Up at the house we unloaded the firewood, but as I finished cleaning out the bed of his truck I saw that his back tire was completely flat. He'd probably put a hole in it when he backed off the driveway and nearly slid down the hill.

I had my air compressor in the garage ready to fill the tire, but before I did anything else I put Burt back in his truck with the engine started. I wasn't sure he could even make it to the tire store, but I filled the tire with as much air as I dared, without exploding the thing, and off Burt went. And perhaps I should have done more, but my situation wasn't much better than his at the time, and staying clear of Burt was most likely an instinctual response at self-preservation.

I had had a peek into a broken world of dysfunction where the only way to rid yourself off one problem is by starting into a new one. And the nearest thing to a good day is when the sum of your disasters at the end of the day is less than what you started with. And though I didn't know it at the time, I was witnessing Burt's world starting to collapse in on him. He stopped driving soon after this, and nowadays his life consists of his daily walk into Igo, his dog, nights spent in the dark on a soiled mattress in the back of the van, and nothing much else.

A particularly kind neighbor of his, a retired teacher, living near Burt keeps a special eye on him. Other neighbors up and down Woods Canyon look out for him too, and sometimes I wonder if there's more I could do for Burt. But there's nothing that wouldn't entail taking him from his place in the hills. It's not Eden but it is Burt's place; it's his home and it's the place he and life seem to have agreed on. Still, even taking the most positive view of Burt's life, his circumstances are bleak and seem to be getting bleaker with each passing year.

He's never asked and never received help from the caring community, who would have made sure that he at least had a small trailer, a place to live in, along with some money for food and heat. His living conditions resemble something from a century or more ago. And it's possible to imagine Burt living in one of the mining camps in Woods Canyon during that time—hard, crude places, with an oilskin tent for protection and an open fire pit to cook on. He would have fit right in, as he does in his own way even now. At least with the rusting equipment and derelict shacks still found in the hills around here. Tucked away, like Burt, in places people rarely visit.

There is a story here, and it's Burt's story. It has very little to do with anyone else or what someone else might think. His story line was laid down a long time ago, and all anyone else can do is watch as it plays out its final scenes.

In the last year Burt's ramblings have steadily gathered more fiction than fact. Not that Burt ever lied, but there was always a friendly mix of fiction with his facts, and as the years have gone by this mix has continued to develop an emphasis on the fiction. When I first listened to his stories, I spent most of the time trying to separate the facts from the fiction, and only then, if there was still time, think about what it was he was actually trying to say. But in this last year Burt seems to be fading, he's looking more and more lost, and his stories have devolved into ramblings. There's no fiction and there's no facts.

It sounds uncaring, but I always thought his worn body would fail him first, that or a really cold snap would pick him off one night. That would be his preferred way to go; never having to surrender the one thing left of value to him, his independence. But it seems his mind is going first, and this makes the situation more difficult. Burt's neighbors keep an eye on him, and if his mind goes much further I'm sure he will be spirited out of Igo and away to a home.

An Ordinary Day

Tornados and divorces have one thing in common in Igo—someone's gonna be missing a trailer. I'm sure Erin didn't deserve it, but while he was helping me build the North Wing his personal life ran into some weather of its own when his girlfriend left him. It would have been bad enough, but one day the family home was towed away. And much as any separation can be an unpleasant experience, it has to be that much harder when you return home from work and find your house is gone. It's no longer where you left it and you return to find an empty lot, with a pile of clothes lying on the ground (approximately where your bedroom window used to be), and a hastily disconnected sewer connection as the only reminder of happier times.

Men are primitive creatures, and just occasionally this trait comes in useful. The trailer might have gone, but Erin still had the plywood shed he had built as a laundry room. It was an eight-foot cube. It had four walls, a floor, and a roof, and all its dimensions were eight feet because that's the exact length of a sheet of plywood. By sticking to those dimensions the plywood sheets don't need to be cut, which makes for a simpler construction and a good chance of getting the whole thing built before lunch. And as this laundry room was the only thing on the property with a roof to it, it became Erin's new home. He didn't even have to move but ten feet.

The first I knew about his living arrangements was when I called to see why he hadn't turned up for work. He sounded different on the phone, he sounded like he was talking from inside a box. I couldn't understand what he was doing, and guessing, I asked, "Erin, are you calling from your laundry shed?" After a few seconds delay there was a plaintive "Yea..." followed by a long pause, "she (his girlfriend) took the trailer." Two hours later he arrived hung-over, having drunk a case of beer the night before, and left after a short and unproductive day. The next day started the same way. So instead of watching Erin regurgitate his way through another day, on my dime, I used the time to talk to him, to encourage him to move on and get himself a new future. Actually, my original suggestion was to ask if I could install a web cam in his tiny plywood house of misery, and that way at least one of us could make some money out of the situation. But later, and more constructively, I suggested that he should get himself another trailer, and quickly, as I needed his help building.

Probably because he had visions of his son moving back in with him, Erin's dad donated $10,000 towards another trailer and the following morning Erin drove into town to buy his new home. The deal was done, and the trailer was scheduled for delivery that afternoon, showing one of the benefits of a house with wheels. With his new home on the way Erin called to invite me over for the house warming and, with construction on hold, I drove over— stopping at the Beer Bar for a house-warming six-pack and wondering if another, newer girlfriend could drive off with this trailer before I had a chance to even see it.

Erin lives in an area south of Igo, down a two-mile long dirt road in an area that's infamous even for these parts. His road lacks the do-or-die slope of my driveway, but makes up for it by having hundreds of potholes your wheels drop into and then have to climb back out of. It's not really a road at all, it's more a winding strip of dirt and rocks that somebody scraped the plant life off and then carpet-bombed. And this is a road the sheriff won't even go down without backup. So when I drop by Erin's place, I make a point not to stop at any of the other dirt driveways disappearing into the heavy brush on either side, or even give them a second look really. The mini-truck isn't equipped with a Motorola and I can't call for backup.

His new trailer was actually better than anything I would have imagined, and I started to think Erin might have the right idea when it came to housing. For an outlay of $10k for the trailer, another $250 for a rifle and a box of ammunition, a careful selection of a home-site on high ground allowing a clear line of fire, and Erin had the American Dream. And considering how much time and effort everyone else has to put into paying for a regular house, which doesn't even have wheels, I'm perfectly serious, I think he's on to something.

When I drove up his friends and family was finishing the electrical, water, and septic connections to his new trailer. I would have volunteered to help, but it didn't feel right to work for free for the guy I paid to work for me, so I decided to support Erin's battered psyche instead. We sat on the foldout steps to his front door, the six-pack between us, drinking beers and talking through his still-mixed feelings about relationships. Fun as this was, the conversation quickly used up any insights I had on the subject, and leaving Erin in good company I said my goodbyes to his relatives and drove straight home. Well almost.

Towards the end of Woods Canyon, the narrow road winds by Rick's house, almost under it really. Rick's a biker, and there are exactly two features worth noting about his house. The first is the wrap-around porch, with its great vantage point looking down on the road. The second, and more important, is the Pit Bull sitting on the porch. A frayed length of string keeps the dog on the porch, mostly, but that would snap like a thread if more were required from the dog than its emotionless gape and its enduring scowl.

Since moving onto Woods Canyon a year ago, Rick spends months at a time, weather permitting, sitting on his porch; normally with an assortment of his biker buddies, drinking and waving at the occasional car driving by along Woods Canyon. And as the sight of people enjoying themselves has always been a magnet for me, if I have time, I'll stop by to sit on one of Rick's plastic lawn chairs, drink beer, and wave at the occasional passing car. Actually, it's a pleasant way to spend an afternoon. There is a small complication to this, though. The wife dismisses Rick as a drunk, and she probably doesn't think much of me either when she sees me sitting with a bunch of bikers, waving at her as she drives by. And I didn't help myself much, when one afternoon I suggested Rick and his bikers drop their oily jeans and BA her. The row of hairy backsides pointing down at her from Rick's porch probably wasn't the worst my wife has ever seen, but it had to rank up there.

For some reason bikers have always got along with me. I don't know whether they sense my anti-establishmentarianism, or think that in a pinch I could be a stand-in for some dwarf tossing. Who knows? Either way, I'd made a point of stopping by earlier that same day because Rick had recently had a knockdown, drag-out fight with his neighbor, a metal sculptor named James. Even for Igo, this had been a bizarre event.

Another recent arrival, James, had taken his shop experience at high school, turned it into a career, and now had a front yard of rusting art ready for sale on the side of the road. And although these two had been living next door to each other, only fifty yards away, they had never actually met. Knowing the two of them it was understandable, but it was still bizarre.

The day the two met, James had been experimenting with something that caused him to stand naked in the middle of the road and waving an ornate six-foot long wooden staff. Rick on his Harley happened along, and being complete strangers to each other things didn't go well. They are both large people and a fight started. First, fists were thrown and then rocks, then an axe, there was some running around and finally shots were exchanged between their two houses. Someone nearly went to jail for that, and the only reason no one went is because the sheriff couldn't figure out who needed to go the most.

I'd been hoping this spat would go away, mostly because I didn't want to take sides when the combatants are large, heavily armed, often drunk, and I had to drive by them on a daily basis. So I'd made a point to stop in and talk to Rick. We had sat up on the porch, waving at the passing cars, joking about how he and James met and, as usual, not petting the Pit Bull. I thought our chat went well, but who could tell?

On my way down Woods Canyon to Erin's house warming, I saw Rick and James standing in the middle of the road. I stopped, out of small-arm's range, and was about to jam the truck into reverse, but on looking carefully I saw they weren't fighting—they were talking. They were talking and their dogs were milling around. It was a picture of bucolic, well maybe alcoholic, friendliness. So rather pleased with myself, attributing the fence mending to my heartfelt words the previous day, I smiled and waved as I drove by, hoping not to distract them.

A couple of hours later, on my way back from Erin's house-warming, it seemed unnaturally quiet at Rick's place. His lawn chairs were empty; in fact, there was no one to be seen. Then, half a mile later, turning onto China Gulch I saw my famously grumpy neighbor driving down the dirt road, chased by a large cloud of dust. He normally drives at a pace that would embarrass a snail, so the cloud pursuing his truck could mean only one thing—there was an emergency.

"There's been gunshots from down the road again," he grumped as he slowed down along side before taking off again. Either Rick and James were at it again, or worse, those damn bear hunters were back poaching again. I had no way to know which, but for some reason the bear hunter scenario won out. I spun the truck around and spitting gravel headed back down China Gulch. Now it was my turn to grump. "Not the mamma bear and her babies, they had better not been hurt. Someone's going to jail if they've been hurt… no… hospital first and then jail!"

I drove up and down Woods Canyon, stopping and starting, head swiveling around in all directions, looking for anyone and everything, but there was no one and nothing. Returning from a second pass through the neighborhood, Dale was leaning against the back of his truck talking to the Mayor.

Not that they gossip, but between the two of them there wasn't much that happened in Woods Canyon that they didn't know about; and not that I gossip, but somehow it often takes me an hour to drive from one end of our road to the other. So I pulled in behind them, pretty sure that I would find out the story behind the gunshots. The answer had nothing to do with bears, but it helped me understand why even the Beer Bar refers to our mountain as Granola Hill.

Having reconciled, Rick and James had spent the afternoon drinking, and the two now friendly drunks had managed to find a common enemy. It was the family that had just moved in across Cow Creek from Rick and James.

Sometimes I think the whole of Woods Canyon is certifiable, and there must be something in the water that makes otherwise normal people behave like imbeciles, but in reality it's the newcomers that cause most of the fuss. And after years of watching it, I still find it astonishing that the majority of people moving into the country, even before they've unpacked, walk over to the nearest fence line and pick a fight with a neighbor. Chances were I would have as well, if I hadn't been so busy trying to survive.

The newcomer on this occasion was a grandmother, a matriarch of sorts, along with a houseful of her extended family. They had made themselves a family compound. That afternoon Granny threw the kids out of the house to go play in the creek, much the same way I do the dogs, and it was the sound of children playing that had disturbed Rick and James. How the row started we'll never know, but granny jumped right in anyway.

On any other afternoon whatever noise the kids were making would have been swamped by Rick's Harley and James's metal working. But as Woods Canyon was about to find out, Granny was a piece of work herself and a discussion between the Granny and the two drunks turned bad early. Welcome to the neighborhood Granny, and by the way... I see you met your neighbors. When the talking was done there were the gunshots from everywhere. Nobody's sure who went first, but it was Rick's rifle that had had the last word or two. It was the loudest.

In the local vernacular a single gunshot is the conversational equivalent of not much more than a common "@!!* you!" It's an exclamation point, a standard part of speech really. But popping off a complete magazine, as Rick did, explicitly states, when words just aren't enough, "I'm drunk out of my mind and I have a box of ammo." And these were the shots heard up and down the valley, nothing more than a neighborly discussion finished off, Igo-style, with some exclamation marks.

I couldn't have cared less about this latest spat. After living here for some years, I find sporadic gunfire almost soothing, and, the way I saw it, the gunfire had stopped the ruckus not started it. But Dale is obstinately law-abiding and wanted to call the sheriff anyway. Not that it would have done much good, as all the parties involved would have denied everything, and firing off a gun isn't in itself a crime.

I like Rick. I like to identify with his bad biker self, but I was worried that another call to the sheriff would get him hauled away, and since there was no actual bodily harm done my suggestion was that I talk to him first. It took some persuading but eventually Dale agreed, "Well, okay then. But I don't want to hear any more gunshots from down here." And with that admonishment, as if I could do anything about it, the crisis was over.

I thought Dale's concern with other people using guns was a little ironic considering his reputation with them, but as any meeting on the road is a chance to gossip (and between the three of us we'd created the necessary critical mass), I didn't rush off. The next topic was more serious, though. "Did you hear that Robbie just died?" Roy asked. "What?" I was surprised. He was only fifty and, as fate would have it, the last time I'd seen him I'd complemented him on how well he was looking.

Robbie had made Igo his home twenty years ago. He was a truly sweet man without a bad bone in his body, and for the longest time I thought his name was Robbie Parker—an easy mistake because that's what everybody called him. In fact, that was Robbie's nickname. Linda had given it to him when she still ran the bar because Robbie had a habit of sleeping off an evening's drinking in his truck, which was parked outside the bar and hence his nickname.

Robbie had left this world the way he had lived it, quietly, without disturbing a thing. I think he had the smallest footprint of anyone I've ever met. He lived off his SSI, alone in his trailer in the back corner of Roy's twenty acres, and it was Roy that had found him the previous morning; sitting on a bench in his kitchen, leaning back against the wall with his head slumped to one side.

"You know when you're on a long road trip with a friend in the passenger seat riding shotgun, and you look over and he's fallen asleep? Well, Robbie looked like that." Roy explained.

It sounded as peaceful an ending as I could imagine, and fitted perfectly the way he'd lived his life. "What about the funeral?" I asked.

"Who knows? We can't find his relatives. He never mentioned any, so we might be all he had."

"That's sad." I reflected.

"Not really. Even if we are his only family, he's been happy here, and we'll put together a really great memorial service for him."

I hadn't attended a memorial since just after moving here, Jim's. I hadn't understood how a community could celebrate someone's death, or realized that most of the locals have known each other from cradle to grave. They die where they were born, their death completing their life's cycle, as they'd lived, among their family. And just like with Jim's wake, I'm sure the community will fill the Inn to overflowing, celebrating the memory of this quiet man. He was without wealth or stature, a very pleasant addition to our lives, but has passed on.

"Will we see you at the breakfast tomorrow?" Dale asked as I turned to leave. He was reminding me that the church was having one of its regular pancake breakfasts. I'd always met interesting people at these breakfasts. People that I would never have guessed would have lived outside the Zone, and were living here long before me. "You bet," I answered.

I didn't bother talking to Rick, as that would have caused me to lose some of my bad boy image with the bikers. And quite content to leave things right where they were, I drove home, past our barn where Thunder saw me coming and, as usual, galloped out of his corral in an attempt to cut me off and demand food. It was a tight race, but the mini-truck out-accelerated the wonky-knee'd old horse, scooting up the driveway and out of his reach.

No day on our acreage could be complete without something unusual happening with an animal. After dinner, the wife and I were walking back from feeding Thunder. Sheila doesn't like to walk in the dark and had brought a flashlight along, which was lucky because behind the barn we noticed two tawny eyes reflecting back in the dark. It was a tiny cat, very frightened, hiding under a bush. But he didn't run away, instead, he allowed one outstretched finger to touch him and then stroke the top of his head, and after a few minutes of petting he let me pick him up.

He wasn't a neighbor's cat, we know all of them, and more than likely it had been a family pet somebody had dropped off, pretending the poor cat would have a happy life in the country. But these animals normally die miserably, as this tiny cat would have, either starving to death or getting sick or being eaten. Still, he couldn't have been abandoned long because he buried himself into my shoulder and purred his heart out.

By the time we walked home, the wife had decided that his smallish size (I would say sensible size) reminded her of me, and named him "Mini-Me". She was just jealous of all the attention I was giving the cat, but the name stuck anyway. The Evil Cat showed enormous restraint and took Mini-me under his arm, quite literally, and although he never grew to have anything like a Shasta cat's usual heft, Mini has stayed just as loving as he was in those first few minutes. It had been over a year since BuggerHead had disappeared, and there was a sorely needed symmetry to Mini-Me's appearance.

There was nothing really remarkable about this day, but it made me realize how much my life had changed. In my former civilized life I couldn't have dreamt a day like this was even possible. And it wasn't just the people and the events that were different, I had changed, I'd become a part of what I was experiencing.

Later that evening I was sitting on the front deck, looking at the outlines of the trees backlit by the rising moon, with the tiny cat asleep on my lap and thinking how far off the Bay Area seemed. I'd always loved the place, but for the first time I was truly perplexed, wondering what all those millions of people were doing there.

It's a Matter of Assimilation

Shortly after we first moved here, while walking round the outside of the mouse-house making an inventory of what needed work the most, I looked up and saw something sticking out from a ventilation hole in one of the eves. It was too far away to make out what it was, so I fetched a ladder and climbed up to see; though I wished I hadn't bothered. It was a mummified paw of a cat; fur and skin over bone, frozen in time, sticking out in a last futile effort to free itself from the attic that had become its tomb. Sometime during the decade that the mouse-house had been abandoned, this poor cat must have climbed into the attic, got stuck and died there. It was a grim scene, and it had a human equivalent in Igo last summer.

This far from the Zone, alcohol abuse is defined as any beer left in the bottom of a bottle. It's a black humor but then there's little chance of the abuse. In fact, as you might have guessed, many of the stories I've told wouldn't have been possible without substantial quantities of beer. And not just on an occasional, or temporary, or accidental basis, but a sustained abuse over decades.

In the middle of a two-week heat wave, a local with a talent for finding the dry end of a beer can went missing, after he and his girlfriend had spent an afternoon drinking and disagreeing. Nothing unusual about that, and initially she was happy just to see him gone. A week passed and she became a little worried, but not to the point of action. That was until her son stopped by the house, walked through the door, and asked the simple question, "What's that smell?"

This was a simple two-room house, built back in the forties with nothing much done to it since. In the summer, sitting in the middle of an acre of dried grass and with no shade to help it, the house baked. And being a small house there weren't a lot of places for a strong smell to hide. Even so, between them, they couldn't find where it was coming from. It wasn't coming from the usual suspects. They had sniffed around under the sink and then checked the sewer line and the septic field, they checked for something dead in the crawlway, or something lying dead outside the house, but without finding the source of the smell. After some more sniffing they decided to look in the attic. They had looked everywhere else.

The son climbed the pull-down ladder into the attic, expecting to find something usual for these parts, such as a dead raccoon, but on shining his flashlight through the cobwebs he found the missing boyfriend instead. He was standing stiff as a board, propped against the chimneystack, quite dead and very bloated. He had climbed up there for who knows what, passed out in the heat, and died of a heatstroke. And in the days since, there had been plenty of time for him to decompose in the oven-like heat of the attic.

After the sheriff, the M.E. and all the usual local agencies had finished processing the scene, it was time to get this now enlarged, ripe corpse out of attic. The task fell to the local volunteer fire department. And since the dead boyfriend was a big boy to start with, and all the more so since he had had a chance to blow up some, the fire department decided they couldn't stuff him back down through the small trapdoor he had entered the attic by. The only way to get him out was through the metal roof.

Country folk are practical. That afternoon, the fire department rented an industrial-sized cherry picker, peeled back the metal roof like a sardine can, tied ropes around the corpse and hoisted it out. The swollen corpse slowly twirled in the air before being lowered to the ground and driven away; the unceremonious departure completed.

I find this story both remarkable and bizarre. Maybe it's just me, but my expectation is not to get so wasted as to inadvertently pass out and die in the attic while my girlfriend, undeterred, watches TV downstairs. But I haven't been able to get anyone at the Beer Bar to see the humor in the situation, not even the black humor they usually find so funny, or even admit to it being the slightest bit unusual. I tried. I pointed out that most people would notice a large dead person in their house, but it made no difference. They take their drinking seriously and must think something equally bizarre could happen to them, and, if it does, they hope people will see that death as natural too.

Unfortunately, it's not really a matter of *if* something happens, but just a matter of *when*. Because I've heard plenty about how alcohol and large family gatherings don't mix, apparently guns don't mix with alcohol either, nor do chainsaws, along with all kinds of heavy equipment and just about anything that is powered and has moving parts. The list goes on, but all of these alcohol fueled *accidents* seem to be treated with a type of impersonal inevitability that I normally reserve for next week's weather. Apparently, things just happen, and obviously I'm just not acclimated to the place yet.

Alcohol might be scourge of Igo, but crime surely isn't. And considering the near absence of law enforcement, and, what I like to euphemistically term, the well-equipped militia in the area, Igo is not a high crime area, or really a crime area at all. There's none really. This might be because the local miscreants are not the brightest kids in the one-room schoolhouse, but it's also because they end up in front of one of Shasta County's judges: Each one a hanging judge, who would if they could, but settle for handing out the maximum on every occasion.

An occasional body does turn up, but even then it seems to take a dozen criminal minds to come up with the plan for an otherwise simple murder. It's crime by committee. If a body is found it's strangled, stabbed, shot, and finally drowned—just to make sure. Then, to save the taxpayers the expense of an investigation, the victim is a known associate of all of the little criminals, seen arguing with them just hours before, and the pickup truck used in the crime is a hundred yards from the body in a ditch, where it was driven during the frantic getaway. And even if it's a property crime, the little criminals come from the same gene pool and $50 is considered an excellent night's work.

Being that the Beer Bar is the only place with cash for miles around, it looms large in the dreams of the local miscreants. One Saturday night the Beer Bar was robbed. It was a random event. A week went by and the bar was again robbed, then the following weekend it was robbed one more time. A pattern was emerging. The only things taken were beer and cigarettes, and far more beer was drunk and cigarettes smoked by the regulars sitting around speculating about whom had done it than was ever taken in the robberies themselves. But it showed badly on the community, as the overwhelming majority of locals take pride in who they are. They play life straight, and the few that don't play it straight must really like the prison life because they head back within weeks of leaving it.

I felt badly for Tom and Ray though, this happened soon after they bought the store. They had to repair their front door, twice, reinforce it, then add a video camera and, after the third robbery, live with the realization that their store was the only place worth robbing for miles around. But the bigger problem was for the patrons of their bar. With each passing week there was more time to speculate who was behind the robberies, and with each robbery the suspicions grew. This is a close nit community and it made for an uncomfortable time. The conversations were mostly about this or that relative, who was in jail and who was out, and there was an undertow of old family feuds across the bar. The robbers turned out not to be local kids after all, but kids from out of the other side of the county. They might as well have come from another planet.

Given that Igo sits in the middle of an area the size of a small country, and there's only one sheriff on duty at night to patrol the area, a crook has to try hard to get caught. But the store's young robbers managed it anyway, their crime spree ending after their final daring raid on the store. They were actually home safe, just another car in the night and miles into their getaway, when they saw Shasta's only sheriff's car with its siren wailing and its lights flashing driving towards them at high speed. It was responding to the 911 call from the Beer Bar.

Some people show their talent early. Without waiting for the sheriff to even acknowledge their existence, they decided to do his work for him and drove off the road, crashing their car right in front of him. It was a youthful career cut short. The sheriff found four high school kids, six-packs, cigarettes scattered on the floor, with the cash register in the back seat. And beyond the facts that the robbers were caught and probably given life sentences, more importantly, the air of suspicion was lifted; the patrons of the bar could return to telling each other outrageous lies over a cold beer, or two, or three, or...

Even with plenty of good reasons to go, I try to limit my visits to the Beer Bar until after I've finished an authentic day's work. That way I can establish my credentials by being covered in dirt or something disgusting. I feel even better if I'm smeared in black or brown lumps of things, and best of all when my clothes have rips and holes in them and my hair is matted together with dried sweat, if possible with leaves or twigs still sticking out of it. I still need the disguise of a hard day's manual labor before feeling qualified to have a beer with the locals, and it always amazes me that they've accepted me as well as they have.

Even with this disguise I still have a problem fitting in. I've never been able to convince my brain to stop thinking about several things at once. And though this problem is lessening over time—my mind's turning to porridge—it still surfaces during conversations. It's not that I'm smarter, I'm not, but it's annoying for people around here if you veer off subject, or finish sentences for them, or stare at the wall, or any number of irritating traits I show waiting for people to finish their thoughts. It's taken me years just to stay on topic, and it still takes a concerted effort to keep the required unwavering eye contact during conversations. But with these improvements I'm hoping to avoid hearing the comment, "If he isn't the squirliest %&&%# I've ever talked to..." just as the screen door creaks closed behind me.

Last summer, the water pump in Cow Creek finally gave up, after who knows how many years. It was working when I arrived here and it must have been sucking silt and water from the creek for years before that, so it had a good life. And I mention this because Sheila's daughter, Brooke, and her husband Eric were visiting at the time. I invited him along to go pick up the new pump.

Eric works for "Bill", that's Microsoft, and in spite of techy stereotypes is nothing like what you would imagine. He's calm, polite, thoughtful, smiles, and is easy to be around. I wish I shared his personality. His career was similar to my former career, and when I thought he could do with a break from the girls, I thought it would be fun to take him on a cultural safari, while I was picking up the new pump. The safari started as soon as he opened the passenger door of the infamous mini-truck, I could tell this by the expression on his face.

In my former life the unwashed thing would have appalled me too. At its best it had been a plain ordinary truck, but after years of the country life its cloth seats were stiff with who-knows-what, the floor had a layer of remnants of bits of paper and dirt, plastic things, along with small metal oddments that had lost their owners, all held together in a sheet of dried mud. Still, the safari wasn't about the disgusting mini-truck, it was the drive to town and buying a new pump.

After several years here, I knew about a pump's ratings, its flow and what a head is. In fact, I was also almost authentic. My hands were scarred and my fingernails packed with dirt, and I could talk about pumps. I could talk about fires, construction, and, if I had to, even some about cows; and these were the differences when Eric and I walked into the pump store. Eric, my former self, and my new country self walked into the pump store together. Actually, I swaggered in.

I knew the pace of conversation, when to lend a hand during the disassembly of the broken pump, when to walk off and talk to the guys round the back, when and what to joke about, and when to stand quiet during crucial assembly of the new pump. I knew to hold eye contact while I handed over the check, and give a firm handshake at the end of the business. It was as if I had arrived after five years in the remaking; I had made the change from an urban life to a country life. Well, maybe.

As I drove home with Eric I noticed he was unusually quiet. He had known me for several years before the move to Igo, and I suspected he had some unanswered questions rummaging through his mind. He was probably trying to match what he had just seen with the relative he once knew—at least that's what I hoped he was thinking. But he was very quiet, and kept the passenger window down all the way home. I thought about Dirty Burt.

I Just Work Here

I had been living on the mountain for four years before I finally spotted my first mountain lion. All I had ever seen before this had been their scat. Plenty of scat seen up-close while hunched over, head down, in thick brush with no visibility and no way for an escape—places where I wished I hadn't seen scat. And this lion showed up in the last place I would have expected, walking down China Gulch. As I drove around a corner, the cat was sauntering down the middle of the dirt road, not more than 20 yards away. It wasn't large, a juvenile or female, and it didn't even bother to look back before nonchalantly jumping up and over the bank beside the road and was gone. By the way the cat had discounted my presence it obviously didn't expect anyone to try following, but it might as well have handed me a written invitation. I stopped the truck, tiptoed over to the bank, and ran up to see the lion glance back and then lope into the undergrowth. It was gone in a second. I never expected a sighting to be such a thrill, even such a brief sighting, but it was.

It looked like every cougar on every nature show ever seen. But seeing first-hand the fluidity and self-assured ease of this top predator, I was reminded that grace is just excess power. Even so, having spent time alone in their hunting range and with good reason to think about these animals, I don't think their greatest weapons are their power or their speed. Somewhat counter-intuitively, I think it's more their patience and stealth that make them dangerous. And that's what I keep in mind when I'm walking alone in their world. I try to imagine what a very patient and very stealthy lion would do, and then go out of my way to make it a little more difficult for it to do it.

I've only had one other encounter with a lion. Even that was a non-encounter because I never actually saw the lion, in spite of it setting up shop only fifty yards from the house. It had made a temporary den in a shallow gully, and there was no reason to think it was there until one day a buzzard sat in a tree directly over its den. I walked over to find out what had died, and found bits and pieces of several deer in various stages of dinner.

Lions like to set up temporary dens as they move through their territories. They drag in kills, eat what they want, and then do what they think is a good job of burying the rest for later. It made for a messy graveyard, with little hooves left sticking out of the ground. And you would think that our two silly dogs would have said something about the new arrival, but there must be an agreement between the two species. In the week the lion was there, the dogs never mentioned the fact that a lion was camped just yards from my backdoor!

To avoid encouraging the lion though, all our pets became indoor animals and I found fewer reasons to crawl through thick brush. Apart from that, nothing much changed in our lives. Once a day I grew as tall as my sensibly sized frame allows, arms swinging wide to the side and boots stomping on the ground, and swaggered over to the den to see who came to dinner last night. After a grizzly week there was no new animal debris, and a day later the neighborhood's other scavengers had picked the place clean. There was nothing edible left; even the flies had moved on.

After four years of looking, and only the one sighting, I was pretty sure that the few lions in the area hadn't the slightest interest in me. I'd finished clearing the land, anyway, so I wouldn't be as readily available, head down in thick brush unaware of everything around me. Essentially all the time-consuming work on our thirty acres had been done, but there was one last chore. I had to bury the water pipe running from the creek up to the mouse-house.

No good deed goes unpunished. By doing such a thorough job of clearing, I had uncovered the PVC water pipe and exposed an impossible-to-miss, uninterrupted, bright white line of plastic pipe from the top of the property to the bottom. The worst of this eyesore was where the pipe had been routed down the middle of our seasonal creek, and the worst of the worst was where it had been put down the middle of its prettiest waterfall. The pipe had been there for forty years, and every time I saw it I asked, "Why would someone do such a stupid thing?" Well that's the printable version, anyway.

The pipe was a festering eyesore but it wasn't my only concern. There were also the two forty-year old, 220-volt cables that carried the electricity down to the pump from the garage. They had been lying out on the ground beside the pipe, and over the years the cables had been chewed on by inquisitive bears. There were literally hundreds of teeth marks pocking them, and in places the insulation had been eaten away, leaving the bare wire exposed. Lying on the ground all summer in the tinder dry grass, the fact that these cables hadn't started a fire was astounding, and proved conclusively that I really do have a kind-hearted, all-powerful being following me around and smoothing out life's little bumps before they become catastrophes.

At the beginning of last winter, after the first rains and the soil had a chance to soften, I rented a walk-behind gas-powered trencher and dug the third of a mile trench down the length of the property. It took a leap of faith to do this. The trencher weighed in at about 300-lbs, and once started on its journey down the side of the mountain there was no way back. I couldn't drag it back up the hill, and once started down the first slope the trencher had to make it all the way to the bottom of the property and out onto Woods Canyon Road. That being the only place it could be loaded into the mini-truck and returned to the rental store, and there was some pretty rough terrain to make it through before getting there.

Starting the trencher below the water tank, I walked along with it as it dug a trench across the relatively flat area behind the house. Which was easy, but as soon as I dropped over the edge onto the first of the thirty degree slopes, it turned into a lopsided wrestling match. The steep slope meant I had to hold the trencher's grip bars above my head, as opposed to the more usual waist height, steering and balancing it while it churned dirt out at me, of course, right at face level. And as the trencher and I slowly fought our way down the hill, it seemed to make a special effort to find

buried rocks and tree roots. It used them as an excuse to leap out at
me, topple over onto its side, trip the automatic cut-off and stop its
motor, which only added to the fun. After pulling the 300-lbs
trencher back onto its wheels, I had to stand down slope under it,
again, balancing it and keeping it level with one hand, while
pulling the rope pull-start with the other hand. It was all very
sophisticated.

After a morning's wrestling, the trencher and I emerged on
Woods Canyon Road, leaving a neat four-inch wide by two-foot
deep ditch running down the length of the property. The trencher
had a few more scratches than it started with, I'm sure I looked my
usual best, and hopefully the last Daring Dan exploit was over.

What a difference four years can make. When I started here
I was an innocent, I wouldn't have thought fighting this machine
from one end of the property to the other possible, let alone have
treated it as routine. The same goes for spending hours under a
shower of dirt. But to show just how much my life has improved, it
was just another day on the farm.

The rest of the project was unexciting. The old plastic pipe
was brittle from decades in the sun, and it would have made no
sense to reuse it and then have it break underground. So I bought a
third of a mile of new pipe from Home Depot. The pipe came in
twenty-foot lengths, which I glued together to make 100-yard long
sections, then dragged each section down the mountain (always
down the mountain), and glued the new section onto the end of the
previous section until the new pipe extended down to Cow Creek.
After that I repaired the two cables, inspecting every inch of them,
repairing the insulation where it was needed, and then laid them
into the bottom of the trench. Finally, I dropped the new PVC pipe
into the trench and the hard work was done, mostly.

All the dirt that the trencher had dug up needed to be put
back in the hole it had left. Shoveling got me so far, but to get the
rest of the loose-packed soil back into the trench I had to jump up
and down on it like a demented troll, and a third of a mile involved
a lot of jumping. I have a feeling that the same local I'd imagined

watching me drive the dozer years before, would have offered yet another opinion, "Now *that's* the stupidest f@#**# thing I've ever seen." And I would have agreed.

The next day, I was working on the trench near Cow Creek, cleaning up my mess and kicking leaves over the disturbed dirt, trying to disguise the fact that a trench had just been dug there. An out-of-towner driving by stopped, looked at the now pristine waterfall, and asked if I owned the land. I've been asked that question before (surprising considering how I normally look), but this time I thought before answering. "No, I just work here." It's pretty much how I've felt for years, though now I have some pride saying it. I've finally come to accept that in the country you don't actually own the land—the land owns you.

Character is Fate

Since first hearing the phrase "Character is Fate", and then actually bothering to think what it could mean, I'd been stalked by an impending doom. What if this was actually true? I might as well resign myself to finishing my days baking in the sun, subsisting in a trailer somewhere east of Barstow; fifty miles down a sand-blown desert road with empty beer cans, tumbleweeds, and the occasional scrub brush as the final trappings to a feckless existence. If character had anything to do with things that would be about right, but, much to the consternation of the truly worthy, good fortune comes to those that deserve it the least. Just before I headed south for Barstow, the square-shooting Sheila swept me off my feet and changed my final destination.

I'm convinced it takes a different mindset to survive outside the Zone of Civilization. This is best seen in new arrivals to the mountain, who often fail the test of living here. Not because it is harder than life in the burbs, which it is, but because living out here seems to relentlessly find flaws in people. And maybe it's the stress of change, or some angst they brought with them, or just who they are, but some people move out here and even before unpacking they pick a fight. They don't last long on the mountain.

I've always enjoyed talking to the ranchers; old-timers, self-reliant with characters as strong as their handshakes. One of these ranchers, Shawn, a young man about my age, with a quick smile that tells only part of the story, runs cattle on a thousand acres. A dispute over an easement started with a new neighbor of his, and the neighbor filed charges on Shawn for trespassing. The neighbor likely didn't understand the point about moving to the country. The dispute had been dragging on for some months, and I had asked Shawn why he didn't hire a lawyer. His answer was typical for him. "Filing a lawsuit wouldn't have been the way I would have handled things, but get a lawyer involved… why would I want to waste the money? I'd have to shoot three or four of my cattle in the head before I even introduced myself to a lawyer. I like my cows."

His logic was good, but mostly what struck me was how calm he was about the situation. I was fooled into thinking he approached all life's aggravations with this godlike equanimity, relying on reason and common sense to find an amicable agreement. I found out later that the last time he had a problem like this he put four men in the hospital. He was probably quite calm about it, though.

A mix of people gets attracted to this area, professionals through to bikers, through quirky artist types and daydreamers. Axles sagging, they pack their characters and personalities, hopes and dreams, along with their photos and home furnishings. And it's hard to tell on a first meeting whether somebody is going to stay, but within a year it's easy to lay odds one way or another. That's if they are still around. But it didn't take a year to know, and this was still longer than we deserved, when a pair of yuppies moved onto the mountain. Yes, the Undead had moved onto Woods Canyon Road. The Plague might as well have arrived.

I don't have anything against young upwardly mobile professionals but I do have a serious dislike for *yuppies*. Soulless things, they would carve up their poor mother, sell the pieces on the Internet, and then whore themselves in Nordstrom's front window if they thought that would get them into the next higher tax bracket. And worse, then boast to their friends about doing it. So watching this smart young couple drive by in a pair of his-and-hers BMW's wearing mirrored sunglasses, they exuded the required delusional self-importance, and, as only an inquiring mind can, I wondered... Why, of all places, would they be interested in Igo? I should have known better but I wondered what their story was. So soon after they moved in, as good and curious neighbors, we invited them over for dinner. That cured my curiosity.

We served a barbequed salmon dinner and in return they served a succession of empty stories. I wish these stories had been interesting, but they weren't, and they were mostly about her. I'll paraphrase, but the common theme to her stories was that she was right and everyone else was wrong. The minor theme was that everyone was envious of her and she was a victim of their envy, though why I wasn't sure.

I'm too old. I've seen too much and know the more emphatically someone declares that everyone else in the world is wrong, the greater the certainty that they're the one that's wrong. And after an hour listening to her talk about herself, I started to think she was mildly deranged—gorged on self-importance and the half-truths that she had bent to her needs. Also, I didn't want to say anything, but I thought she might consider loosening her bun a turn or two, as it was drawing her already hard features into something better suited for chopping wood. I was beginning to worry for my hand-finished redwood dinner table.

I sat across the table from what I thought was her true victim, her husband, watching a weakling's unconscious agreement with his captor. It was domestic version of the Stockholm syndrome. There might as well have been a gun to his head, but most likely it was just the threat of a divorce and having to divide their toys that fixed him in his purgatory. And these were a successful pair. He was a financial advisor and she worked in a lawyer's office, so they both had relatively good jobs, a rarity in this poor county, and which likely added to their view of themselves as movers and shakers. But watching the two of them, I wondered, beyond their signatures on their tax returns, what cold-blooded forces bound these two together, because love surely wasn't one of them.

We live on, what was once, a very large goat ranch. For a hundred years goats had picked the place clean, they were the only domesticated animals that could survive in this terrain, and things stayed that way until the ranch was broken up into smaller parcels, fifty years ago. It's all residential acreage now, and considering the area is residential, a reasonable person would think twice about allowing their animals to roam around on other people's properties. You would think.

Shortly after moving onto Woods Canyon Road, the yuppies bought a herd of alpacas, they called them pets but they were just some more faddish possessions to add to their collection, and naturally one wasn't good enough, they needed a herd. One morning a stock transporter drove up Woods Canyon and dropped off twenty alpacas. A month later, two of the alpacas were dead of malnutrition and confused as to what it took to keep their possessions alive, the yuppies decided what their designer herd shouldn't be fenced and their alpacas should be allowed to roam free, so they could graze in lion country. The lions might have been pleased but the neighbors weren't happy about it.

Their nearest neighbors, a retired couple, were the first effected. While the couple was away one weekend, the alpacas ate their vegetable garden. It wasn't a large vegetable garden but, as with most gardeners, it was important to them. It was the sort of thing that should have been settled easily enough with a phone call and an apology. It should have. But when the elderly couple complained about their garden being trampled and eaten, the yuppies manufactured outrage and used the opportunity to make a point—a deranged point. And instead of an apology they made it their life's work to attack their neighbors, just to show them.

For months, actually most of the time they lived here, the yuppies pulled spiteful petty stunts on their neighbors, threatened them with the sheriff (they constantly boasted that they had one in their pocket), and filed a series of frivolous lawsuits. They never did attack a neighbor that could fight back, not even a hard look at anyone that could retaliate, and their coordinated attack had merely been the well-honed skill of bullies to find someone weaker than them.

I don't like bullies. I grew up as a child in a culture that made a point of not liking bullies, and where I grew up bullies had to be physically large, something, anything, and not merely the calculating cowards these two were. So I drove over to have a talk to them, not knowing what to expect or what to say, and when I lifted the rock I saw what was underneath—it was just a couple of self-absorbed children with paychecks.

What she had merely hinted at previously revealed itself as malevolent. She turned purple as she spat out their case against their neighbor, using language better suited to describe the crime of the century, and boasted how they intended to *annihilate* anyone that crossed them. Halfway through the diatribe her cell phone rang, I was put on hold while she temporarily transformed into a giggly girl. Finished with the call, she dropped the smile and continued her rant, abruptly finishing with a line in the sand: "I thought you liked us!" And I suppose I could have erred diplomatic and dribbled some weasel speak, but it's not in my nature, I didn't see the point and, more importantly, I can't resist one-liners.

"Like you? You're yuppie f@@*s!" It was a phrase I hadn't had to use in years, but it resurrected itself just in time.

"Yuppies!" They cried out in unison. It was like they had never heard the word before, or heard it too often. Who knows, but either way I must have hit a nerve. Her face seemed to swell to twice its original size, and taking a step forwards she made a point to come within inches of my face, "You're dead to us!" almost in way of an excommunication. Not being catholic this was wasted on me, but I was worried whether her spittle was infectious—she was starting to bubble.

The average death march has to have warmer feelings than their marriage. And you would think they would have picked up on something else I said, but I guess the greatest insult to a yuppie is to be called one. It must be a reminder to them that they're the Undead. Irrespective; I had erred, I had failed to worship, I had suggested imperfection in their perfect lives and now I was the enemy. I was dead to them.

Sensing this was as good a time as any, the husband poked his head around from behind his fuming wife. It was his chance to act like a male of the species, but all he did was fumble for his cell phone and bluster, "Do you know who we are?" then dialing, "I'm going to call the sheriff on you." What a girl I thought and left. There was nothing to be gained, and I had had enough of their peculiar lives.

I've been thrown out of better but not for less, and as I was getting in the mini-truck she apparently had some more to say on the subject: "You're just like the other redneck ar*h%#les on this road! Get off our property! Get off our property!" Her purple head looked like it was about to explode.

I've heard somewhere that a marriage is supposed to bring out the best in two people, not the worst. But these two equally broken people were mangled together in a marriage I ordinarily wouldn't have wished on an enemy. And so it was with mixed feelings that a week after my excommunication I learned he had lost his job.

The very next day, with their sacred bond broken, she stormed out with the newer of their BMW's, while she still could, to seek out another host organism. And after that, alone and debarked, the worst Woods Canyon had to endure were his sour faces as he drove to and from their house. Poor bastard, being weak isn't much of an excuse for anything. He sat in his house alone for another month and then he left: walking away from their house in foreclosure and making a perfect closing statement to their short stay here.

Although a blind man could have found their faults, I still prefer to think it was the mountain that had. And it probably had in its own way. The yuppies were out of their element, and without the Zone's hall of mirrors to constantly confirm their bloated opinion of themselves, without the distractions, the quiet between them must have become deafening.

Their neighbors held a potluck dinner, in celebration. And sitting around with some of the other redneck ar*h%#les living in the canyon, I realized that I must have become a local of sorts. The unlikely day had come when I had been called a redneck, and, considering where the slur had come from, it had been an honor, a sign that just maybe I was becoming a part of the community.

A Man and his Derelicts

We had hardly finished celebrating the yuppies departure when another brief visitor to Woods Canyon arrived. His was a different story. He came from out of state on a personal mission; "Getting back to the land," as he explained it to us. He seemed genuine, though a little fussy to be getting back to anything too real, and the very first time Sheila and I met him he let us know that he was more than a mere chiropractor, he was in fact a highly advanced practitioner, and preferred the title of Doctor—even though he wasn't. But the title stuck, and from then on we referred to him by his preferred title and made sure to include an exaggerated emphasis along with it.

Woods Canyon has always had an attraction to people wanting to hide out, and we immediately were suspicious about why The Doctor would abandon his goldbrick profession to experience life in a travel trailer on a tract of land without water and electricity. But then, doing our best to find a positive side to his story, we thought what a man of vision (certainly larger than our own) to give up a promising career; reject the false values of society, and live here as one with Nature. That was the thought, however unlikely.

He arrived in an old moving van that he had bought for the purpose, stuffed full with his worldly possessions. The van had sunk up to it axles in the first muddy hollow, only a few yards up his dirt road, got stuck and then become his base of operations. But in spite of his sad-looking slab-sided mar to our landscape, The Doctor was welcomed with handshakes, offers of help should he need it, along with plenty of free advice—which he ignored, while making it clear to everyone he thought we were all bumpkins.

Months went by and suspicions started to fester about The Doctor, and then the Internet revealed his past. He had lost his chiropractic license (an achievement that must take considerable talent in itself) and arrived here chased by lawsuits. Everybody deserves a second chance, but soon our mountain community began to realize there was little correlation between what the Doctor said and what he did. Yes, The Doctor seemed to misspeak, and on a regular basis. The grace period given to any new arrival to get their country legs under them was being badly used and then things got worse.

It's not The Doctor's fault, entirely. What with the lawsuits and outstanding judgments he couldn't have wanted to financially surface, not in any legitimate way. And not being a rancher or a farmer, and few options to help finance his life, The Doctor started to cut down his trees and sell them for firewood.

He must have had a little money left over from his more prosperous days, though, because in his short time here he bought more cars than I had owned in my whole life. He would have been better off if he had just bought the one car and looked after it, and no matter how many cars he bought they all shared the same fate. They didn't work for long, and over time ended up scattered across his property, where they had died or got stuck, but either way were abandoned. His property became a place where old cars came to die.

The one vehicle that did manage to keep moving didn't do that well though. It was a fairly new Chevy Heavy Duty pickup, the flagship of his fleet, but it lost most of its newness after the Doctor parked it conveniently close to a very large oak he wanted to cut down. It showed a certain kind of genius to do this, but he allowed his pickup truck to cushion the tree's fall: leaving a tree-trunk sized indent across the bed of the truck, bending its frame, and giving it the look of a sway-backed horse. That was the look the truck stayed with, and if I ever wondered how The Doctor got his chiropractic credentials in the first place, this helped me understand how he lost them.

I was surprised that he'd tried his hand at all, but after this first attempt, being that it was such a success, he decided to have his trees cut down for him. Maybe he was short of cash, but The Doctor tried bartering. He allowed people to live on his land and hunt in exchange for cutting firewood, which The Doctor could then sell. But that then there was The Doctor's downfall.

The only people that would go along with such a deal were derelicts. The Doctor scrounged up as many as he could from around the county, and when that wasn't enough he used the Internet to find more, even from out of state. It was just a matter of time before something bad happened. Tattooed paroles started driving up and down Woods Canyon, trailing clouds of smoke behind their beater cars. And as our over-worked sheriff once told us, "We expect you guys to take care of your own problems." Up and down Woods Canyon, shells were put into chambers.

The game-changing mistake came when two of the Doctor's derelicts shot a buck. There were several problems to this, even ignoring that they were in the middle of a community of rabid animal lovers. First, it was out of season. Second, they had the foresight to do this beside the road, and in broad daylight. Third, being the incompetents they were, they might as well have been using the poor deer for target practice. Only a few rounds could have hit the poor animal, none squarely, and it had staggered off to die. So the derelicts followed it until it dropped, and then resorted to sawing through its neck with a hunting knife to finish it off.

There are those that hunt for food, and though I would point out Safeway's meat department to them, I don't have an argument with them. But I don't understand the "sport" of hunting, even under the best of circumstances. If one of these *sportsmen* were to run naked into a moonlit forest with a Buck knife in his teeth to grimly chase down a five hundred pound wild boar, something mildly challenging, I might call that hunting. I could even respect a sportsman for doing that, and though I'd think him nuts, I could respect him. But stepping out of a truck, looking down a laser sight and squeezing off a round from a high-powered rifle at a deer minding its own business, is about as sporting as beating a baby chick to death with a baseball bat, and then calling that a sport. It's just a little too one-sided for me. And unless the idea is to put every scrap of the animal on a dinner plate, then these sportsmen need to rise up as one, and tell the world the truth: "We're powerless, frustrated, middle-aged white guys. We're over-weight, our wives hate us, and we need something to take our miserable lives out on." I think that would about cover it.

The shooting had alerted the entire community, which, apart from one throwback, thinks we've done enough damage to the Earth's wildlife without trying even harder. By the time the Fish and Game Department arrived on the scene the derelicts were dragging the perforated and mutilated carcass back to the road with a length of chain behind The Doctor's sway-backed pickup. It was a sight to remember and a catalytic moment. The community rose up in a collective anger. We had had enough and The Doctor had to go.

This might be a scofflaw community (with more than its fair share of cantankerous people who would ordinarily be busy interfering in each other's lives) but when an outsider behaves worse than we do, we unite as one. At 9 a.m. the following morning, a caravan of cars streamed out of Woods Canyon and coalesced as an angry mob in the lobby of the county offices. They demanded action but the county moves slowly.

The county has to get past the annoying legal burden of a property owner's rights, and until there was something more than anecdotal evidence, The Doctor had a legal barrier he could use to his advantage. The county needed more. So early one morning, while his derelicts were still fast asleep, a retired bank president and I accidentally dropkicked a "No Trespassing" sign high into the air and crept onto The Doctor's land. It must have been a sight; two old men crouched over, skulking around with digital cameras.

Hiking through The Doctor's hundreds of acres we found the mother lode of infractions: illegal trailers, illegal sewage dumping, illegal trash dumping, illegal roads, illegal grading, illegal everything. Two little old men, tiptoeing around at dawn's first light, all eyes and ears (or what was left of them), on a mission for Woods Canyon. Strangely, it was a small detail that I remembered the most—an occasional waft of stale cigarettes hanging in the still morning air. We left undetected an hour later and by noon the digital photos were processed. We had a stack of eight by ten glossy photographs, with circles and arrows and a paragraph on the back of each one, which Sheila dropped off to the county. Finally the county had the proof it needed, but the law grinds slowly. There were motions and hearings and more motions, and months later, after his day in court, The Doctor was fined. This did nothing.

It wasn't the county that finally caught up with The Doctor, though. The Doctor had been recruiting from a pool of people that likes to settle its disagreements directly, and the day came when the derelicts had a disagreement with The Doctor. Shortly after a call to respond to a disturbance, several patrol cars arrived filled with full-sized Shasta County sheriffs. The derelicts scattered and the next day so did The Doctor, back to something called civilization, where it was safe for him to be who he was.

Admittedly, life here is a little different, but I still don't understand why personality failings have such consequences. The yuppies were nasty and The Doctor wasn't very smart, but they would have been fine if they had just stayed in the Zone. And out of the hundred or more people living on the mountain we have our fair share of difficult people—deliberate curmudgeons, misfits and outcasts—and why being difficult isn't a failing, when spiteful and stupid are, I haven't a clue.

Nothing's Ever Easy

I'm not sure when my feelings about living here changed, and maybe they didn't at any one moment, but they did over time. And like the start of a new season, when no one-day means too much, it was spring and not winter, and without knowing exactly when my feelings had changed, they had. I was no longer in hunkered down in survival mode, and found myself enjoying my funny little life on the mountain, quite content to be here and not somewhere else, and even discovered a little enthusiasm for it all.

With each improvement to the mouse-house, the screen porch looked sadder and sadder. It had turned into an eyesore. And even if it had once been the best looking structure on the property, things had changed, and now it looked the worst. I started to think about building an addition to the mouse-house in its place; forgetting how I felt about pounding nails and going for it anyway.

It was a little late in the year to start construction and have it closed in before the winter rains, but an almost certain chance of failure has always been an attractant to me. I was missing the excitement of a self-imposed disaster and decided that there was still time to find an architect, float the plans by the county, and get it built in time. Even with inevitable delays and my increasing disinterest in building, it could be done. So we pre-named the addition the East Wing, because of its location and all the other usual reasons, and it became my last construction project. But before any construction could start, the thing that had spawned the insanity, the screen porch, had to be demolished.

The screen porch was elevated over a steep slope, off to the side of the mouse-house. It was supported by a mere handful of posts up to its flimsy plywood floor and even fewer posts from the floor to the roof. Its roof was solid though, overbuilt if anything, and between its top-heavy design and its inadequate underpinning, the screen porch had always gently swayed with the wind; only adding to its charms.

My demolition plan was to chainsaw through some of its few supporting posts, until the whole thing was ready to collapse, and then pull it down using the Warthog. That was the plan, and if the screen porch was wobbly to start with it was downright scary by the time I finished cutting out some more of its support posts, of course, while standing underneath it. With the screen porch teetering, I drove the Warthog into position, tied one end of a rope to the back of the truck, and then climbed onto the roof to tie off the other end to the main roof beam. You see the problem here. As I tied the rope to the beam, thirty feet up in the air and wobbling on top of the wobbling roof, it occurred to me that I should have done this before I had cut through the support posts. Details.

Hurrying down from the roof, with an occasional glance back at the teetering structure, I fast-walked over to the Warthog and started it. I eased the truck forwards, taking the slack out of the rope, and the screen porch leaned towards the truck. The Warthog pulled some more and the porch creaked and groaned and leaned some more, but it didn't collapse. Only after it was pulled over to a seemingly impossible angle did it give a last protracted groan and pancake onto the ground behind the truck, along with the usual satisfying cloud of dust. It had gone exactly as planned and, more importantly, it hadn't fallen on top of the truck or started sliding down the slope after the truck, both real possibilities.

With the screen porch on the ground, it was easy to salvage the forty-year old 2 by 6 pine boards from its roof—to recycle as the floor of the new addition. What little that was left I dragged into a nearby gully, ready for a burn next winter, leaving the site clear for construction to start.

Not exactly the manager type, I've always preferred to let people do what they're meant to do, but having the hole dug for the East Wing's foundation showed me my mistake. The job needed a mini-backhoe, one able to fit in the cramped building site, and I'd found the mini-backhoe and its driver in the local rag. There wasn't much to the job. The spray-painted and impossible-to-miss florescent orange lines in the dirt showed clearly where he was supposed to dig, and I left him to it, which was a mistake. When I came back to see how he was doing, he had missed the marks literally by a foot. And adding insult to injury, he then made a point not to understand that he had dug the holes in the wrong place.

I stood in front of him and pointed at the impossible-to-miss florescent orange lines in the dirt, where the holes should have been dug, and then re-marked them to make sure. The backhoe guy scraped another few inches here and there, then I went through some more pointing and some more spraying, but with every redo it seemed more of an effort for him. I began to suspect that, in his mind, he had already dug a hole and therefore his job was done. His lack of understanding was deliberate and he won in the end. I gave up and paid him to go away.

The thing about digging a hole in the wrong place is that even after you dig the hole in the right place, you end up with more hole than you were hoping for. And as concrete is not cheap, pouring it into a hole that's twice the size it need be becomes expensive. So I went through the time-consuming and money-wasting process of building wooden forms to pour the concrete into. But before the wooden forms could be built, I had to dig the holes where they should have been dug, of course, by hand, which was the exact thing I had been trying to avoid in the first place. It should have been so easy.

It took a week of digging and building the forms before I was ready for the concrete. So tired, fed up, and behind schedule, not only did I have the concrete delivered but I also had it pumped into the forms. I was able to stand around and chat with the crew boss rather than mixing tons of concrete and humping it two buckets at a time into the forms. It was civilized, if a little expensive.

The foundation's completion brought the construction "out of the dirt" and next step was the rough carpentry. So I called Erin at his new home, and together we laid down the floor and framed the walls. In a few days a wooden skeleton for the new addition stood in the spot where the old screen porch had teetered only three weeks before. The walls were up but the roof had some complications to it.

The East Wing's pitched roof was designed around a large load-bearing ridge beam because I'd wanted to keep the look of exposed beams in the original mouse-house, even though it would mean some extra cost and effort. The beam was thirty feet long, twenty inches deep, four inches wide, and it was heavy. The problem was that it had to be raised from the floor, up fourteen feet, and bolted on the top of two large posts, one at each end. But after the North Wing's near catastrophe, I didn't feel like getting underneath another beam and trying to lift it. The solution was simple though—my automotive floor jack.

Using the jack, I raised the beam a foot then nailed new blocks under the beam to hold it in place, then put a longer post between the floor jack and the bottom of the beam and jacked the beam up another foot, and kept going until the beam sat on top of the posts. It took less that an hour, and it would have taken that long just to explain what needed to be done to a team of the unwilling. With the heavy lifting done, I bolted the beam into place, tore out the temporary blocks I had used to help raise it, then cleaned up the place and even put my tools away. I flipped an empty plastic bucket upside down in the middle of the floor, and sat down to admire my achievement; proud that I had implemented the lift flawlessly.

This was the first time I'd had a chance to really look at the beam since taking off its plastic shipping wrap, that was just minutes before starting to jack it into place. At the time I'd been thinking about the upcoming lift and didn't pay much attention to whatever nonsense the factory had stenciled on the beam. And without my reading glasses I couldn't have read what it was from that close, anyway. But sitting underneath it, looking up at the bottom of the beam above my head, in poorly stenciled black ink, I slowly read a 'T' followed by an 'O' and finally a 'P'. "TOP" I murmured to myself, followed by a stunned silence that ended with a stream of expletives.

I had never heard of this! How could a piece of wood have a top and a bottom? But this one did. So I spent the rest of the day building scaffolding and a temporary platform to stand on at each end of the beam, and the next day, with Erin's help, I turned the beam over and bolted it back in place.

The rest of the work went quickly. Erin and I installed the windows and doors, and nailed up the plywood siding and the roof ply. Then the roofer came out and the addition was sealed up. And just in time, the rains started just as the roofer was finishing and the next day it poured. I had made the deadline, we were closed up before the rain, but winter was setting in fast and I was getting bored with construction. The East Wing languished. By Christmas, only the sheetrock had been hung, and then it snowed. The scary steep driveway iced over, and with that all the supply runs stopped. What little work I had planned to do, came to a halt.

I worked off and on for the next couple of months, pretty much when I felt like it, but even at this disinterested pace it didn't take long to finish, and with the final inspection by the county my construction career was finally over. The mouse-house was effectively a new house throughout, I had built two additions, two master bathrooms, a kitchen, a guesthouse, a garage, acres of decks, arbors, pergolas and a barn, and as I put my tools down for the last time I hoped never to lift another hammer again. Off and on, the construction had taken five years, but if I had to stand in front of the mouse-house and explain why it had taken that long, I couldn't. I was also five years further down an increasingly steep slope into old age, and I was glad to be done.

However hard it had been, the combination of construction and working on the land had one benefit. After thirty years of nearly constant pain, I had a healthy back again. And I'm sure if I had held onto a desk job and been encouraged by a generous health insurance plan, that I would have had a million-dollar titanium spine by now. So I missed having multiple operations, a metal back that would have been less than useless, and Christmas's spent boring the relatives with details of my latest painful surgery.

On the subjects of great luck and extravagant amounts of money, we couldn't have finished building the mouse-house if our investments hadn't finally started to come through for us. Not a vast amount but enough to get by, which was lucky, because even though there's no way to make any, it still takes money to live in the woods.

Within a few weeks of finishing the East Wing, the flush of success was over and I was bored again. It was late spring, and one of the few remaining areas of thick brush on the property became all the excuse I needed to get back into some manly work. It was a chance to run the chainsaw and sneak in one more burn before summer.

I like to start a burn with a *starter pile*. A starter pile is pretty much what it sounds like, a small pile of brush used to start the burn. I try to keep them small and build them out of whatever brush is already there. This has the advantage of clearing an area for the starter pile and at the same time creating it. After lighting a starter pile I wait for it to burn down, giving me enough time to get a feel for the burn conditions for the day, and only then do I start cutting more wood and throwing that into the fire. So you can see, I am responsible.

The brush I wanted to clear was in a steep gully, and was particularly dense just where I needed to build the starter pile. I started to cut the brush and build the starter pile, but there was so much brush I began to worry that the pile was getting too large. It was growing into something more the size of a full burn pile. So I cleared a larger than usual area around the pile, just to stop the fire crawling out, which in turn made the pile bigger.

It was in steep-sided gully that needed clearing just because it was packed full of manzanita. There was a combination of new growth over the top of dead and dried out old growth, and it made for a mix of brush ten feet high, too dense to even fight a way through. Adding to the problems was the inevitable layer of leaves under the bushes, waiting to catch fire and ignite everything else in the area, if it ever got the chance. Still, I had meticulously cleared the ground around the starter pile, leaving a four-foot ring of unburnable dirt without a leaf on it, so my precautions were as good as they could get.

With the usual trepidation I lit the starter pile. The trepidation should have counted for something, but one minute later the starter pile had turned into a solid-red roaring flame twenty feet high (I had been hoping for something in the two to three-foot range), and its heat was so intense that it forced me to scramble out of the surrounding brush. This wasn't a good start, but I had to know what was happening with the fire. So I got down on hands and knees and crawled close enough to check on my carefully cleared circle of dirt. What a relief, the fire wasn't crawling across the dirt. After all, how could it?

It didn't have to. The heat was so intense that the brush surrounding the starter pile, several feet away, had burst into flames. In less than a minute, my carefully constructed starter pile had engulfed the bottom of the gully. The fire was now coming up the sides of the gully, very angry, with a lot of fuel to make sure things got worse by the second.

For once my Daring Dan chainsaw came in useful. Arms locked out in front of me, holding the chainsaw in a death grip with the throttle wide open, I started cutting through an area across the top of the gully, where the brush was thickest, frantically trying to cut a new firebreak before the fire reached me. This might sound almost clinical, but it wasn't. The entire gully was on fire, and if there hadn't been a solid wall of brush between the fire and me, acting as a heat shield, I couldn't have stayed long enough to cut a new firebreak. Then there was the smoke, and it's always this way. Just when you need to suck huge quantities of air, it comes at you as thick smoke and you can't.

I finished the firebreak along the top of the gully and then cut firebreaks along both sides, completely surrounding the fire. Again, there was nothing clinical about this. It was a fight to the finish, and one more time that I had been at my max. I had been gasping for every breath without a thought of letting up, for longer than I would have thought possible. And at the end of the self-induced disaster, I lay collapsed on the ground, swearing I would never ever do something that dumb again. The day had started out so peacefully.

I should have learned a lesson over the years, and maybe I have, but probably not the right one. I started out trying to control fire by stomping at it with my tennis shoes, not a great start, but through a few too many experiences I found out what it actually takes to control a fire, or at least control it better. And not wanting to get too metaphysical, that's the only lesson I want to take from this.

The Unimportance of Importance

Being tucked away in Woods Canyon, life is different from the rest of Igo, especially from the ranchland in the softly rolling hills that fan out from the bottom of our mountain. In contrast, Woods Canyon squeezes tight as it winds up the side of the mountain, and with steepening sides what little level land there is becomes rarer, until there is none. Which makes it useless for farming or ranching, but it gives the reason for the canyon's small community to live here; even with all the inconveniences. The landscape is inspiring. It's an intrusion into the wilderness and very peaceful apart from the occasional gunfire. And although historically the canyon's remote location—with its front door a long narrow road in and its back door an open escape route into the wilderness behind it—was an invitation to people wanting to keep a distance from the law, nowadays a more thoughtful bunch lives here. Well, maybe.

"Does Howdy Doody have a wooden dick?" A simple "Yes," would have been a perfectly good answer to my simple question, but Alice has her own way with words and it needs some getting used to. I've lived next door to her, a half-mile away, for five years now and I'm still getting used to her. But even I can tell that she's someone very special.

Hers has been an extraordinarily tough life. Born sixty years ago into poverty, and (if it were possible) in an even more primitive Shasta County, living with a father who burned down their family home three times in drunken rages. She survived through her lesbian life in a bigoted time in a bigoted county with a few good friends, but no good breaks; so chances were that she would never become an important person and make her mark publicly. For most of her life she worked for the county, on a road crew, and when she was interviewed for the job she was asked what she thought her qualifications were. She answered with the now famous quote, "Well I don't bake cookies and I don't give head, so you tell me... do I have the job?" She got the job.

Those were early days, and her social skills haven't improved much since then. And you have to see past Alice's chain smoking, her bottomless glass of vodka, the profanities strung together with an occasional thought, and ignore (if that's possible) the holstered sidearm on her hip. But what lies behind the façade, packed into a five-foot nothing frame, is a gutsy life-affirming celebration of humanity.

Still, appearances are seldom the whole story, and though I will live in mortal danger for even suggesting it, under her tough exterior beats the softest heart that she insists on denying having. She will do anything for a friend, is one of the most remarkable people I've ever met, and someone I'll remember for life.

She has lived in Woods Canyon for as long as anyone left alive out here, having bought a large parcel of land nearly forty years ago when Woods Canyon was a lot further out of town than it is now. She lived in a one-room log cabin, built during the area's mining past, and it became her refuge. The same smooth-talking real estate agent that sold me the mouse-house would have described her moss-roofed cabin as "rustic". Which it was, built out of rough-cut planks of wood common to that period. It had no indoor plumbing, no electricity, one meagerly window, and a crudely fitting plank door. Over time, she upgraded her miner's shack with a small bedroom, a water supply, a wood burning stove, and finally electricity. It didn't have many conveniences, but it was her home.

Her cabin is set idyllically under a grove of cedars beside Cow Creek, and would be anyone's idea of picturesque. So picturesque in fact that when a bed-and-breakfast, called "The Castle", was operating for a time at the end of Woods Canyon, the lost guests would often turn into Alice's driveway to ask if her moss-roofed one-room cabin was "The Castle". This would happen at all times of the day and night, sometimes catching Alice naked in her homemade hot tub and forcing her to stand up, rudely illuminated by the visitors' headlights, point in exasperation at her one-room miner's cabin, and ask the simple question: "Does that look like a f%*$ castle to you?"

There is another side to Alice, though. (And for the sake of the rest of humanity, there had better be.) She married her girlfriend in August. The ceremony was held at the Igo Inn on, what was for Igo, a warmish Saturday afternoon. Most of Igo attended, packed too tightly into the large parlor-style front room, and a few people did faint, but that was from the heat. Their lesbian wedding was a first for Shasta County, and their love for each other is something most of us could only wish for. And though I've never been a fan of weddings, at least the ones that I wasn't the center of attention, this was beautiful and perhaps the only one that I've sat all the way through. But the real benefit of Alice marrying, at least from my perspective, was that her sharper edges were smoothed off some.

We've lived as neighbors for years. Initially we scrapped, I was far too busy surviving to get to know her, or anyone else for that matter, and our friendship only started after I found out that she's a horse whisperer. Anytime Thunder saw Alice, the old horse would miraculously grow light on his feet and trot over to her, then press his head softly against Alice's cheek and just stand there. The two of them would stand around like this for as long as Alice had the time—the horse would have stood there all day.

This always puzzled me. I did all the work, took care of and fed the silly animal every day for years, and I couldn't get a response like that, whatever I did. So I asked the question, not expecting an answer I could do anything with, but asking anyway.

"So Alice, how do get Thunder to stand there like that?"

"I talk to him with thoughts. I just don't say the words," was her paradoxical answer, stated self-evidently as if it made perfect sense to anyone with a brain.

Don't *say* it just *think* it? Could it really be that simple? I had always thought that I had a knack with animals, having looked after just about everything small and cute since I was a kid, but horses had always been a mystery to me. I thought of them as giant rodents, though a lot clumsier, not nearly as smart, and with an evil side to them.

Alice's words stayed with me, and over time and in small ways I found her insight worked. Thunder and I just stood together. I wouldn't say a thing, which was difficult in itself, and in a horse sort of a way we communed. Well at least Thunder stood there, which was an improvement, though he never managed the same soppy look on his long horse face that he had for Alice. So maybe Alice was right, there really was something there, though I still had no idea what.

The real test of Alice's insight came the day Thunder had colic. The old horse had been in trouble all afternoon, and by late in the day he wanted to lie down. As with all our horse emergencies I called Alice. She met us at the barn, where she and Sheila tried walking Thunder, to keep him moving, even though he didn't want to. He wanted to lie down. After an hour that's what he did, and once down he stayed down, outside his barn. His breathing became so shallow it was almost indiscernible, his eyes were blank and he seemed to be lost inside himself. Later that evening, when Alice had to leave, her final somber thought was that Thunder was likely going to die that night, and unfortunately Alice knows horses.

Thunder is an old horse, a very old horse, and eventually something like this is bound to kill him. There's not much to be done with a worn out old horse that's already living on the margin, there's only what's left of the horse's will to live to pull him through. But live or die, we wanted to make sure that Thunder's last moments were as good as they could be. So Sheila stayed with Thunder through the evening and about midnight I took over.

Sitting with Thunder, I had a feeling that I was beginning to understand him. And though I would not have thought it possible, I was sure the old horse was very aware that people cared for him, and more than that, our love was important to him. As I might have mentioned before—I didn't understand horses.

With a full moon for company, in the long quiet of the night and without words, I talked thoughts to this proud shape as he decided to live or to die. I lay beside Thunder; his great bulk unnaturally sprawled out on the ground, and swept my arm gently back and forth, rubbing his swollen belly. He had only the shallowest of breathing and not a muscle moved for hours, yet there wasn't any of the fear that I would have expected from a sentient animal like a horse that can show the shock of life so easily.

Then, just before dawn, the old horse just stood up as if he had woken up from a long sleep. A little shaky, but he was back on his feet with what appeared to be a renewed spirit. He must have been lying low, waiting-out the problem in his gut. Or, he had had enough of delusional people whispering in his ear about his imminent death. Either way, within minutes he was pretty much his normal self. Still weak, but wandering around sniffing at tufts of hay on the ground and rolling his big tongue around, as he always does when he's hungry, and with that I knew he had made it. I stayed with him until I was certain he would be okay, then put out some more food for him and walked home: Taking my time, thinking about our old horse, and glad that we still had him around. Till the next time.

In the winter, especially during long rains, I like to walk down to the barn and sit on an old Adirondack chair we keep tucked under the overhanging roof. I enjoy listening to the rain on the metal roof and staring out through the sheet of water pouring off it. It's very peaceful looking out at the gloom. Nothing moves when it's raining, the animals all hide and leave behind them an empty stage.

One gray afternoon, I was sitting under the overhang with a heavy rain rattling on the roof, when Thunder sauntered out of his stall to join me. He looked like a particularly wet and sad Eeyore. First, he wandered around near me; then deliberately squeezed his bulk right by me, causing me to pick up my feet so they wouldn't be trodden on; then stopped right beside me to sniff at my face and breathe on me; then snuffled my bald head with his big rubbery lips; then rested his chin on top of my head; then drooled grass-stained saliva down my jacket while he tugged at the collar. When he wasn't trying to torment me, he stood beside me under the overhang and looked out at the same rainy day I was looking at. And this time I took the words from my thoughts, and looked out at the scene as I imagined Thunder's eyes might see it. I experienced a world of here and now, a world with no right or wrong, not even too hot or too cold, nothing judgmental. It was just the way it was, straight forward and simple, there weren't a lot of complicated ideas piled on top of yet more complicated ideas; I was in the world as it was, in the here and now. I thought this was the way this big old horse saw the world, and I had been missing something by not having seen this before—thinking thoughts without words.

My favorite (printable) of Alice's enumerable maxims is "If you look after the Mountain, the Mountain will look after you." I remember hearing this shortly after moving here and dismissed it as so much quasi-spiritual nonsense, hapless musings from someone who has lived out in the woods a winter too long. But after five years I must have been here too long too, or something must have happened in the meantime, because nowadays I sense some truth in those words. I think the truth is found behind the maxim, not so much in the words themselves but the person saying them. Perhaps if you are pure of heart, if you are straight with yourself and straight with others, then, in spite of whatever life throws your way, you can always find a place you can call home.

Alice reminds me of many old-timers from around here, there's no trace of self-importance to them. So there's no chance of hearing Alice's ego bellow the inane question, "Do you know who I am?" as the yuppies had. She states her case, a little colorfully, and the rest is down to you. I saw this during our early squabbles, while I was still settling into a life on the mountain. Not that I was pleased about it, because I knew something was different in the way she stood toe-to-toe and the way I did.

I've always been perfectly willing to make a public stance of standing tall, but privately I'm busy thinking of ways to get out of the situation and hoping the appearance of a firm stand will be good enough. But Alice doesn't just make the appearance of standing toe-to-toe, she actually stands up for what's right. On the other hand she carries a sidearm, and that probably helps her position some.

The last time someone made the mistake of poaching a deer on Woods Canyon, the word went out over the community's walkie-talkie network. Getting the call, Alice immediately drove onto our narrow road, turned her pickup sideways and blocked it. She stood there alone, confronting three well-armed hunters as they tried to drive back out, and kept them there until Fish and Game arrived.

Maybe I should but I don't have a walkie-talkie, so I didn't hear the call. If I had, I wouldn't have minded helping to seal off the road, after carefully timing my arrival with everyone else's. But Alice took on whomever and whatever was driving back out of the canyon that night, by herself, and probably thought nothing of it.

We all work for someone in some way, we all have to compromise, the choice is what and how much. But not having much to lose in the first place, and with no interested in social status, Alice hasn't had to compromise. There's a pioneer spirit to her, and although her life is Spartan it's not uncomfortable, at least not so much recently. And over the years she's been joined by an influx of artists, writers, and retired professionals who have also chosen to make the mountain their home. Leaving what they had, they've chosen the minor sacrifices required to live simply away from distractions. Much like Alice, really.

She arrived here from a different place, took a different path from most of us, and spent her life building character and a gritty self-reliance. So there aren't any public displays of spirituality from her, but just by being who she is, I think she's helped to preserve the mountain. And unimportant or not, considering the extraordinary person she is, "If you look after the Mountain then the Mountain will look after you," just might have some truth to it after all.

It's a Good Life After All

The wife and I have kept a tradition of starting the day with coffee in bed. It's a small thing, but as with most emotionally healthy things in my life (balanced diet, clean underwear, balanced checkbook, etc), I have her to thank for it. Even when we were living in the back of the garage and the bed was a just mattress on the concrete floor, we drank our coffee while propped up against the unfinished wall, scraping away occasional cobwebs and talking, Sheila mostly. We talked about anything and everything; one another, events, our lives, and other people's lives, just whatever was on our minds. It was probably a healthy thing to do in the best of times, but considering our circumstances it was probably a necessity.

The dogs have a morning ritual of their own. It starts with me walking out of the front door and yelling "Horsy". They seem to live for this moment because it means a walk down to the barn. It's an opportunity to bark, run, chase each other, chase sticks, chase things I don't want them to, stop to dig up things, and lastly eat horse poop at the barn. It's all very grand. The two dogs turn up like magic, from whatever they shouldn't have been doing, running deliberately straight at me and testing my fragile belief that they wouldn't dare run over the top of me. But sometimes, even this simple routine of a walk to the barn is complicated by one or more cats trying to tag along.

The cats aren't allowed. It has been part of an ineffective campaign I've had to convince them that it isn't safe out there, at least no further out than a short hurried dash for their cat door. And not being allowed to start the walk with me, they learned to wait until I've walked a good way down the hill before running past me with their tails puffed up in the full flagpole position, convinced it was all great fun. A cat's arrival means that I have to scoop up and carry the offender, or, if there's more than one and then with great difficulty, herd the offenders back to the house.

One particular morning I had walked halfway down to the barn when Mini-Me ran by me at full scamper. He stopped and waited for the praise, which wasn't coming, and was then scooped up and trudged back to the house, drooped over my arm and apparently thinking this was the best fun. After dumping the little offender back in the house, I took off again on a route that Mini-Me and the other cats couldn't see so easily.

The dogs and I started back towards the barn and halfway there were met by Thunder, ambling slowly up to meet us, head-down in his near-perfect imitation of Eeyore, complaining as he often did that his breakfast was late. Our little group grew by one sad looking horse, which used the opportunity to aim his customary warning nip at the Sheepdog. The Sheepdog stayed walking a step in front of the horse, glancing furtively over his shoulder, and so far this had been an average walk to the barn.

While I was taking care of the horse, and with no one to amuse them, the dogs used the time to play in the seasonal creek. They like to make sure they sop up as much grit and mud in their fur as they can, so once back in the house they can shake off another layer of grime onto the floors. With Thunder taken care of —fed, watered, and his corral cleaned—and his head buried in his feeder, the dogs and I started home. We took another trail back for variety.

The dogs took off, which was a relief, as I wouldn't be pestered into constantly throwing a stick for them, but the relief didn't last long. I had only gone a few steps when Prissy gave a quick sharp growl, followed by a silence. Suddenly she and the silly Sheepdog popped over a bank pursued by a deer. Yes, *pursued*. Now my reaction to Prissy's growling at anything is not to that dog's benefit, and when some "innocent" animal is involved the wrath of the heavens descends on her. She's part Lab so anything small enough to eat appeals to her. I don't care. There's nothing worse than walking along enjoying Nature and have a dog eat it. So the dogs, meaning her, are trained on the idea that if they should see something they think might be edible, to look the other way. This hopefully gives the smaller animals living on the property a better chance of making it through the day, and makes my day a little more pleasant, as well.

Still, this scene had to be an embarrassment for all dogs. I had never seen a deer chase two full-sized dogs before, or one small dog for that matter, but what surprised me the most was that the deer was doing a good job of it. I had a worry, though. Why would this deer give chase in the first place? Whatever the reason it couldn't be good, and the most likely explanation was that the deer had a fawn hidden near by. So I called the dogs to me, *call* being an understatement. I yelled at them and, between the tone of my voice and the attack deer behind them, they ran over and sat right at my feet. Any other time this would have been a miracle in itself, but the deer was not satisfied. It had followed the dogs over and had begun to circle our little group.

I had never been circled by a deer before. It peered into our huddled group fixated on us, as if looking for an excuse to rush in and continue the attack. She seemed to be looking for a weak spot. At this point, to add to this already strange scene and with perfect timing, Mini-Me came flying down the hill, ecstatic that he had managed to re-find me. He zoomed through the middle of our group, stopping his downhill rush by shooting straight up a tree behind us. He waited for some praise (which didn't come), jumped down, walked calmly over to the two dogs and rubbed on them with his tail in the air; only adding to their humiliation.

At this point we were about a quarter of a mile from the house. There were two stupid dogs, a wacky cat and an irate attack deer circling, when the deer seemed to forget its dislike of the dogs and seemed to become fixated on the cat. It circled even closer, this time with its head down staring at the cat. The cat was oblivious, being immersed in its own wonderfulness and still walking from dog to dog rubbing on them with its tail in the air.

It didn't make sense. Why would the deer be mad at the cat? The cat hadn't done anything to the deer; it was the dogs that had done whatever it was. So expecting the deer to keep circling the dogs, I told them to stay, in a voice that said: "... and I mean it," then called the pint-sized cat and started walking back to the house. The idea was that the deer would stay circling the two oafish obnoxious dogs, but I was wrong. As soon as I had taken the first couple of steps the cat ran after me and the deer ran in for the cat.

I've seen a deer explain its feelings to one of my cats before, but that cat was big, fluffed-up, its back arched, prancing sideways at the deer and hissing. But Mini-Me is not much bigger than a squirrel, and not even in its little Mini-Me dreams could it appear threatening to a deer, even if it had wanted to. What did that matter this morning? The deer charged.

Mini-Me took off with the deer in hot pursuit and only just made it to the nearest tree, half-a-hoof in front of the deer. Ordinarily, I would have been chasing the deer away from our little group, but I was feeling guilty. I was sure the dogs had done something to the deer in the first place, and was disinclined to victimize the giant rodent anymore than had been done already, whatever that was. And I was definitely not interested in picking up a cat with a strong possibility of it getting spooked while I was holding it. A cat four-wheeled over my shoulder once before, and I am not about to repeat the experience. Point being, I wasn't a blocker for the cat when I really should have been.

While I dithered, feeling responsible but confused, and trying to make sense of what was going on, Mini-Me was still working under the delusion that this was all a great game. He clambered down backwards, partway, and then jumped to the ground. The deer charged right back at him and a new chase started. This time from one side of the meadow to the other with Mini-Me running serpentine, the deer chasing and doing its best to stomp the cat, and me running behind the two of them in hot pursuit, waving and yelling.

Again, the cat kept half-a-hoof in front of the deer and wisely shot up the first available tree, which left the deer circling the tree and me panting for my life, deciding that this was enough.

The deer seemed to have proved its point though, and as I walked up to Mini-Me's latest tree to finally protect the miniature cat, the deer circled wider and headed away. But not without stopping to give one more menacing stare at the cat. I used the truce to call the two stupid dogs, who were still sitting where I had left them wearing looks of disbelief, then scooped the cat under my arm and carried it back to the house. Hopefully, giving the deer some time to calm down a bit.

I was still worried about what had caused the deer to go into attack mode in the first place. Most likely there had been a fawn hidden nearby and I had to know if the dogs had harmed it. With the dogs instructed to stay by the house, in a tone of voice that clearly said: "Be prepared to die if either of you moves," I had just begun the walk back to the spot where the little adventure had started, when I noticed that the deer must have followed us back to the house. It seemed to be paralleling me. It was keeping pace about fifty yards out to the side and matching every move I made. The deer was stalking me!

Having the larger brain I decided to out-stalk the deer, and cleverly ducking out of sight I circled around it. Only to find that the deer had had used the time to circle me, and once again it was staring at me rather than me staring at it. This went on for a couple more rounds before I gave up; before this reversal of roles got any worse. But it made me even more certain that I had to know why the deer was so agitated. So I retreated back to the house, again, and waited another half an hour.

The attack deer was nowhere to be seen and I walked down to the spot where it had all started. It was mostly tall grasses, low bushes, and shrub oak, which made the ideal cover for a mother deer to leave her fawn. With an occasional check for an irate mom, and in full stealth mode, I quietly crept through the area till I saw it. The prettiest spotted baby fawn I had ever seen, tucked under a bush with its ears as big as its body, curled up into a ball and pretending not to be there. I couldn't believe my eyes, but it was all I needed to see. Life was good. I tiptoed out of there with the biggest smile on my face and a sense of relief that, at least for today, Nature was in a kind and generous mood.

It just comes with living in the country. One cranky horse, two stupid dogs, a wacky cat, an attack deer, the most precious fawn I had ever seen, and it wasn't even breakfast yet. Maybe tomorrow the dogs and I will cross paths with some overly-sensitive squirrels, and end up being surrounded by a gang of enraged rodents making menacing chattering noises and bouncing acorns off our heads. As apparently nobody seems to have heard that there are rules.

Life's Little Unpredictabilities

With the house finished, the land cleared, and something resembling a social life, I had time on my hands. Ordinarily, this would have been an invitation to do something stupid but for a change of pace I started to think, instead. I found myself thinking about unpredictability. That's probably because I'd been experiencing a little too much of it lately and it had been puzzling me. There seemed to be a paradox to it—we're surrounded by it but at the same time it really doesn't exist.

Last June, an old friend, Don, showed up unexpectedly for the weekend. He, of anyone, should cause anyone to think about unpredictability because on too many occasions his appearance seems to precede it, and his latest visit was no exception.

We had met thirty years ago at a county airport, north of the Bay Area. It was a small airport with a grass strip for a runway, and once a year it held a competition in which small single-engine airplanes (the same type we flew) came by flying low and slow, dropping bags of flour out of their cockpits at a target painted on the ground. These were perfectly ordinary 1-lbs bags of white flour from the grocery store, but we upgraded them to 5-lbs bags and changed targets.

We originally dropped our flour bombs over uninhabited areas, aiming at safe but uninteresting things like trees and rocks, but when that lost its thrill we needed more. The "more" became a mutual friend, Badger, who lived alone in an unassuming house (shack), squirreled away in the back of a canyon and conveniently only a short flight from our small airport.

The thing about a 5-lbs bag of flour, especially when it's dropped from a great height, is that by the time it hits the ground it's traveling at an ungodly speed, and though it explodes in a large and very satisfying white cloud, it's flat out dangerous (trust me). An though it's hard to believe, we actually thought through the downside of hitting someone, even someone we knew, and although still fixated on groceries we came up with safer ammunition—containers of a dozen eggs. Eggs were safer, and the idea was that when a box of them gets thrown out of an airplane window, the slipstream blasts the box open and its contents are scattered. We didn't know how far, though.

We took off for the bombing run, circled over our target then dove down with the motor cut back to an idle, in full stealth mode. There was no reaction to our small plane as it glided quietly overhead, and unlike the flour bombs we had no idea where the eggs had landed. It was a bust, the experiment hadn't worked, and we flew off to find some other nonsense, forgetting about eggs.

Some weeks later, while we were visiting Badger, he happened to mention a neighbor and his girlfriend were splitting up.

"What neighbors?" I asked with little or no interest, having no idea that Badger lived near enough to anyone he could call a neighbor.

"Oh you don't know them, they live down the road. They've been doing some organic farming." Pointing down the hill from where he lives.

"What happened?" still disinterested.

"Pete was working in his back garden a few weeks ago and his girlfriend threw an egg at him."

"What!" Egg... egg... I thought. No, it couldn't be.

"Yeah, she threw an egg at him. She was cooking breakfast right by the kitchen window and not ten feet from him, there wasn't anyone else around but she still won't admit it." And yes, they were already in the middle of a row and I imagined the conversation.

"Did you just throw an egg at me?"

"What egg?"

"Don't pretend you didn't!"

"What egg? You're crazy!"

"That egg!"

And on and on; both sides with perfect logic and all the available facts supporting both sides. The one missing and highly improbable fact was that a low flying airplane, gliding silently overhead, had dropped the egg.

I keep this in mind, not to remind me of the consequences of my actions on others (which it should), or a reminder of a careless youth squandered (that too), but because the most improbable really does happen in life. It mostly reminds me that ultimately life is unpredictable. In this rare case there was a thread through time that could be followed: Starting with a chance meeting at an airport and finishing years later, and miles away, with an egg spattering at feet of a complete and total stranger who just happened to be in the middle of a domestic spat. A sometimes wonderful, and sometimes not, connection of accidents and the unlikely, turning events in and out of our favor on the whim of things we could know nothing about.

A larger example of life's unpredictability, which wasn't in anyone's favor, happened the day after Don left. It had been a perfectly ordinary spring day. Sheila and I had been hoping to spend the summer living a more normal life after years of struggle. We were just beginning to enjoy our country life. We were looking forward to a year of small pleasantries, little adventures, time off and, now that summer was here, time on the lake. We had in mind late starts in the mornings and relaxing days, just to see how they felt. That night, a little unpredictability arrived in the form of an outermost band of a distant weather pattern swirling a thousand miles off the coast in the Pacific Ocean.

"I'll get some sleep sometime tomorrow." At least that's the lie I use to console myself in the middle of the night. I might as well considering that I spend most nights lying awake, rummaging through a head full of stubborn nonsense, my mind more active than anytime during the day. This particular June night wasn't any different. I might have been asleep or not, but either way a faint flash of light involuntarily opened my eyes.

Could that have been lightning? Propping myself up in bed I stared out the window at the night sky, looking for a repeat of what I thought I might have seen and wondering what it could have been. It was 3 a.m. There was another. It was lightning, which was interesting but it was a long ways off. Still, this was more than enough to keep me awake, and I watched, interest building, as the storm grew in size and moved closer until there was a constant rumble along with the lightning. It was a good-sized storm and we could use a late rain after a very dry winter.

The storm continued to grow as it moved north along the Sacramento Valley towards Igo. It seemed strange that it hadn't started raining yet, and at first light I looked out at the leaden sky, expecting to see rain hanging from under the dark clouds. But there was none, anywhere, and this was no ordinary storm. Without a drop of rain the storm had continued to grow and now dry lightning was bombarding the hills and mountains around Igo. Looking at the lightning hitting the hills, I knew this could well be the end of our life in Igo, at least as we had known it. The place was going to burn.

By midday the storm was directly overhead. Each brilliant flash was accompanied by a simultaneous shock of thunder, rattling the house and echoing up and down the canyon. The thunder maintained a constant rumble, one into the next, as the lightening crashed into the hills. I didn't even dare venture outside, to raise my fist to the heavens and call upon the gods to strike me down, my usual reaction to a lightning storm. I stayed well indoors. The power went out with one flash. A few seconds later there was another lightning flash and the phone literally exploded off the wall. I found myself standing in the middle of our downstairs room, looking for ways to make myself safer, and only occasionally peaking out the corner of a window to see what was happening outside.

Feeling very small and powerless, I was watching a slow moving natural disaster unfold in front of my eyes, on a scale that I had no idea existed before.

Summer of Fire

Nearly two thousand fires had started in the mountains that morning. Something abnormal had just occurred but we couldn't know what. We didn't know that wildfires peppered the mountains behind us, and we didn't know this was the beginning of a month of fires, coming from all directions to burn us out. We knew something had gone terribly wrong, though.

By mid-morning there wasn't much to see. There were thin columns of smoke rising, not by the house but over distant ridges, and further down Woods Canyon there was a single column of smoke. Even if I couldn't see any flames, it was time to start evacuating. I had often thought about what to do in case of a forest fire, but now there was one all I cared about were our animals.

Being the hardest to locate when you need to the most, I rounded up the cats and locked them in the spare bedroom, along with their cat carriers so they were ready to go. The dogs were not a problem, being harder to get rid of than to find, which left only the horse to take care of.

Up to then I'd had several evacuation plans in mind, but those clever ideas went up in smoke when faced with a real fire. The grimmest threat was from a fire closing off Woods Canyon's narrow road. If the road out was closed Sheila and I might be able to make it over the back of the canyon driving the Warthog, with the dogs and the cats in their carriers, but that wasn't an option for the old horse. So Thunder had to be moved off the mountain, at least out of the canyon, and forgetting everything else the horse became my first priority. I ran down to the barn to lead him down Woods Canyon to safety, but Thunder had other ideas.

Thunder had it pretty good. He had never been ridden, there was always plenty to eat, he had thirty acres to roam on, and the last thing on his mind was leaving. And why should he? It had been years since anyone had asked anything of him and, from his perspective, there was no reason to change things. So it didn't matter how desperate his little human became, Thunder had no intention of leaving.

I tried coaxing, I tried threats, and I tried pulling as hard as could, but Thunder didn't even bother to take a hard stance. He simply allowed my tugging to extend his head a little further forward than usual, something he might have done to clear his throat, but nothing too obvious. If I hadn't been so frustrated I'd been embarrassed. So with a parting, "You're in trouble now... you %%&& horse," I stomped back up to the house and did what I did whenever there's trouble with our horse, I called Alice.

I was sure Alice was busy throwing her own life into the back of her pick-up truck, but she came right up, anyway. She walked over to the obstinate old horse, picked up the lead rope, and without another word said or a moment's hesitation that miserable ruminant put on the same soppy expression he always does when he sees Alice, dropped his head, and trotted along after her without a word said. The two of them walked onto China Gulch and down towards Woods Canyon Road, as if it had been the horse's idea all along.

I watched this show from the bench and made use of the time to purge some pretty negatives thoughts I was harboring about our horse. But once done purging, I took over leading Thunder away. Which I did, with the occasional help of a stick and a lot of yelling, "Thunder, youuu, I'llll, if you don't... Thunder!" But, one way or another, the horse and I walked the three miles down to the beginning of Woods Canyon. I left him safe in a rancher's very wet and very green irrigated field, where he joined the several other Woods Canyon horses already there taking refuge. With my main worry taken care of, I started to run back up Woods Canyon, hoping nothing bad had happened while I'd been gone.

Over the following month, I walked Thunder to this field three times. A sensible person would have just left him there until the winter rains had started. I would have done that too, if Thunder hadn't spent all day, every day, standing conspicuously in the corner of his field next to the road staring back up at the mountain and his barn. Every time I drove by he was standing there, staring. So I had no choice, and as soon as it was safe, well safer, I walked him home. I did this three times, but if you had seen that horse standing forlornly, and Thunder can look forlorn even on the best of days, you would have agreed—I had no choice.

There had been no need to hurry Thunder to safety. The one fire that looked like it could block off Woods Canyon was only slowly crawling its way through still-damp undergrowth. It hadn't picked up any speed. If this fire had started later in the summer it could have taken out the complete canyon by now, but this was mid-June. The ground vegetation and the tree canopy still had some retained moisture from the spring rains and, with no wind to push it, the fire was just crawling along. In fact, the only thing that could be seen of the fire was a column of smoke rising from behind a ridge half way up Woods Canyon. Still, this was a fire in a box canyon and it was relief to see a line of fire trucks drive by.

By the afternoon the wind had come up and the plume of smoke from the fire had grown larger. I drove down to see who or what was getting the upper hand—the firefighters or the fire. It looked like the fire to me, but it was a very busy scene and not wanting to clutter up our one-lane road, I turned around and went home. There was nothing to do anyway, and, like everyone else, I became resigned to watching and waiting. Something we were about to be accustomed to doing.

That evening, Sheila and I drove down Woods Canyon for one last check, towards an impressively large cherry-colored glow filling the evening sky. We rounded a corner in the road and got our first view of the fire. "Holy s**t!" The whole place was on fire, and at night it didn't have that cool smoky look to it, it looked angry. There were bulldozers and Battalion chiefs, reserve fire fighters and fire equipment lined up and down Woods Canyon Road. The wind had picked up, and in the steep terrain, in places impossible to reach, the fire had taken off.

This was my first up-close experience of a wildfire. A year earlier, and from miles away, I had seen a fire nuke several square miles in less than an hour, taking out a small town with it. The difference was this was close to home, and that made it scary—adrenalin scary. And though in my youth scary was fun, now scary was simply scary and there was absolutely nothing fun about it. But as there was nothing we could do, except get in the way, we turned around and went home for the night.

The wife can sleep through anything, and often does, but I'm the opposite and unless I'm convinced that everything is right with the world I stay awake indefinitely. So Sheila went to bed and I stayed up, staring out of our floor-to-ceiling picture windows, no longer looking at our stately ponderosas but at the cherry red glow filling the sky behind them. I spent the night staring past the silhouettes of our trees, watching and waiting for what the fire might do next. And though I didn't have a clue that this would be a pale imitation of the fires to come, I was making the worst of what there was.

I might as well have joined Sheila and slept the night away. By noon the following day, the California Department of Fire (CDF) had the fire contained. We drove down to watch the fire fighters complete the last of the back burning, burning out the area inside the containment lines they had made with their dozers. The excitement was over. The other two fires in Woods Canyon seemed to have put themselves out; though that was impossible to know for sure because the smoke from other fires, further out, was starting to fill the air and we couldn't see more than a hundred yards.

Behind us in the hills, literally hundreds of fires were burning, and they were growing unchecked. Ordinarily, CDF fights a few fires at a time, but nearly two thousand fires were on a scale that hadn't been seen before. CDF didn't have the equipment to fight this many fires. And as we learned more about what was happening in the hills, in places the CDF couldn't reach, the community of Woods Canyon began to realize that whether their homes, and indeed their entire mountain community, was going to survive or not, was outside their control. All we could do was sit and wait for the fires to come this way.

So Sheila and I started planning for the inevitable. It didn't take much planning. Maybe it was the impending doom, but when confronted with loosing everything we could only think of a few things worth saving. There were some important documents, every photo we had, some mementos and every stick of artwork, but that was about all. We put what little there was into cardboard boxes, lined up in the hallway, ready to be thrown in the back of the truck and driven out when the time came.

Thick smoke filled the air, and without the resources to control them, the hundreds of smaller fires had coalesced into one huge fire. By the end of the first week, sixty square miles of forest were burning in the mountains behind us, and each day the fire moved closer; some days a little and some days a lot. Some days we were told to be ready to evacuate and the next day nothing, and if a flame front looked as if it had stopped for a day, it roared back to life the following day. We watched helpless as the fires consumed the mountains behind us. It was inexorable. It might take days or it might take weeks, but however long it took, it looked like we were doomed.

During the second week of the fire there were several days of a mild south wind, and the fire looked as if it might burn itself to a standstill, trying to get past what it had already burned. We got our hopes up. But the next night the winds switched direction, the air temperature rose, and the fire exploded again. The complete western half of the county was put on a mandatory evacuation. During the day, helped by a heat wave, the temperatures rose to 110 degrees and the fire came out of the hills along an eight-mile front in a wall of flame, sometimes a hundred feet tall.

At the end of that day, Alice and I drove to the top of a nearby hill. Mile after mile, mountain after mountain, as far as we could see was blazing from top to bottom. During the night, the winds died down and the fire took a break, but it was far from done.

Whether it was the sight of the fires, or the smoke, or the lack of sleep, I don't know, but it felt like we were living in a war zone. After the first few nights of living in the shadow of the fire, I couldn't close my eyes without waking with a start. Woozy from lack of sleep, I would walk up to the top of the rise behind our house where I had a view of the fire. I couldn't not look. In the distance there were hundred-foot walls of flame moving relentlessly, occasionally at an astounding speed as they roared up a slope, literally incinerating everything in their paths, and then slowing while they finished off anything they might have missed. I think it's impossible to know the fear a wildfire can induce unless you've actually seen and heard one. It isn't just the sight of the fire, or the blizzard of burning embers preceding it, or the choking smoke mixed in with the hot air swirling by, or the heat from the flames that even from a distance seems unbelievable; it's the mayhem, the sounds of furious destruction that half an army couldn't duplicate. It comes at you with the force of a freight train, and at some point something primeval takes over your feelings.

Trees on un-burned ridges stood out in relief, backlit by other ridges burning further out. Then there would be a few flickers and another ridge would explode in flame, brightening the bloody sky with the death of a hundred more trees. And with each ridge burned the fire crept closer.

During the days the fire hid behind the smoke. It left the Sun hanging, a dull red orb, a flat disk painted on a sky of smoke that was busy entombing us. The community became united. And even though each of us was worn out, nerves in tatters, permanently on the edge and not at our best, there was nothing we wouldn't have done for each other. The fires had fused us together.

For the locals who had lived here all their lives this was nothing unusual. Tough and self-reliant, they had been fighting wildfires before air tankers and helicopters. They were used to this, and used to turning up at neighbor's houses to fight a fire and then rushing on to the next house to save that, too.

They met at Igo's community center, the Beer Bar, which didn't disappoint its customers with the fires only a mile away. And really came into its own after the sheriff set up roadblocks stopping all traffic in and out of the fire areas. The Beer Bar became the headquarters for Igo's version of an Underground Railroad, with Tom organizing.

No one was allowed past the roadblocks. The west half of the county, including Woods Canyon, was "inside" the cordoned off area, and though we hadn't been forced to evacuate, anyone that walked or drove out past a roadblock wasn't allowed back. You were in or you were out. But with the fires burning for literally weeks, we ran out of food in a couple of days and needed provisions to stay on the inside. So we took turns sneaking around the roadblocks, and as the Beer Bar was on the "outside", just past the roadblock, it became the starting point for our underground supply route.

The sheriff had strategically placed a roadblock near the Beer Bar, on a rise to allow surveillance of the fields around it. It was there to stop just what we were doing, but we lived here and had home field advantage. Once out the Beer Bar's back door, under a couple of wire fences, through the blackberry bushes, down into a shallow gully, and a couple of hundred yards later we were past the roadblock and gone. .

It was a game, and with nothing else to do except be stressed, running the gauntlet became a way of keeping busy. It became a form of defiance, not against authority but the helpless state our lives were in, and it also became a way of keeping our spirits up. So, if anything was going to be brought in, it had better be good. I remember that the most popular order was for Chinese take-out, closely followed by pizza, which was driven all the way from the Zone, delivered to the front of the Beer Bar, paid for and sent along the Underground Railroad—with a six-pack of beer, of course.

The camaraderie helped. Our sense of community helped. Tom running the railroad from the Beer Bar helped. It all helped, but we'd become empty shells. Running on instincts, with failing faculties trying to make sense of things we were powerless to control. In fact, I started to think there might actually be a hell—because I was in it! How could a fire last a month? How could we be in the same wretched situation day after day and week after week? How could we stand helpless outside our houses staring at yet another mountain burning? Or spend another night watching a bloody glow fill the sky, giving Igo all the appearance of being on Mars. With what was left of my faculties, I wasn't sure what planet we were on, not that it mattered much at the time.

It was the helplessness I remember the most. Woods Canyon was told to evacuate on several occasions, but along with most of our neighbors, Sheila and I didn't leave. Ridiculous as it might seem, we didn't want to leave the mouse-house. It had become our home, and we had years of our lives invested in it. The cats were boarded at a vet, the horse was safe in its waterlogged field, and even the mini-truck was safe, parked miles away. We kept the Warthog with us, and who cared if that burned up, but our home was important.

The community used telephone trees to keep each other up to date about the fire, but I thought that there were just too many uncertainties, too much confusion to be deciphered in the middle of a night, and too much reliance on rational thought at a time that I knew there wouldn't be any. So I simplified things, and came up with some trigger points. If the fire reached any one of these trigger points, Sheila and I would leave. It wouldn't be a time for thought, we would just leave. And with the trigger points in mind, we put off abandoning our home and put off living out of the back of the mini-truck. When the fire came, the truck would be all we had left, and there would be plenty of time to experience just how much fun that would be.

The most obvious of these trigger points was the fire coming over one of the ridges surrounding Woods Canyon. Three weeks into the fire, in the middle of night, I walked out of the house to see trees exploding on the ridge across the valley from us.

I could see the fire was starting to drip down into Woods Canyon; it could be just minutes away. I ran back into the house, phoned the neighbors and told them what I had seen, grabbed the boxes in the hallway, threw them into the back of the pickup, and lastly the dogs. We turned off the electricity, the gas, shut the windows, closed the front door, and abandoned the house.

I stood in the dark and took one last look at our empty home; a brooding shape outlined by the unnatural glow behind it. With the sound of trees exploding across the valley and heated air swirling unseen in the dark, the old house seemed to cry out, or was it just me. Then we were gone into the night, chased out of our home like thieves with the fire the new owner.

Three weeks into the fire, three weeks of hoping that this moment would never arrive, but it had. We found ourselves hurrying down a smoke filled canyon in real fear, worrying if we had left it too late and the fire had already cut us off. As we drove out an orange glow illuminated the valley in a menacing half-light. There were fingers of flame already visible through the trees and I thought we would have to drive through fire to get out, but we were lucky, and one long mile later the fire was behind us.

I hadn't a clue what we were going to do or even where we were going, and I had the oddest feeling that I had never seen Woods Canyon before. It must have been shock. I didn't recognize the road I had traveled up and down for years, but coming towards the end of Woods Canyon Road, I saw Alice in the headlights. She was standing in the middle of the road and waving me down. Good old Alice.

"Where do you think you guys are going?" She asked as I came alongside her.

"I haven't a clue," was the honest answer.

"Well you're not going anywhere. Find yourself a place to park and join us over there." She waved at an encampment of Woods Canyon refugees, sitting under a porch light outside a farmhouse. It was the modest home of the rancher who allowed us to leave our horses in his field. And that's where we stayed for the night; as close to home as we could be and needing all the companionship we could find.

During the night we watched what we thought was Buckhorn Mountain burn. It seems quite ridiculous now (and was even more ridiculous then), but in the smoke and the dark and from miles away, we had been looking at the wrong mountain. We had been looking at a mountain just to the west of Buckhorn Mountain! We had suffered through a night of lost hopes, lost dreams, wringing of hands and wailing, only to stare as the morning light revealed that the fire had stopped at the ridge above Woods Canyon. It had only singed one side of our valley and had spent the night finishing off the mountain next door to ours. In my sleep-deprived brain there was disbelief that I could have been that stupid and enormous relief that I was.

That morning the CDF poured in. We waited until the afternoon, when there was a lull in the fire equipment streaming into Woods Canyon, then drove up in the Warthog. We found that the house hadn't been touched. So we packed up our encampment and went home, feeling like intruders, until the next time.

CDF finally had the resources to throw at our fire. Fire equipment had driven from across the country to help, and with that we shared our house with firefighters, the road with fire trucks, the skies with fire bombers and the air with even thicker smoke. It was heavy equipment against the fire and we were in the middle of it. China Gulch became a creaking thoroughfare for dozers, water trucks, and the other heavy equipment heading up into the mountains behind us. For the first time in my life the sounds of helicopters, bombers and dozers were reassuring, and for the first time in weeks I fell into a deep sleep. I had finally worn myself out.

The fire kept coming though; there was nothing else left for it to burn. It was literally all around us and was trying to get into Woods Canyon from three separate directions. Each time the fire surged towards Woods Canyon, CDF held it back with days of bombings and a sky-train of helicopters working a non-stop bucket brigade. But I remember clearly the evening the fire came over the back of Buckhorn Mountain. It was on its last attempt to burn the valley.

A structure protection engine and its crew had been stationed at the mouse-house for several days. Sheila had gone back to the beginning of Woods Canyon and camped out again, but I stayed with the house. Goodness knows why, maybe as a way of making myself feel a little less useless. One evening, an angry black cloud of smoke had been growing, boiling thousands of feet in the air and obviously being thrown up by a very hot fire on the far side of our mountain. The fire was at least a mile away but it was headed this way.

The fire was growing and, to complicate things, it was getting dark. Then pieces of still-smoking bits of trees started to fall out of the sky, making noticeable thumps when they landed on a vehicle. Lastly, the wind started to pick up. At first, it was just an unnaturally warm breeze, and then a wind swept down from the mountain that felt as if someone had just opened a giant oven door. I thought the fire was coming to burn us out.

I had been getting accustomed to being around a fire and thought we were safe, up to that point. But one look at the fire fighters' faces told me all I needed to know. This was serious, a firestorm could be headed this way, and in an instant all that mattered were lives. I was out of there, and with a final plea to the crew not to risk their lives, and thinking that they would to be right behind me, I jumped in the Warthog and left; not expecting to see the house or our forest again.

Incredibly, this was the fire's final push. The winds that I ran away from were the last for that night, and in the still air that followed the fire fighters used the slope of the mountain to back burn into the fire, stopping it halfway down Buckhorn Mountain. Once again, the fire had singed the ridges but it hadn't made it down into the canyon. And after four weeks of burning everything in its path, the fire was stopped, less than a quarter-mile away.

Our emergency was over, but miles away, further out in the wilderness areas, other blazes continued to burn all summer, and along with smoky skies, an emotional aftermath lingered in Woods Canyon. Even months after the fires, when we talked to each other it was more as a way of leaning on each other. We spoke in tired flat voices about what amounted to nothing, affirming the simplest facts and calling it conversation. The fires had left us empty and we stayed that way for the rest of the year.

It was astonishing that Woods Canyon had been spared, singed at the edges, but it had been spared. Alice still confidently states that it was the mountain's energy that saved us, and looking at the improbability of our canyon surviving, she might be right. Of course, the CDF might have had a hand. And if I have failed to detail the skill, hard work, dedication and bravery of the fire fighters, it is because they deserve more than a mere mention.

We all owe are homes, our way of life and probably some of our lives to what they accomplished during this time. I would not have believed it possible for mere men and women to effect, let alone to stop, a fire of this intensity and size. It had been out of all human scale. But these brave men and women, day after day and night after night, for weeks on end, in awful conditions and awful heat, always in personal danger, kept fighting the fire. Bit by bit they fought it to a standstill. Then they left our fire and did the same to other equally dangerous fires. All these men and women deserve, and have, our lasting respect and admiration.

A Quiet Worth Hearing

After the fires I hiked the burnt areas. Some of the mountain was unrecognizable as ever having been forested—areas where there had been so much brush and so many downed trees that a firestorm had developed and incinerated everything that could possibly burn. The fire had left behind an expanse of still smoldering stumps, starkly black against acres of fine white ash. In other areas the fire hadn't burnt as hot, it had cleaned the brush out, killed the small trees, and left the largest trees untouched. It's surprising that there was anything left alive.

One of our reasons for buying where we did was that our property backs onto National Park land. In fact, Whiskeytown Lake is only five miles away as the crow flies, and if I was a crow that would have been fine. I've run it on several occasions and found that it's more like fifteen of the hardest miles I have ever made the mistake of running. But irrespective of its steepness, there's more open space than anyone has the right to expect, literally, outside my backdoor.

Buckhorn Mountain itself keeps going higher another fifteen hundred feet behind the mouse-house, and a walk up this mountain is a walk past the last signs of human existence, into a wilderness that could rarely if ever see a human. The last activity there was some logging sixty years ago, and the rough logging roads cut in then are now hardly discernable. They are eroded and overgrown or swept away in slides, hard to distinguish from the average animal trail, and considerably more miserable to try following.

These forgotten dirt roads had become excuses for Nature to fill in with every type of fast-growing inter-twangled brush it has available. And only after the brush has had years to fight itself, and then choke itself, do the trees start taking a hand. Then they take over and start choking themselves. So, even if these logging roads had at one time been an access into the mountains, they had returned to wilderness, but worse. And the reason I used them at all was that they were comforting reminders of my species existence, and also so I would know where I was... except I didn't.

My first time exploring the mountain, and early on into it, I started down one of these likely looking remnants of a road and later realized that I should have taken the other. I won't admit to being lost, but I was pretty confused for a day. At the end of that day, made all the longer by my not having brought any food or water, and only after I had walked and crawled through most of Northern California and had not seen a thing I recognized, I finally came across my mountain again, by accident.

Up to then I had no idea it was possible to get lost anywhere, especially so close to home, and I would have thought it impossible to lose a large mountain. But take the wrong trail early enough on a hike and anything becomes possible, especially in the chaotic jumble of peaks and ridges that make up the backcountry in this area. It's a place where every view looks the same, except when you see it again, and then it looks different. So I took a compass on my next exploration, though I didn't need to, having had the opportunity to get to know the terrain pretty well the first time.

In my early Igo years, being the inquisitive type, I explored the wilderness. Initially, I ran where possible. After a year, I ran some and walked some, and nowadays I prefer just to walk. This is partly because the mountains have grown steeper with each passing year, and partly because I worry more about breaking an ankle while running down one. That would be bound to happen hours out, in what is truly the middle of nowhere with no chance of help. And, as I spend more time in the wilderness, I'm realizing that these desolate mountains are very different from the well managed county parks and open spaces that I had been used to. There's some danger to being alone in a wilderness area and, as a token to the danger, nowadays I explore protected by a feeble attempt at self-defense.

Sometime into a hike, soon after hearing what sounds like a twig snapping behind me, I would start looking around for a broken branch of manzanita to use as a spear. My preference is something two to three feet long with a particularly jagged break to it, but depending on how scared I am at the time, anything will do. There's no pretending a stick could stop an attack, and it's never meant to. The idea was deceptively cunning, a typically British attempt at self-defense, lie perfectly still until after the initial attack (with a set of large fangs sunk into the back of my neck), and fool whatever animal has me in its teeth into thinking that I'm bleeding out. Only then, when my attacker is completely relaxed and comfortable with the way I'm dying, stab it in the eye with my nifty manzanita stick. Anyway, that's the best I can come up with, and it's a lot better than the thought of my soft pink hands flapping around, pathetically trying to ward off a lion or a large hungry bear.

A giant Bowie knife might have helped, but I didn't want to be spotted wandering around the hills looking like the Mad Slasher. Not that I've ever seen anyone else on these hikes, but just the idea of coming across even one peaceable bird-watching tree-hugging hiker, with me wielding a foot-long blade—I'd prefer to be eaten alive by a wild animal.

I had no idea anyone knew about my habit of exploring the hills until about a year after we moved here, when a lighting strike started a fire on Buckhorn Mountain. It was several miles away and uphill from us, and although Sheila and I kept it in mind, the fire wasn't exactly a reason to panic. But an hour after first noticing the fire the dogs start barking, it's their job, and I looked outside to see a CDF truck grinding its way up the scary steep driveway.

My first thought was, "What have I done now?" This is my usual reaction to seeing anyone in authority, and, with all the burning I had done and all the possible infractions I could have committed, it was a reasonable reaction.

"Does the runner live here?"

"Well, I run a little." I replied, hedging my answer.

"Oh good, jump in, you must be the runner we were told about."

"You were... told what?" Still not convinced.

"We need somebody to mark a trail up to the fire. You know the mountain don't you?"

"Oh, oh yes." And silently relieved, I climbed up into the cab and we were off. I was splattered in sheetrock mud from surfacing a wall in the mouse-house, but no one seemed to care.

We drove up to the far end of China Gulch, up an old fire trail as far as the truck could make it and stopped. The CDF captain gave me a large roll of fluorescent pink tape and the instruction to tie a piece to a bush every now and then, so a dozer could follow the route up to the fire. No more explanation necessary: I knew dozers and I knew running. Simple. With an unprecedented expectation of common sense on my part, I took off.

I suppose it was lucky the fire crew found me for the job. They could have easily ended up as I had during my first exploration, on the wrong mountain or in the wrong place on the right mountain. But I knew precisely where the fire was and which trails to use to get there. In less than an hour, I was close enough to the fire that the CDF bombers were flying directly over me as they finished dropping their load. So I was close, in fact, too close.

The brush had been getting thicker, and added to the difficult mix were the trees that had been pulled down by a snowstorm the previous winter. I was clambering up and over and through a three-dimensional maze of thick brush, when I had the disturbing image of the fire racing up-hill towards me. So with a parting "Close enough for government work," (something I've always wanted to say for real) I tied the last ribbon of pink tape and turned back the way I had come. First scrambling out of the brush, and then running down the mountain like a little kid, rather pleased with myself.

By the time I got down to near where I'd started, I met the dozer coming up, following the flags, with a crew trailing behind cutting and clearing the mayhem that the dozed was leaving behind as it made its way up the mountain. A little further down were the fire crews walking in and finally the fire crew captain. I let him know I had made it back, and while standing around getting some water to drink, I overheard a fire crew talking about a horse that had stopped them on the way in. "Thunder!" I thought. The old horse must have stood in the middle of the road and demanded food before he would let the fire trucks get by.

Thunder had learned to extort food from passing vehicles because he wasn't fenced and was free to wander onto China Gulch anytime he felt like it. Everybody fed him, including the UPS driver, who became his favorite. At the first sight of Brown, Thunder would come galloping out of his corral and chase the UPS truck, all the way to the end of China Gulch if he had to. He had learned that anything with wheels meant food, and now he had specific knowledge that fire trucks come with apples and carrots, from the fire crews' packed meals. So the same thing happened during the Summer of Fire. The first convoy of fire trucks started their grind up China Gulch and met an expectant Thunder blocking the road, and not about to move. A couple of fire fighters owned horses and they knew exactly how to solve the problem, but after that we had to lock the old horse in his corral for the duration.

During the Summer of Fire it was serious business. Early on, I spent a couple of days hiking around the mountain with a CDF captain. His job was to update their maps, assess fire roads and mark escape routes for the fire fighters. Then came the fires, along with the dozers cutting firebreaks, which changed the mountain.

I've heard the rumor that life is but a dream, which isn't my experience, but during the fire I wouldn't have minded a bit if it had all been a dream. Before the fire, I had used the mountain as my touchstone. It had been a place where I could leave whatever nonsense I had been worrying about behind, a useful thing to do on any day. And since the fire, I still make a point to walk through the devastation to spend some time on the top of Buckhorn.

For some reason the summit didn't get burnt, singed on the one side but not burnt out, and although it's a long circuitous hike to get there, and the journey isn't what it used to be, the quiet at the top of mountain is still a quiet worth hearing. A walk up the mountain sheds the last sights and sounds of people, and though I would never have thought it possible—living in a quiet place for there to be an even quieter place—I'm always struck by the difference.

Once at the top of the mountain the quiet is huge, it seems to become a part of the expanse of mountains and sky stretching from one distant horizon to the other. And it's humbling to be a mere speck in the midst of something so vast and timeless. Sometimes, I've sat alone on top of this brooding mass of stone and felt as if something is looking through me.

There's a feeling that only a mountain can give. A bonding, a feeling that no matter how insignificant and impermanent we might be, there's something shared with this massive unchanging entity. And maybe it's because the mountain needs life to express itself and life needs the mountain as a form of expression, but as I get older I'm perfectly happy to be no more and no less than a part of the world around me, and this mountain in particular.

A Part of the Community

Poor old Thunder passed away. Passed away is too kind of a term, we had to have him put down. But whatever the good reasons I felt responsible, and at the moment the vet completed the act and euthanized our old horse, I felt like an executioner. I stood in front of him holding his harness, looking into his eyes as the anesthetic was injected. It was a moment of betrayal, even if for all the right reasons.

His mark is all over this land, he helped to give it life, and with his passing I've felt my connection to it grow cold. I had no idea he was my link to the land. Even the trails worn over the years while walking to and from his barn are his trails, and in a moment they seem to have gone silent, too. This was the old horse's land to walk.

No one knew Thunder's age. All the guestimates were between thirty and thirty-five, which is a long life for a horse. But when he lay on the ground, his life gone, it didn't seem long enough. I wished for immortality, for the impermanence of life to be suspended. I wished fateful moments could be reversed and greater efforts made, and that the cruelest reality, that we all live on measured time, wasn't.

The following day, with a weight hanging on me I drove to Whiskeytown Lake and paddled out in silence to my favorite island on a mirrored surface that reflected perfectly the mountains in sentinel around it. It was late in the winter's afternoon and most of the lake had already fallen into shadow. As the last of the sun arced behind the western peaks, it selected the island with a shaft of golden light and held it there while I finished my paddle to its bank. With tears in my eyes I walked to the top of its small rise and released Thunder's spirit into the light of the setting sun. I wished him well, and asked only that on occasions I be able to call on his quiet strength.

In three weeks time it will be Christmas, and Sheila and I plan on having a great bonfire near the barn and toast this wonderful old horse, sharing his memories with our friends arriving for the holidays. We'll invite our neighbors, too. Thunder was such a character; he was known to all in Woods Canyon and will be missed by everyone. Happy trails, Thunder.

∞

This has been our fifth winter on the mountain, and during our time here we've morphed, sometimes seamlessly and sometimes awkwardly, into something that's better described in terms of a lifestyle. So after five years on a mountain, a pickup truck stirring up a cloud of dust on a dirt road seems perfectly normal, along with always wearing work clothes, being covered in a light layer of dust, or mud, and doing anything and everything that needs to be done ourselves. And having made the change, I could never ever fit back into a tidy life on a city-sized lot.

Our property is at about two thousand feet, which is beneath the snowline in this area but high enough that it still gets cold, and several times each winter our scary steep driveway turns into a toboggan run. I've never fully understood why, but it's always my responsibility to make sure there's a truck parked down at the barn (beneath the scary steep part of the driveway) before it snows. Even if you try, which I seldom do, it's hard to be right all the time, and each year I make the mistake of second-guessing the local weather forecaster. I wake up in the morning to find our vehicles marooned on top of our hill, and whether I'm in the mood or not, my job is to dig out a quarter-mile of however-much snow fell during the night. I try to think of it as just so much healthy exercise, followed by the thrill of driving the mini-truck down our near-vertical driveway. Creeping the truck over the top, staring down our icy driveway at the creek waiting at the bottom, knowing that the brakes might not help that much, gets my attention every time.

Off the mountain and in the flats, where there there's no snow to speak of and saner people lead happier lives, Christmas brings the largest event in Igo—the Christmas Parade. It's promoted as being held in "Beautiful Downtown Igo", a statement that is completely accurate but also entirely misleading, as "Downtown" consists of only three buildings—the Igo Inn, the Beer Bar, and the Post Office. There's the school, but that's another hundred yards further down the road, which places it safely in the outskirts of town and hardly counts.

The Post Office hasn't been mentioned before, but it deserves to be. It might or might not be, the oldest continuing operating Post Office west of somewhere, but I'm sure it's smallest. It's located just a few uncomfortable feet from the Beer Bar, and barely distinguishes itself from its neighbor by being painted on a regular basis. It is the only official entity in Igo, though it's difficult to conceive that it's actually a part of the US Postal Service, and its undignified location in this scofflaw community makes it the postal equivalent of Fort Apache.

Still, the Post Office is the end of the road for mail out here; there's no actual mail delivery in Igo. Most of the population lives scattered, often miles down uninviting dirt roads, and a fair number of them don't want to see someone in uniform, anyway. So anyone that wants one gets a free mailbox at the Post Office. This should have been an agreeable arrangement, and probably would have been anywhere else. But there were some Post Office regulations that had been overly enforced, at least that's how some locals have seen things, and over the years this had led to a few resentments.

It was a tradition for the locals to reach through the open back of their mailboxes and make a delivery of their own. It was a form of community feedback, and was only limited to whatever could be stuffed through a mailbox. The arrangement had worked well, for the most part, but there was one simmering feud that needed something more.

One Labor Day weekend, chosen because it was a three-day weekend, an unknown someone stuffed a dozen chickens through one of the larger parcel-sized mailboxes. A bag of chicken feed and a bucket of water were slid through too, just to make sure that the chickens were happy, active chickens. Three days later, when the Post Master opened the door to his tiny Post Office, chickens came flying out. There were chickens rushing under his feet and chickens flying by his head. They had perched on the shelves, laid eggs in the mailboxes, and covered everything in chicken feathers and chicken poop. What galled the Post Master the most was the strong likelihood (judging from the laughter) that the scofflaws responsible were standing a few feet away on the Beer Bar's lopsided front porch watching the whole thing. But this pristine zone of government officialdom had been defiled for the last time. Security cameras were installed in the tiny Post Office, courtesy of Homeland Security, and what had been an Igo tradition was banished to history.

Every town changes, but during the few years we've lived here we've seen Igo's scofflaw personality diluted. There's nothing to put your finger on, but the old Igo seems to be fading away at about the same pace that the old-timers die off; with the void they leave being filled in by the expansion of the Zone. There is one notable exception to this though, it's the Igo Christmas Parade, and it keeps growing with every passing year.

The Mayor started it twenty years ago, along with some of his drinking buddies, staggering around "Beautiful Downtown Igo" on Christmas Day. This was when Linda still owned the bar. Back then, if she felt like it, she would turn off the bar's outside lights at closing time and however many of her customers (friends she had known her whole life) could sit in the back of the bar and drink through the night if they wanted to. They often did, and when Roy and the others staggered out that Christmas morning, it wasn't a parade at all, and the only connection to Christmas was the date on the small, grubby, well-scribbled, on-it's-last-page calendar hanging on the wall behind the bar's cash register. But by the following year, Roy had built a float and the Igo Christmas Parade was born.

Even then their float had nothing to do with Christmas, though it did attract attention. Roy and his crew aptly named themselves *The Igo DT's* (Delirium Tremors), and acted, or not, being drunk—sitting on bales of hay, swigging moonshine, playing fiddles, and banging on a base drum. It wasn't much of a stretch for them. Somehow, the parade went on to become the wholesome family affair it is today, drawing what appears to be the entire population of Igo, either to watch or to participate, and making the parade the social event of the year. It even draws people from the Zone of Civilization, though probably not for the right reasons.

As with any public event in Igo, the town closes the county road through town. There's not a lot of traffic in the first place, and what there is need take only a short detour. Even so, this has to be one of the few towns in the U.S. where a main road can get shut down whenever the citizenry (the Beer Bar) feels like it.

The parade assembles at the Igo Inn and then waddles, staggers, and drives past the Beer Bar and out the other side of town to the school. It reassembles itself in the school's parking lot and makes a return pass on its way back to the Inn. In total that's only about four hundred yards, which probably makes it the shortest parade in the world, but that's long enough anyway.

A few months after we moved here, Sheila and I were chosen to play the parts of "Beauty and the Beast" in an upcoming parade. We didn't even know there was a parade, but we'd walked in on its annual committee meeting (being held, of course, at the bar), and as we were overly anxious to become a part of the community, we were happy to be selected to play the parts. We were probably the first people not to have responded, "No *%^* way," but at the time we thought it quite an honor.

We might have known better. My costume was the "Beast", though it was actually just a monkey suit that had seen better times. "Beauty" didn't fare any better. Her costume was a wedding dress dating back to the thirties, and it was probably a white dress at the start of its long life, but now it was a shade or two off. And as I write about this I see how some, with more jaundiced eyes, could see our honor differently, but this was an opportunity to show the community we weren't the stuck-up Bay Area snobs that we were, so we jumped at it.

The day of the parade it was raining, and a cold rain at that. Both of us are practical types, so we wore wetsuits under our costumes and happily stomped (at least I did) and splashed around in the puddles oblivious to the weather. At the end of the short parade, with encouragement from some on the Beer Bar's front porch, I rolled around in a large muddy puddle, then stood up and shook the water off like a dog. Wearing a wetsuit I didn't care, and it's probably what got me an invitation to play the Beast again, though Sheila has stayed slyly unavailable for the part of Beauty ever since.

She had been walking dutifully in the rain the entire time, looking very, very wet and, without any further explanation, rather than looking like Beauty, she looked demented. Her long wet hair lay flat against her face and the now saturated dress clung to her. Between the expression on her face and the off-white dress, she looked like she had been left at the altar about the time the dress was made and sadly hadn't changed out of the thing since. And having someone in a muddy monkey suit laughing uncontrollably at her can't have improved her mood much, either.

It hasn't rained on the parade since, and this last year, being a relatively warm winter's day, made for the biggest parade to date. There were even more vintage tractors, more restored fire engines, and a few classic cars for the first time. The church expanded its turnout to include a trail of baffled children wearing cardboard boxes on their heads, with hand-written slogans on the sides extolling the basic virtues. There were lots of horses and ponies, goats dressed up in Christmas decorations, just the one politician (looking extremely awkward), and a mishmash of costumed people, like me, wandering around and in and out of the parade, waving, and handing out candies to the kids waiting by the side of the road. No, it wasn't the Macy's parade, but it was country.

We walked the hundred yards to the Beer Bar, where the Mayor was announcing the passing floats on his PA system. Past the families sitting on their lawn furniture, with their small children standing eagerly in front for the best view of the parade, when I noticed Nathan. I'll be kind, but he's not exactly the handsomest man in the county, though he is interesting to talk to, as you never know what he's likely to pull out of his beard and proudly show you. I spotted him as he crossed the road, beer in hand, on his way over to talk to yet another pickup truck full of his extensive family. His family has been in the area long enough to have a relative in every other family, so wherever he went and whomever he talked to, it was pretty much with family.

The monkey suit wasn't comfortable, in fact just holding it together took up most of my time and energy, and the only advantage to wearing it was that it gave me a disguise. It allowed me to approach Nathan, who would have been on his guard if he had known who was in the costume, but Christmas must have lulled him into a friendlier mood than his usual. He didn't see anything strange about a monkey walking over to him with a friendly rubber monkey hand outstretched in greeting. Hard to notice, but the rubber hand was craftily turned away, and filled with a dollop of recently retrieved and still warm horse poop.

One firm squeeze later and Nathan's face turned to a look of disgust—to an untrained eye it would have been hard to tell the difference. Giving no visible reaction, and care for what's important in life, Nathan carefully put his beer down, and only then was the chase on. But he couldn't catch the monkey (even with its size-19 extra-floppy monkey feet flopping chaotically) as it ran away as fast as it could: hairy arms waving, right through the middle of the parade, dodging around floats, out past the Girl Scouts leading the parade, and gone. We were past the school before Nathan finally ran out of breath, leaving me sprawled a few yards in front, trying to catch my breath and laughing hysterically. The monkey suit is optional, but if I ever needed a quick (innocuous) summary of my life, this would be about it.

The final float in the parade was Santa's. He sits on a pony-drawn sled with Santa's helpers, and as the float passes by the line of parked cars and trucks, Santa stops at each to hand out presents. Every year, every child gets a present—which is the point to the parade and the several fund-raisers the community puts on during the year to support it.

It's a wonderful tradition, and typical of how this community supports itself. The shame is that most of Igo's traditions are being replaced by the inevitable expansion of the Zone. Security gates have started to pop up at the bottom of driveways leading to country estates, and even our tiny Post Office gets occasionally busy with important people and expensive cars left idling outside. There are still the forty-year old pickups (my mini-truck's getting there!), but I'm guilty, I'm part of the change just by not being born here. I've helped to dilute the community that has been Igo for the last hundred years. It's fading, along the locals who've reached the end of their days, who were here when there was only a one-lane road through a dusty town, and a handful that even watched the Low Bridge being built. They are the living proof of another time that's being swept away by a thing called progress. It is a loss. I've never seen a place quite like Igo, and it's hard to imagine it being repeated anywhere soon.

The last event of the year is the party at the Igo Inn. The Inn has had a speckled past, not marbled but speckled, as Roy has had it open sometimes, but mostly not, as a restaurant. It's always just launched, trying to stay afloat, or recently closed and rumored to be preparing to reopen with a new theme. But whatever its current status, and as Roy doesn't need much of an excuse to enjoy himself, there's always a party at the Inn around Christmas.

These parties are never large, twenty or thirty people at most, and they are unannounced. The invitation is simply the Inn's lights being on late in the evening and a collection of cars and trucks parked outside. Anyone driving by with the time to waste is welcome, and since these are all friends, family or neighbors that had known each other for most, if not all, of their lives, they usually stay.

It only happens once a year, and it's an opportunity for some hopelessly bad dancing, some falling down, some silliness, too much alcohol and, of course, a small quantity of medicinal herb. And I remember getting some air during the last party; stepping outside into the pitch black there wasn't another light to be seen, and there wasn't a sound to be heard either, apart the nonsense coming from inside. A little unsteady on my feet and swaying slightly, I inhaled a lungful of chilly night air and thought there couldn't be another place like this town, anywhere. It was a place to be juvenile for a while, away from consequences and responsibilities, where the nearest adults were some long country miles away. And considering that with every passing year, each of us was getting a little older and a little stiffer, both in mind and in body, what did it matter if for a couple of hours we didn't have a care in the world, and acted like the children we could never be again.

As we left this last Christmas, Roy gave us each a T-shirt he had made for the occasion. It was typical of Roy, and a reminder of both the kind thoughtful man he is and the unique little community we live in. Printed on the front, under a simple line sketch of the Igo Inn, was printed:

> If you're **famous** you live in Hollywood.
> If you're **rich** you live in Malibu.
> If you're **lucky** you live in Igo!

Burning Bears

"Find a job you like and you'll never work another day in your life." It's an adage I'd always had trouble with. I've seen it as a cleverly worded misrepresentation, a half-truth designed to mislead. But in yet another strange reversal, weather permitting, I now spend weeks at a time clearing brush—lost in the hardest work I've ever done in my life and enjoying every exhausting minute of it. On its face that's nuts, but there's worse. Since I've run out of brush to clear on my own property, I volunteer to clear the evil manzanita from my neighbors' land. And I must look nuts, an old man struggling with a giant chainsaw, a mere speck on the side of a mountain, periodically flopping onto the ground exhausted before getting up to cut down another tree-sized bush, and then another, and another. Something in my core must have changed.

Even the bane of my life, the mouse-house, is no longer the endless project it was. After five years it's become a home. It reliably keeps us warm during the winter and cool in the summer, and during spring and autumn the windows are flung open, allowing the outside inside and filling the house with the sounds and scents of our very private forest. There's artwork on the walls and cats sleeping, stretched out on the back of the couch. There's time for books and music, and time to have found out that we actually live in a community of artists and writers (sensitive types compared to our other neighbors) tucked away in these hills. Sheila keeps finding them, I keep being surprised by them, and (with Sheila's personality paving the way) we've become a part of that extended community. After what feels like a lifetime in a war zone, I'm enjoying the difference.

Our acceptance has been a reversal from the isolation we felt when we first arrived. Then we thought all of our neighbors were gun-toting hillbillies, dotting the top of every hill as far as the eye could see, but that turned out not to be the case. We've since found that only half the hilltops have a gun-toting hillbilly defending them, and even they add to the lumpy texture of life around here. They help to make up this distinct community, a geographically large neighborhood where people are mostly friendly most of the time, and are more like a family—warts and all.

I can (and do) find things to gripe about. The summers are still too hot and the winters here too long, the trees have yet to learn the art of conversation and it's a long ways to town—but then nothing's ever perfect. And more than balancing out all these minor shortcomings are the benefits of a country life; with its peace and quiet, and, of course, the land. It's become a part of me, drawing me into it every day, fussing with seedlings and pulling the worst of the weeds, tending it as if it were a back garden while hoping to bring out the best in it. And though I'm sure it looks feeble-minded, I often find myself smiling for no apparent reason. And why shouldn't I? I have all the time I used to long for. There's time to relax, read a book from cover to cover, be astonished at the richness of Nature around us, hike in the mountains and, as conclusive proof of a restored normalcy, make the wife explode "What!!" on a regular basis. Yes, the struggle is finally over.

Still, in spite of this relatively happy ending, I can't pretend the last few years were that easy, and it took some time to recover from the events. But after thinking about them, and throwing away the worst of them, I decided to write about them. Actually, Sheila decided for me. She talked about a book in me, and, after my jokes about passing a large rectangular object fell flat, her relentless encouragement caused me to put down my chainsaw and start writing. And though writing could never compare to the satisfaction of a day spent cutting brush, surprisingly, it was only through writing that I found out what had happened to us (actually me) since moving to Igo.

It the middle of all the adventures and unexpected events, it turned out that this had been a time to learn. And of all the things I could have learned about—how to build a house, fix old cars, drill for water, fix water pumps, clear land, drive a bulldozer, make burn piles, horses, poop and more poop, scary steep driveways, dogs and cats, tools, shovels, chainsaws, rattle snakes, vermin, gun-toting neighbors, baby deer, good folks and bad folks, community, bears and lions, wilderness, fires, wildfires, mountain life, summer heat and winter freezes—there was one thing, one single thing, that stood out like a beacon. I learned that life is about character.

It took several too many humbling experiences, but that's the lesson the mountain seems to have had in mind for me. And maybe I'm seeing things this way because I didn't have much experience of it before, and maybe character's not everything, but it's far more important than I had ever realized. I just don't understand why it has to be found at the end of such a long hard road, and in my case probably longer than most.

In my former life, I had been a well-oiled cog in a fast moving world where character had become obsolete. And between the pace of life and an urban life's anonymity, there wasn't any need for it. But the little community of Igo brought me face to face with a different world; one that is unimpressed with importance, or years spent in school, or diplomas or credentials, or careers, or salaries. Instead, it taught me about something that should have always been a part of my life, and I should have known about it earlier, though just a small taste would have been fine. Now it sits on my shoulder with the grip of a bad tempered parrot, vetoing my best ideas with the same abandon I used to reserve for well-meant advice.

We've changed since moving here, we had to, we've adapted to a world where even the simple things can be difficult. Not impossible but still difficult. As an example, Sheila has been trying to recreate the garden she had planted in our more civilized lives: Seeing which of her plants survive from year to year, sifting through what was left alive after the summer heat and the winter snows, then replanting a new round in the spring. She keeps everything she doesn't want eaten by the deer behind a six-foot high stake fence surrounding her garden. The same fence we repaired when we first moved here. The fence keeps the deer out, but there's another animal living in these hills that doesn't seem to understand the concept of a fence. It adds a small thrill to her tending of herbaceous borders.

In the autumn, when there's too much fruit to eat or give away, bears use the opportunity to clean up anything we might have missed. It's the time of year that they're busy eating everything in sight to help them through the winter months, and they climb onto the fence, clumsily crushing it under their substantial weight. After they've finished eating (leaving behind just about as much as they ate, though in a different form), they walk out through the hole they made on the way in. The two dogs decided some time back that a large hungry bear is none of their business, so now the bears break into our garden whenever they feel like it.

I don't have a fear of bears. If it existed at all it would be found way down at the bottom of a long, long list of more justified fears about people. And this casual attitude about a large and wild animal could only have come through personal encounters that have all had happy endings. Respect I have, but not fear. Well that's not entirely true, there is this one bear. It has to weigh seven or eight hundred pounds, and even watching it surreptitiously from a hundred safe yards away, sends a primeval fright through me every time. Still, from my encounters I think they're mostly peaceable animals, seemingly unaware of their enormous strength, and although they have a large and intimidating presence they tend to stay on their side of the street.

Even so, a chance encounter with a large bear (and just to add to the mental image, alone, several miles from anyone or anything) is likely going to be a fright. Every instinct is to run like hell, because up close it's easy to see that these mountains of meat are actually wild animals. Not pets and not institutionalized zoo animals, but wild animals that are completely unaware of laws and regulations, and that have no sense about our inflated importance. So the first few times I was close enough to a bear to really care I wished I wasn't there, and it was only after many, many encounters that I learned to be (mostly) at ease with bears. This can't be said about mountain lions.

My first, unexpectedly, close encounter with a bear came about a year after moving here. It was a summer's evening, just as the last gasp of twilight was giving way to night. It looked as if it might rain that night but I'd been avoiding going back out outside to put the coffee can over the top of the dozer's exhaust, to keep the rain out of it. This was understandable, because the dozer was parked where I had left it, at the far end of the property, and by the time I did make it out of the door, the last light had gone. I stumbled out into a world of barely distinguishable silhouettes, disappearing into a background of almost complete darkness.

Not expecting visitors, all I was wore was a pair of heavy-duty work boots, and feeling free expansive and natural I walked out into the warm night with my overly inquisitive cat, BuggerHead, tagging along behind. We were nearly to the dozer when all of a sudden my naked body stopped dead in its tracks—literally. I didn't know why it would want to do that, but I knew I was frozen in place. By the time every hair on my body had stood straight up, a pint of adrenalin had flushed through me, and my heart had restarted, I understood why.

Not ten feet away a huge black shape silently moved in front of me. It was a Black Bear, a big one, easily four hundred pounds, and apparently unaware of me as it made not the slightest sign it knew I was there. And thank goodness, because I had never felt so completely deeply and utterly naked, or such a defenseless thin-skinned small-boned fragile white-boy in my whole life. I suppose a mountain lion walking in front of me would have made this situation seem positively reassuring, but no matter, this wasn't exactly a Disney moment. I had absolutely no problem in not moving, not an inch, and not even taking a breath.

Not even my eyeballs dared move. I stared straight in front as the bear ghosted its ponderous bulk into the night. And even though it didn't make any signs that it knew I was there, I knew it did. It had to know! That gave the bear an amazing dignity and only added embarrassment to the mix of more primitive emotions I was trying to keep a lid on.

The whole time I'd been balancing on one leg, caught in mid-stride, and I stayed this way until the bear was far enough off that I was sure it had forgotten what it had just seen. Very slowly and very, very quietly I lowered my foot to the ground. Then just my eyeballs, as far as they could swivel, and only after that my head, I turned to see where my silly cat was and what it had been doing all this time. I was expecting to see her long gone and find her at home cowering under the bed. But there she was, right behind me, and still standing on three legs with one front paw held up motionless in front of her. She too had stopped dead in her tracks.

If nothing else I am an animal lover, so for the cat's sake and not mine, I changed plans and headed directly home—I'd become convinced that it wasn't going to rain that night. BuggerHead and I made off like ghosts into the night, silently spiriting ourselves out of there, and only breaking into a run as we neared the house.

Later that same summer, I was propped up in bed in the middle of the night, half awake and half asleep, and looked out of the bedroom window, south down the valley. I saw what looked like a string of lights. There was no reason for any lights to be there, it was fields, and my feeble eyes couldn't tell much except to place the lights at the beginning of Woods Canyon. I stumbled around in the dark, found the binoculars, focused in on the scene, and yelled: "Fire!"

I didn't know much, but I knew if you live at the back end of a box canyon, a fire is not what you want to wake up to—even if it was miles away. The "lights" I saw were the front of the fire flaring up as it burnt across a grassy field. I called 911. Strangely nonchalant, the operator said they already knew about it, but thanks anyway. Thanks nothing! I was in full panic. This was my first sight of a fire and I had no idea what happened next. But the fire never had a chance to get going. It was a calm night and as cool as it gets around here in the summer, which isn't saying much, but it was enough to make the difference, and being only a grass fire the fire fighters put it out in an hour.

Curious, I drove down in the morning to find out what had happened. The fire had started in a field behind the Volunteer Fire Department and, with irony to spare, it was a field the fire department had recently mowed to keep the fire danger down. Nobody knows for sure how the bear ended up where it did, but most likely this unfortunate juvenile bear was chased into the field by some neighborhood dogs (left out at night to stand guard), and the bear did what small bears do when chased—it had climbed a tree. Except in this case the tree was a utility pole. It had climbed to the top of the 12,000-volt pole and was electrocuted. With so much electricity flowing through its body, the now very dead bear burst into flames and fell to the ground, which is what the Fire Department found that night—a burning bear sitting in the middle of a field of burning grass.

I was told that this had happened before, but the image of this poor bear falling from the sky has stayed with me. It seems in part to be a metaphor for the unpredictable world found outside the well-planned Zone of Civilization, but it's also a reminder (after too many well-planned years of my own) that unfortunately life requires a little disorder to thrive: A reminder that even our exalted self-congratulatory species seems to be at its best somewhere in the middle, in a balancing act, halfway between stupefying predictability and complete chaos. An uncomfortable truth maybe, but something I needed reminding of.

In the end, the small town of Igo wasn't so much a place after all—it was more of a journey. A journey packed with adventures that tested my limits to their limits, at an age that I would have been quite content to have sat back, smugly bemused, watching life's comings and goings. Instead, I was tossed back into the middle of the fray with the flippant advice: "Start over!" And in spite of this, I'm (almost) grateful for the non-stop jaw-dropping experiences thrown at me during these last years. Experiences that at times have stripped me to the bone, but then balanced the transaction by giving back just enough strength to get by. Experiences that even gave a little wisdom to a pair of dimming eyes, wisdom that they would have never known otherwise.

In truth, there has been something mystical to my time on the mountain, and I sometimes sit and wonder if I had played into the hands of a cosmic joker by moving out here. A someone or something that wanted to remind me that life is at its sharpest when we are seeing things never seen before and doing things never done before. But whether there was anything mystical or not, I'm sure that my life is far, far richer for having lived in a place where burning bears fall from the sky.

It had been close run race though, and I often thought this mountain had finished me off. I thought this had been my last grand folly and one day I would find myself slumped in a torn Naugahyde recliner, with a beer in one hand, the remote in the other, wearing week-old underwear, staring sullenly fixated at the TV. But in another of its Machiavellian moves, the mountain hauled my recliner away and replaced it with a cruel case of selective amnesia.

There's another equally large acreage further up Woods Canyon, just as derelict as this place ever was, that's practically begging me to build on it. And I'm sure it won't be as difficult a second time around, but should my delusions of "architectural significance" lure me into repeating this last mistake, I'll bring all the experiences from the mouse-house along. This time I'll follow Sheila's example and call it an adventure; I'll borrow her enthusiasm, as well. Because chances are that sometime in the near future I'll be gasping for breath and cursing, wondering how I could have gotten myself into another fine mess, struggling to remember which way was up, and, though I wouldn't have believed it remotely likely before moving here, somehow be all the better for it.

Made in the USA
Charleston, SC
30 June 2010